Pictures

Originally published in 1989 *Pictures at an Exhibition* brings together a rich collection of essays, representing the diversity of views and approaches among professionals towards art and psychoanalysis and art therapy. The editors, both of whom are practising art therapists and art therapy educators, have arranged the contributions so that they may be read in a way similar to looking at pictures in a gallery: they can be glanced at briefly or lingered over, read consecutively or dipped into at random. Artists, art therapists, psychotherapists, psychiatrists and art historians will all find something of interest, and something to stimulate thought and discussion.

Contributions include innovative papers on the relationship between artists' lives and the subject-matter of their work; the work of Kandinsky, Picasso, Magritte, Moore, Lear and Genet is looked at in particular. Generously illustrated, the book also highlights the importance of language and culture in attempting to understand imagery. Each contribution is linked by editorial comments drawing together the threads of concern which are common to art and psychiatry.

Pictures at an Exhibition

Selected essays on art and art therapy

Edited by
Andrea Gilroy and Tessa Dalley

Routledge
Taylor & Francis Group

LONDON AND NEW YORK

First published in 1989
by Routledge

This edition first published in 2013 by Routledge
27 Church Road, Hove, BN3 2FA

Simultaneously published in the USA and Canada
by Routledge
711 Third Avenue, New York, NY 10017

Routledge is an imprint of the Taylor & Francis Group, an informa business

Publisher's Note
The publisher has gone to great lengths to ensure the quality of this reprint but points out that some imperfections in the original copies may be apparent.

Disclaimer
The publisher has made every effort to trace copyright holders and welcomes correspondence from those they have been unable to contact.

A Library of Congress record exists under ISBN: 0415001366

ISBN: 978-0-415-83991-4 (hbk)
ISBN: 978-0-203-77005-4 (ebk)
ISBN: 978-0-415-83993-8 (pbk)

Pictures at an Exhibition

Selected essays on art and art therapy

Edited by Andrea Gilroy and
Tessa Dalley

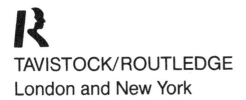

TAVISTOCK/ROUTLEDGE
London and New York

First published 1989
by Routledge
11 New Fetter Lane, London EC4P 4EE
29 West 35th Street, New York, NY 10001

Typeset by Witwell Ltd, Southport
Printed in Great Britain by
Butler & Tanner Ltd, Frome and London

British Library Cataloguing in Publication Data
Pictures at an exhibition: selected essays
 on art and art therapy.
 1. Art therapy
 I. Gilroy, Andrea, *1949–*   II. Dalley, Tessa
 615.8'5156

Library of Congress Cataloging in Publication Data
Pictures at an exhibition: selected essays on art and art therapy/
 edited by Andrea Gilroy and Tessa Dalley.
 p.   cm.
 Bibliography: p.
 Includes index.
 1. Art therapy – Congresses.   2. Art–Psychological aspects –
 – Congresses. I. Gilroy, Andrea, 1949–   . II. Dalley, Tessa.
 RC489.A7P53 1989
 616.89'1656—dc19   88–31911
                                       CIP

ISBN 0–415–00136–6
ISBN 0–415–00137–4 *Pbk*

Contents

Part two: From theory into practice

Illustrations

Notes on contributors

Tessa Dalley is a registered art therapist who works part time at a mainstream primary school and lectures on the Art Therapy Diploma courses at Hertfordshire College of Art and Goldsmiths' College, University of London. She is editor of two previous publications on art therapy; *Art as Therapy* (1985) and *Images of Art Therapy* (1987).

Andrea Gilroy is Lecturer in Art Therapy at Goldsmiths' College, University of London. She was formerly a Council Member and Officer of the British Assocation of Art Therapists (BAAT), and has worked primarily in acute psychiatry in the NHS. She is currently engaged in doctoral research focusing on the occupational motivation of art therapists, and the influence of professional training and clinical practice on their work as artists.

Peter Fuller is a writer and critic. He is the editor of *Modern Painters* and contributes regularly to a number of magazines, including *The Burlington* and *New Statesman and Society*. His books include *Art and Psychoanalysis, Beyond the Crisis, Images of God,* and *Marches Past*. He is currently working on a book about Henry Moore, and has just completed another about John Ruskin.

Brandon Taylor is Reader in History of Art at Winchester School of Art. He has published many articles on modern and contemporary art, and his book *Modernism, Post-Modernism, Realism* was published in 1987. He has a particular interest in the relationship between psychoanalysis and modern art.

David Maclagan is an artist and an art therapist. He has worked as an art therapist in a therapeutic community within the NHS, and teaches on the postgraduate Art Teachers' Certificate Course, and on the MA in Art Education and Art Therapy at Birmingham Polytechnic. He is the author of *Creation Myths* and of many articles and papers on art and art therapy.

John Birtchnell is Scientific Officer and Hon. Senior Lecturer, Medical Research Council, Social Psychiatry Unit, Institute of Psychiatry, London, and his principal research interest is in the familial causes of mental illness. He is also a member of the Clinical Advisory Committee of the Art Psychotherapy Unit at Goldsmiths' College, University of London, Tutor to Leeds Polytechnic Spring School in Art Therapy and author of several articles on art therapy.

Annie Hershkowitz trained in art therapy at Goldsmiths' College, University of London. She has been teaching in Adult Education, and works as a freelance art therapist. She is also a practising artist, with work in private collections in Britain, France, and the USA.

Joan Woddis trained as a teacher and worked for many years as an art teacher/therapist in mainstream and special education. She teaches on the Art Therapy Diploma course at Goldsmiths' College, University of London, and practises as a group analytic psychotherapist at a West London clinic. She is also Chairperson of the BAAT.

Michael Edwards was until recently Professor of Art Therapy at Concordia University in Montreal, Canada, and practises privately as an art therapist. He was formerly Chairman of the British Association of Art Therapists, and is the author of numerous articles and papers on art therapy. He is completing training as a Jungian psychoanalyst in Zurich whilst conducting research in the Jungian archives.

Roland Littlewood is a psychiatrist and social anthropologist. He is Senior Lecturer in Psychiatry and Anthropology, University College London and consultant psychiatrist at the Middlesex Hospital. He is co-author of *Aliens and Alienists: Ethnic Minorities and Psychiatry* (with Maurice Lipsedge), and has written over thirty papers on cultural psychiatry, epidemiology and medical anthropology.

Roger Cardinal is Professor of Literary and Visual Studies at the University of Kent at Canterbury. He is an authority on Surrealism and Outsider Art, and is preparing a book entitled *The Primitive*.

John Matthews is an artist and art educator who has taught at Nursery, Infant and Secondary level. He is Senior Lecturer in the School of Education at Goldsmiths' College, University of London, where he teaches in the Nursery and First School Section of the B. Ed. Dept., and also on the Art Teachers' Certificate Course. For the last fifteen years he has been studying the origins and nature of representation and expression in early childhood, focusing special attention on very young children's drawing, and has written and lectured extensively about his work.

Mary Levens is Head Occupational Therapist in an Eating Disorders Unit. Since training in occupational therapy and art therapy she has completed an MA in art therapy and has been involved in analytic psychotherapy, specializing in personality disorders. She has published a number of articles and lectured in England, New York, and Israel.

Joy Schaverien is an artist who became an art therapist. She has worked as an art therapist in the NHS in a wide variety of clinical settings, most recently in an out-patient psychotherapy department. She teaches art therapy at St Albans College of Art where she is course leader of the MA and advanced training in art therapy. She is involved in doctoral research in aesthetics and psychotherapy, focusing on the role of the picture in the therapeutic relationship. She is in private practice in Leicestershire.

Gerry McNeilly worked at the Ingrebourne Centre, a therapeutic community, as both an art therapist and a psychotherapist. He trained as a Group Analyst at the Institute of Group Analysis, and from 1980–7 worked as a part-time lecturer in art therapy at Goldsmiths' College, University of London. At present he is setting up and directing the development of a new Mental Health Centre for counselling, psychotherapy, and family therapy at Bromsgrove, Worcestershire.

David Edwards has been employed since 1982 as a Senior Art Therapist by Wakefield Health Authority Mental Health Services, and since 1984 as a part-time tutor on the Art Therapy Training programme, University of Sheffield. He is a member of the Training and Education Committee for the British Association of Art Therapists, and of the Editorial group responsible for the publication of *Inscape*, the journal of the BAAT.

Diane Waller is Head of the Art Psychotherapy Unit at Goldsmiths' College, University of London. Her main research interests are in the history and development of art therapy as a profession in Britain, and in cross-cultural issues in art therapy and psychotherapy. She is consultant to a project sponsored by the World Health Organization to establish art therapy within the Bulgarian NHS, and is also involved in developing training in Yugoslavia and Italy.

Rosemary Gordon is Editor of the *Journal of Analytical Psychology* and author of *Dying and Creating: a Search for Meaning*. She was formerly Senior Psychologist at Knapsbury Hospital while training with the Society of Analytical Psychology. She is now in private practice.

Michael Donnelly has a degree in Fine Art and has worked as an art therapist, specifically in family art therapy, for many years. He regularly lectures on the Goldsmiths' Art Therapy course and has written several papers on this innovative area of family work. For four years he served as Chair of the British Association of Art Therapists, and continues his involvement with the professional association as an elected member of BAAT Council, and as Chair of the BAAT Training and Education Committee.

Paola Luzzatto has an MA in Education and a Ph.D in Comparative Religion and did her art therapy training at Goldsmiths' College. Currently she works as an art therapist in adult psychiatry at St Thomas' Hospital, London, and the work presented in this paper was carried out at ACCEPT.

Muriel Greenway has worked as an art teacher for many years. She trained as an art therapist at Goldsmiths' College, and has since worked in the school at the Park Hospital for Children, Oxford.

Foreword

In the first of this fascinating collection of papers on art and art therapy, Peter Fuller unequivocally proclaims 'Art is not a symptom.' Many of those who most value the arts, whether or not they are artists themselves, may question the need for such a statement. Who ever thought that art *was* a symptom? The answer is that Freud did, and it is because Freud's influence on the way we think about ourselves has been so crucially important that the psychological significance of art and the motives which impel artists to create it are still seen as controversial.

Freud himself had a deep interest in sculpture and literature, some appreciation of painting, but virtually no response to music. He valued artists and thought that they were ahead of ordinary mortals in psychological understanding. His paper 'The Moses of Michelangelo' bears witness to his knowledge of art history and to the acuteness of his powers of observation. Yet Freud was so wedded to his view of the mental apparatus and its functions that he could not avoid treating artists as partly maladjusted and art as if it were a neurotic symptom, even though he sometimes appears uneasy at doing so.

Freud's ambivalence springs from his categorization of mental functioning into 'primary process' and 'secondary process'; a dichotomy which, one is glad to say, has been abandoned by those psychoanalysts who look forward rather than backward. Amongst the most important of these writers are Marion Milner, Anton Ehrenzweig, Charles Rycroft, and Donald Winnicott. Freud's original view, which he never modified, was that primary process is governed by the pleasure principle; that is, by wish-fulfilment, a disregard of external reality, and the desire to avoid pain or obtain immediate satisfaction, even if this proves illusory. Secondary process is under the direction of the reality principle. It is characterized by conscious planning, rational thought, the ability to postpone immediate satisfaction, and an appreciation of real conditions in the external world. Primary process is used by the child, the primitive, and the immature or neurotic. Secondary process is employed by the rational adult, who, ideally, should have put away childish things.

Freud laid it down that 'a happy person never phantasies, only an unsatisfied one'. He believed that phantasy was derived from play, and that both play and phantasy were essentially childish activities which ought to be outgrown. He linked together play, phantasy, and dreaming as escapist, wish-fulfilling techniques of compensation for the unsatisfying nature of reality. In Freud's view, the artist is 'originally a man who turns away from reality because he cannot come to terms with the renunciation of instinctual satisfaction which it at first demands, and who allows his erotic and ambitious wishes full play in the life of phantasy'. Works of art, in this view, are sublimations of infantile conflicts, and can be interpreted psychoanaly-tically in the same way as phantasies, dreams, and neurotic symptoms.

It follows that, in an ideal world in which everyone had matured sufficiently to replace the pleasure principle by the reality principle, there would be no need for art. It also follows that, although a psychiatric patient's artistic productions might justifiably be used to expose and interpret his psychopathology, using art as therapy is a misguided enterprise. Regarded through old-fashioned, fundamentalist Freudian eyes, art therapy must surely be deplored as a technique which can only reinforce the patient's failure to adapt to the real world by encouraging him to persist in an activity which is basically escapist.

This book bears ample witness to how far the limitations of Freud's original formulations about art and artists have been transcended by modern theorists and practitioners. Art certainly reveals something about the psychology of the artist, but artists are not necessarily more neurotic than other people, and the drive to create works of art is often an effort to explore and understand both the natural world and the inner world of the psyche rather than a wish to escape from either.

Amongst the originators of dynamic psychology, it was Jung who most convincingly rebelled against Freud's negative view of phantasy. When his patients felt unable to progress, Jung encouraged them to make positive use of phantasy. He urged them to set aside part of the day in which they were to enter a state of reverie and allow their phantasies free rein. Then they were enjoined to take note of what occurred and, if possible, to record their phantasies by painting them, drawing them, modelling them, or writing them. In this way, Jung affirmed, patients might be able to rediscover hidden parts of themselves as well as portraying their psychological condition. Jung stated that, in dealing with patients who were 'stuck', his aim was to bring about a state in which the subjects made use of their creative imaginations to experiment with their own natures instead of remaining in a condition of immobility and sterility. Jung may justly be called the founding father of art therapy.

In writing a brief introduction to such a rich and varied collection of papers, it would be invidious to select any individual paper for special consideration. As a psychotherapist I found it particularly heartening that the use of art in therapy seems to have the effect of reducing the differences between Freudians, Jungians, Kleinians, and adherents of other schools. One of the characteristic features of human beings is the possession of an inner world of the imagination which is different from the external world. It is the discrepancy between the two worlds which motivates the use of the creative imagination and which ultimately accounts for man's inventiveness. Art not only bridges the gap between inner and outer worlds but also seems to span the gulf between different theoretical positions. For example, we find therapists who are predominantly Freudian taking the Jungian point of view that the images produced by patients not only represent infantile wishes and conflicts but may also contain material pointing the way to a new and better adaptation.

Another function of art therapy which clearly emerges from this book is its importance in bridging the gap between cultures. Today, therapists are often required to work with patients whose original language may be different from their own, or whose cultural background is so unlike theirs that purely verbal communication may be difficult. It is also the case that children, from whatever background they may come, often find it hard to express their feelings in words, but may produce drawings and paintings which vividly convey them.

Recurrently, one is made aware that the production of paintings or other work by the patient alters the transference/counter-transference situation in an interesting way which demands considerable personal insight on the part of the therapist. The use of the couch in psychoanalysis has a number of positive advantages, but it does create an artificial distance between patient and analyst which is abolished in art therapy. When patient and therapist are studying a picture they are together on more equal terms than if one is lying down and the other is out of sight.

Encouraging patients to paint, draw, or sculpt has another analogous effect. Those who seek help with their emotional problems are usually driven to do so because they feel overwhelmed and unable to cope. Patients who feel like this often find that painting and drawing both objectifies their conflicts and also restores their faith in their own ability to deal with them. Art, even if one is totally unskilled, can become a sword with which to confront the dragons of the unconscious.

This stimulating and richly varied collection of papers can be confidently recommended, not only to those who have a particular interest in art therapy, but also to anyone who is concerned with the manifold psychological meanings and functions of art.

Anthony Storr, F.R.C.P., F.R.C. Psych.

Introduction

Our original intention was simply to publish the entire proceedings from the conference 'An International Review of the Arts in Therapy' held at the University of London, Goldsmiths' College, in September 1985, sponsored by the British Association of Art Therapists and the International Society for the Study of Art and Psychopathology. The conference attracted delegates from all over the world who presented papers, videos, workshops, and exhibitions of their own or their patients' artwork. It brought together people from a variety of professions all of whom had some kind of interest in the arts and their use in therapy, be they artists, art, music, drama, or dance therapists, art historians, psychiatrists, psychologists, occupational therapists, as well as students of any one of the aforementioned.

However, the variety of presentations was very wide and distilling the essence of the whole conference proved well nigh impossible. Somehow we had to limit the number of papers as the diversity of views across international boundaries seemed to broaden rather than focus the central issues. The differing health systems and cultural contexts the delegates represented varied enormously; from Italy, where the Psychiatrica Democratica movement is well established but art therapy barely recognized; to France and Hungary, where art is used largely as a diagnostic tool by psychiatrists without the mediating influence of art therapists; to the United States of America, where art therapy flourishes as a profession without formal recognition at government level and with a rather different philosophy and practice to that of British art therapists; and other countries such as Chile, Iceland, Holland, and Germany where there might be the occasional, somewhat isolated, art therapist, or psychiatrists who value the artworks of their patients. All of these represented such different approaches to art therapy than that in the United Kingdom – the only country where the profession is recognized, practised, and taught within a state system – that, regretfully, we decided to include only those papers from the British delegates.

The decision to forgo the publication of so many interesting papers has been a hard one, but one which subsequently enabled this book to take on a life of its own, in some ways separate from its origins. Many of the papers in this collection are as they were originally presented. Some have been reworked and some rewritten and updated, but all are based on the ideas spawned at the conference. The papers are in the same form as we received them from the authors, our editorial task being the choice, collation, and commentary on the book as a whole. Our aim in choosing these particular papers has been to demonstrate both the diversity of views and the common concerns as they were expressed at the conference; many explore similar themes, others are complementary, and some contradict each other – one or two are controversial. But, as we hope the reader will appreciate, all address the way in which art therapy and psychiatry, and the arts and psychoanalysis, can either collide with or mutually inform one another.

We were interested to see the way the papers themselves reflected the particular professional 'culture' in which they had been written, be it that of the art historian, the psychiatrist, or the art therapist, and how each in some way not only reflected their particular ideology *vis-à-vis* the arts and psychoanalysis, but also highlighted issues discussed in art therapy circles today. Broadly speaking, there are two strands to the present-day approach to art therapy and the artwork of the mentally ill. First the focus is on the products of art therapy. The artifacts themselves are used in various ways: to illustrate particular feelings or dynamics and to aid verbal interaction; as tools in assessment and diagnosis; some are elevated to 'the art of the insane' and join the realms of galleries and exhibitions. The second approach emphasizes the process of making art and of therapy. Some therapists view the activity of making art as healing in itself; others work with the dynamic processes that are engaged as images are made within the therapeutic relationship between art therapist, the patient, and their imagery.

This philosophical and practical divergence of views was reflected in the conference by the delegates' presentations and occasionally by their affiliation to one or another of the sponsoring bodies – were we discussing art therapy or the psychopathology of artistic expression? Do they have much in common? Whatever the conclusion may be it is helpful to be aware of the origins of each author's interest in art and madness, and to reflect on the way in which these origins influence their work.

Both the editors are practising art therapists and art therapy educators, and our commentaries before each part of the book are based in these professional roots. Our comments are responses to the papers, not explanations; sometimes we agree with the authors and at other times we disagree. The aim has been to make links and pull together differing aspects of an argument, drawing attention to similarities and differences. Reactions to the papers, once assembled, reminded us of looking at paintings; in a gallery one may just glance, or stop and linger, allowing levels of meaning to unfold as one gains familiarity with the picture. Similarly, some of these papers need repeated reading and often contain the message that there is more to an image than may initially meet the eye. Being open and available to aesthetic, emotional, and intellectual responses and looking into the multidimensional layers of an image is the issue that lies at the heart of this book, and at the heart of our practice as art therapists.

We have divided the papers into two broad sections. Part One of the book is primarily concerned with the different ways in which the theories of psychoanalysis may be used to assist an understanding of imagery, including that of particular artists, writers, and cultures. Part Two is based in the theory and practice of art therapy, and includes very different casework-based papers. At the conference the papers were presented to an audience familiar with the theoretical frameworks of art therapy and the psychopathology of expression, and this collection, of necessity, assumes a similar knowledge on the part of the reader.

Part one
Psychoanalytic views of the arts

Commentary

These papers cover many aspects of the psychoanalytic views of culture and the arts. Several papers in this first part have an immediate sense of being in touch with childhood experience and with the process of making art, which for us demonstrates the duality of art therapy – the importance of working with the early experiences of our patients whilst maintaining the awareness we, as artists, bring to the art therapy process. A dominant theme is the degree to which it is necessary to allow space for the voice of the artist him/herself when using analytic theory to understand the nature and content of an artist's imagery.

The first chapter, by Peter Fuller, is one where the tension that can exist between art and psychoanalysis is successfully negotiated. Peter describes how early infant experience and the relationship between mother and child were subjects that preoccupied the sculptor Henry Moore and the child psychoanalyst Donald Winnicott, and by drawing parallels between the central concerns of both men illustrates a sense in which Moore visually expressed Winnicott's theories. What is significant about this paper is that whilst making it plain that it is not his intention to interpret Moore's work – 'Art is not a symptom' – Peter none the less uses Winnicott's developmental theories to enhance our understanding of Moore as an individual and as an artist whose work reflected both his life and the preoccupations of the society in which he lived and worked.

As one might expect in a collection of this nature, there is considerable interest in mother and child relationships and their influence on the production of art in all its forms. Annie Hershkowitz (Chapter 5) explores similar ideas to those in Peter Fuller's paper and illustrates how this first and most important of relationships influenced, and was indeed the subject of, the work of several writers and painters. She shows how, for these men and women, their art became a means and a medium through which they and, significantly, their audience could relive their early experiences in the present, the 'here and now' of art. Despite the brevity of the material there is clearly substance to the author's argument about each of the individuals she discusses, and about the significance to them of the 'performance' of painting, writing, or of theatre itself.

The importance of acknowledging and understanding the artist's language and experience of their work is clearly seen in Joan Woddis's sensitive appraisal of the work of Edward Lear (Chapter 6). She argues that much of Lear's work was a defence through which he could explore his lost childhood and early separation from his mother, and the consequent depression and isolation. Lear's diary descriptions of his daily life are used to draw attention to the recurring but obscured themes in his poems and drawings, constrained as he was by the repressive values of Victorian England. This approach, while utilizing analytic theory, also listens to the artist and creates a sympathetic framework within which reader may engage with both artist and author.

All the papers in one way or another address the issue of interpretation. How do we see the images and what is our understanding of them? What is the influence of the society in which the piece is made and viewed, and is the spectator's experience necessarily the same as the artist's? Is it possible for any viewer to make a judgement about a painting or sculpture which is unsullied by personal projections? Peter Fuller made the point that works of art can, and do, reflect not only the artist's preoccupations but those of his or her audience, the society at large. Brandon Taylor extends this discussion in Chapter 2 and argues that the audience should be aware not only of the context of the work, but also of the manner of its making.

Brandon uses the work of Kandinsky, Matisse, and Picasso to describe how they each, to some extent, embodied in their painting the crisis through which Europe was passing in the years immediately preceding the First World War, whilst at the same time either consciously or unconsciously exploring conflicts they, as individuals, were experiencing at the time. His thesis is that the broader implications of their work can be clearly seen in the surface of their paintings, in the ways the materials were used – the process of painting itself. Surfaces are fragmented, the objects in the paintings sometimes being substitutions and intentionally misleading or secretive. Brandon argues that in these instances substitution was about fusion, not sublimation, these artists being at one with the society in which they lived, and therefore reflecting it.

Making an interpretive statement in this way highlights the significant influence of the environment and the discipline in which a picture is being discussed – whether it be that of art history, art therapy, anthropology, or analysis. Brandon speaks of the viewer's ability to risk recognizing what the artist is saying, and of being able to cope with what he describes as the 'radical incompleteness' of our understanding of imagery. In a gallery context it is perhaps acceptable to acknowledge the marvellous uncertainty of a Henry Moore sculpture, whilst in an art therapy session it may be difficult to stay with 'not knowing' what a painting is about. Working with this tension can create a temptation to 'fill in' a picture, to use Brandon's term, with too many interpretations. At its most extreme this can lead to a quasi-scientific approach to art and art therapy. Unfortunately this is one which art therapists can fall victim to, perhaps in an effort to gain credence as a profession within a predominantly medical environment.

Something of this 'filling in' can be seen in John Birtchnell's controversial examination of Chagall's paintings (Chapter 4). John begins and ends with clear indications as to how he believes art therapists should work with their patients' imagery – by entering into and sharing the patient's world in order to be able to communicate within the patient's language and symbolism. John's thesis is that Chagall's symbolism was disguised but nevertheless showed his preoccupation with eroticism. One recognizes the relationship to the other authors' suggestions about the oblique exploration of issues too intimate to be overtly described, but in this chapter the interpretations seem at times too simplistic and reductive, and, surprisingly, there is a noticeable absence of Chagall's voice. Attempts to (in John's words) 'dissect' and 'decipher' paintings and their apparently 'innocent' symbols, whatever the reason for their production, must take account of the several meanings which any one symbol may hold simultaneously. For example, we would not disagree with the sexuality and glorious romanticism of many of Chagall's paintings, but could it not be that there were also references to folklore, to childhood, and elements of sadness arising from his separation from his native Russia? Some of the universal resonance and beauty of many works of art can thus be lost in our need to understand and articulate visual images in verbal language.

David Maclagan (Chapter 3) asks that we pay attention to the dangers of such narrow vision, of 'interpretive straitjackets', and the pitfalls to which they can so easily lead. He explores the psychoanalytic understanding of fantasy and the products of the imagination (dreams, fantasies, images, art), and suggests that art can confirm a split between reality and fantasy, inner and outer. He argues that art does not simply record what is present in reality or in fantasy, but that it can actively create and serve as a conductor for experience. David believes that trying to 'translate' fantasy into reality can inflict a sense of 'otherness' on to it, a set of rules and conventions which serve little purpose other than the aggrandisement of the translator.

As art therapists we are then left with the question 'Who are the translations or interpretations for?' This is not to say that art therapists and all those who attempt to verbalize their understanding of the products of the imagination and of the art therapy process should not try to communicate their understandings both to the patient (when appropriate) and to colleagues, but, as David concludes, there are times when we should be able to be content with images and let them speak their own language.

Many art therapists are uncomfortable with reductive or projective interpretations of fine art and art therapy. Others work successfully with the diagnostic and problem-solving aspects of art therapy as a treatment. These differing models of art therapy and attitudes towards art and psychoanalysis are traced back to their origins some 200 years ago in Michael Edwards's paper (Chapter 7). By describing attitudes towards art and madness in the eighteenth and nineteenth centuries Michael demonstrates how ideas from other areas of enquiry, such as the use of art in rituals, religious customs, and anthropology, form a 'more elaborate and enduring context' for art therapy that was in existence way in advance of its establishment as a discrete profession.

It is interesting to see how history in general, and art history and the history of psychiatry in particular, have given rise to certain models of present art therapy practice. Michael postulates that the roots of the codified, diagnostic attitude towards imagery are in eighteenth-century Neoclassicism, and in their 'rational' belief that a person's state of mind could be 'read' from a picture. The depiction of feeling in art was formalized, and enabled the painter and his audience to remain uninvolved. By contrast, the nineteenth-century romantics embraced a positive conception of the imagination and valued the artistic representation of inner experience; this attitude relates to a belief in the natural healing capabilities of art. It would be interesting to trace further the evolution of one of the modern practices in art therapy of utilizing a psychodynamic framework (the consideration of boundaries and transference relationships for example) and the shift away from both the romantics and the neoclassicists.

Roland Littlewood's interest (Chapter 8) is in madness as a social phenomenon. He identifies a number of examples where the 'imitation of madness' could provide psychiatry with a model for understanding the meaning of psychotic behaviour. He argues that politically influential individuals who become psychotic are validated initially by the inertia of political structures, although it is rare for an individual to maintain influence if actually insane. Alternatively, an individual may be only periodically insane and in between episodes of madness may live in the same social reality as other members of the community, where his delusions are validated as acceptable communications if they have meaning for the community of which the individual is a part. Roland's paper overtly has little to do with art and art therapy but is nevertheless important in its affirmation of the significance, once again, of the context in which imagery, symbols, or behaviour occur and are interpreted.

Chapter One

Mother and child in Henry Moore and Winnicott

Peter Fuller

There was a moment to which Winnicott referred more than once in his writings, when he found himself bursting out at a meeting of the Psychoanalytical Society, 'There is no such thing as a baby.' 'I was alarmed to hear myself utter these words', he was to comment later, 'and tried to justify myself by pointing out that if you show me a baby you certainly show me also someone caring for the baby, or at least a pram with someone's eyes and ears glued to it. One sees', as he put it, 'a "nursing couple".'[1]

But Winnicott later went on to draw conclusions from this moment of insight which went beyond what could be immediately seen with the eyes. Winnicott began to write of a 'condition that it can be assumed exists at the beginning of the individual's life in which the object is not yet separated out from the subject'.[2] For those not used to the psychoanalytic jargon, 'object' means 'other person' – usually, from the baby's point of view, the mother. Winnicott says that, from an observer's point of view, the baby may seem 'to be object-relating in the primary merged state'; but he adds that it has to be remembered that, at the beginning, the object is a 'subjective object', as distinct from an 'object objectively perceived'.[3]

Now, more than any other psychoanalytic writer, Winnicott respected 'the delicacy of what is preverbal, unverbalized, and unverbalizable except perhaps in poetry'. And yet when he attempts to describe such things as the infant's experience of a 'subjective object', we feel that language is being strained to its limits. If only there was another more visual way of expressing these sentiments and ideas. Consider, for a moment, the sculpture, called 'Mother and Child', which Henry Moore carved out of Ancaster stone in 1939. This piece is now in the British Council's collection. I do not feel that I need to offer any further commentary on it.

Now some of you may be thinking that there is something forced, or fortuitous, about the comparison I have invited you to make between one of Winnicott's theories about the nature of the infant's experience in the infant–mother relationship, and a particular sculpture by Henry Moore. If you are, that is understandable. But I hope to be able to dispel at least some of your doubts.

But I feel I should make one point absolutely clear, right now. I am not, I insist, going to use a body of psychoanalytic ideas derived from Winnicott's theoretical writings as a means of 'interpreting' Henry Moore's sculpture, and telling you what it is 'really' about. Such 'applications' of psychoanalytic ideas to art were always misplaced; today, they are quite obsolete. Art is not a symptom. Indeed, I am reminded of how, in his clinical practice, Winnicott grew increasingly sceptical about the value of making clever interpretations to his patients – even if they happened to be right. As I get older, I find that something similar applies in the appreciation of art, too; the clever interpretation – and I'm not only thinking of psychoanalytic interpretations – can be an impingement, something which distracts from, or even detracts from, a deeper aesthetic response. The good critic, too, knows when to withhold clever interpretations. What I want to do runs, I hope, a little deeper than that.

I want to suggest to you that there are vital resemblances between D. W. Winnicott's pioneering psychoanalytical insights and the vision which Henry Moore has expressed through his great sculpture and drawings. Do you know the Henry Moore drawing of 'Women Winding Wool' made in 1949, and now in the Museum of Modern Art in New York? It is, I think, one of our century's very greatest drawings. As the wool passes from one woman to the other, the lines through which the two figures are drawn seem to merge, and fuse inextricably. And yet each remains separate – monumentally so.

I think we can say without doubt, it is a drawing Winnicott would have appreciated had he known it. Just think, for a moment, of the importance which imagery of mothers, string, and mergence has in his own work. But I am offering this image to you because it seems appropriate in both form and content as an illustration of the relationship between two quite distinct but also intimately related bodies of work which I now wish to sketch.

At first sight, D. W. Winnicott's achievement does not seem to have much in common with that of Henry Moore. Winnicott was born in 1896 into a prosperous middle-class family. His father, a sweet manufacturer, became Lord Mayor of Plymouth. Winnicott himself studied biology, became a doctor, and specialized in paediatrics, the treatment of children. He soon started an association with Paddington Green Children's Hospital, which was to last for forty years. Winnicott also underwent training with the British Psychoanalytical Society, and, in the late 1930s, began to emerge as a prominent figure within the psychoanalytic movement. Outside it, too, he was to become known for his radio talks, and popular articles, about mothering and babycare. As Masud Khan, one of Winnicott's editors, once put it, he displayed 'a militant incapacity to accept dogma'. Although he always acknowledged his debt to Melanie Klein, when the British Psychoanalytical Society was torn by theoretical and organizational controversies after the Second World War, Winnicott aligned himself neither with the Kleinians nor with the followers of Anna Freud.[4] Rather, he became a leading light of the so-called 'Middle Group'. This should not be taken as a sign of weakness or woolliness. Rather, Winnicott began to formulate and to explore highly original ideas about the nature of the infant–mother relationship, which were a challenge to existing psychoanalytic orthodoxies. They also led him far beyond the nursery and the consulting room to a tentative new view about the nature of human creativity, and indeed of culture itself.

Henry Moore was born two years after D. W. Winnicott, in Castleford, Yorkshire. As far as I know, they never met; but it amuses me to remember that they were infants at the same time. Raymond Moore, Henry's father, had been a miner; however, his sight was injured in a pit accident, and he was retired by the time Henry, the seventh of eight children, was born. Raymond was an exceptional, nonconformist autodictat, and he did nothing to discourage Henry's improbable ambition to become a sculptor. Moore studied first at Leeds College of Art, and later at the Royal College in London.

Moore was a natural carver. In the early 1920s, under the influence of Roger Fry's writings, he steeped himself in the so-called 'primitive' art to be found in the British Museum and other public collections. His interest in Aztec, Assyrian, and African work was evident in his own early carvings which often brought down upon him the charge of 'primitivism'; but these works also manifest the sculptural obsessions which were to dominate so much of his life's work – the reclining figure and the mother-and-child group.

In the 1930s, however, Moore became close to the Surrealist movement; he produced his most 'abstracted' pieces, including the 'Stringed Figures', of which he was later rather critical. Although he contributed to the major Surrealist exhibition held in London in 1936, he could never have been described as being a whole-hearted member of the movement. It isn't just that, like Winnicott, Moore had a 'militant incapacity to accept dogma'; his imagination also always possessed a poise, balance, and, in the best sense, an ordinariness which the Surrealists lacked. Indeed, I would suggest that his relationship to European Surrealism had much in common with Winnicott's to classical psychoanalysis. Moore himself once explained that with the outbreak of the Second World War he 'felt it was silly to start a large sculpture';[5] and so he concentrated on drawings. As an official war artist, he produced his famous 'Shelter Drawings' of Londoners sleeping on the platform in the underground.

His return to sculpture came in 1943 when Canon Hussey invited him to carve a Madonna and Child for St Matthew's in Northampton. After the war, Moore's reputation grew steadily. At various times he produced family groups, helmeted heads, studies of hands, animals, and fallen warriors. He also made a number of neo-abstractions, based on organic forms – especially bones. But the themes laid down in the prewar years continued to dominate his work; the majestic reclining figures appeared at regular intervals, although after 1960 Moore began to fragment them in extraordinary ways. Moore began to become the most widely distributed sculptor in history; major works were erected throughout the western world. In the 1970s he returned to drawing. He also began to make an exceptionally fresh and intimate series of small maquettes of mothers with their children. 'There are three recurring themes in my work', he once explained, 'the "Mother and Child" idea, the "Reclining Figure" and the Interior/Exterior forms.'[6] He added that some sculptures combined two, or even all three, of these themes. But, in 1943, he emphasized that of these, the mother and child had been the most 'fundamental obsession'.[7]

The mother–child relationship was certainly the most fundamental of all D. W. Winnicott's concerns. All that he said and wrote was rooted in his extraordinary empathy for the mother and her child, an empathy which, of course, was based on exceptional empirical experience; it was estimated that 60,000 mothers with their children consulted Winnicott at Paddington Green. Winnicott broke decisively with Freud's concept, inherited also by Klein, of the baby as an auto-erotic isolate, driven by the need to experience pleasure through the reduction of instinctual tension within a hypothetical 'psychic apparatus'. Winnicott simply did not accept the idea that a 'one-body relationship' precedes the 'two-body relationship': he stressed that in the beginning 'the unit is not the individual, the unit is the environmental-individual set-up'. Winnicott described the infant as being enveloped within, and conditional upon, the holding environment (or mother) of whose support and succour he becomes only gradually aware. 'I would say that initially', he once wrote, 'there is a condition which could be described at one and the same time as of *absolute independence* and *absolute dependence*.'[8]

Winnicott thought the infant made his first contact with reality through what he called 'moments of illusion'. Through such moments, the infant gradually became aware that he was not everything, that he was contained by a limiting membrane, or skin, and possessed an inside. These 'moments of illusion', Winnicott thought, arose when the infant's fantasy and external reality coincided – most notably when the mother offered her breast at precisely the moment when the infant desired or imagined it. In this way, the infant acquires the illusion that there is an external reality which corresponds to his capacity to create. Later, Winnicott thought, it was the mother's task to take the infant through a process of 'disillusion', associated with weaning, during which the infant gently relinquished omnipotence, and learned there was an outside world which was not his own creation.[9]

But Winnicott spoke of a continuing need in the developing and growing child for a space which could not be clearly categorized as inner, or outer, as fantasy or reality, a continuing need, if you will, to make use of 'subjective objects'. Thus he was led on to his famous theory of 'transitional objects and transitional phenomena'. He began to describe 'the third part of the life of a human being, a part that we cannot ignore, an intermediate area of experiencing, to which inner reality and external life both contribute'.[10]

Winnicott emphasized the child's use of 'the first possession', that is those rags, blankets, cloths, teddy bears, etc., to which young children commonly become attached. He saw that, for the child, such 'transitional objects' belonged to an intermediate area between the subjective and that which is objectively perceived. Winnicott regarded play itself as a transitional phenomenon. Clinically, he made use of these ideas through such techniques as 'the squiggle game', in which he communicated with a child through an open-ended process of transformation of the given. Winnicott would draw a line on a piece of paper; the child would turn it into something; then he would complete a line, or squiggle, made by the child ... and so on.

Winnicott talked a good deal about the importance of not challenging transitional objects and phenomena, of not impinging upon them. One simply had to accept the paradox they offered. He repeatedly drew a comparison between these ideas about transition and Christian doctrines about the eucharist. How can the host be, at once, both ordinary bread and the body of Christ? The controversies of transubstantiation arose from the attempt to resolve a paradox of which there can be no resolution.

Towards the end of his life Winnicott became increasingly aware of the wider cultural and artistic significance of his ideas. He came to talk about what he called 'a potential space', which, he said, arises at that moment when after a state of feeling merged in with the mother, the baby arrives at the point of separating out the mother from the self – and the mother simultaneously lowers her degree of adaption to her baby's needs. At this moment, Winnicott says, the infant seeks to avoid separation 'by the filling in of the potential space with creative playing, with the use of symbols, and with all that eventually adds up to a cultural life'.[11] He pointed out that the task of reality acceptance is never completed: 'no human being is free from the strain of relating inner and outer reality'. The relief from this strain, he maintained, is provided by the continuance of an intermediate area which is not challenged; the potential space, originally between baby and mother, is ideally reproduced between child and family, and between individual and society, or the world.

Winnicott saw the potential space as in direct continuity with the play area of the small child 'lost' in play. He felt it was retained in the intense experiencing that belongs to the arts and to religion and to imaginative life of all kinds. Indeed, he described the potential space as 'the location of cultural experience'.[12]

Winnicott's ideas about the 'potential space' were certainly tentative. *Playing and Reality*, the book in which he puts them forward, is not entirely resolved. We know that Winnicott was working on his formulations about the 'potential space' immediately before his death and still felt he had not got them quite right. None the less, I believe Charles Rycroft was absolutely right when he said, in 1972, that Winnicott's concept of a transitional reality mediating between the private world of dreams and the public shared world of the environment was 'perhaps the most important contribution made to psychoanalytical theory'[13] since the Second World War. He was also right, however, to say that this insight was not entirely original – as it appeared synonymous with what poets and artists described in terms of the imagination. The association of Winnicott's psychological ideas with artistic vision is not fortuitous. As Madeleine Davis and David Wallbridge point out in *Boundary and Space* (an excellent introduction to Winnicott's work), 'Underlying Winnicott's writing is a sense of balance and proportion – an aesthetic sense that often seems to take a visual form, just as his favourite method of communication in his work with children took a visual form in the Squiggle Game.'[14]

Moore has always been a sculptor for whom 'form experience' is paramount. 'Complete Sculptural expression', he once wrote, 'is form in its full spatial reality.' But Moore has also repeatedly insisted that no 'real or deeply moving art can be purely for art's sake'. He has insisted on 'a spiritual vitality ... which goes deeper than the senser'.

A good work of art, according to Moore, is 'an expression of the significance of life, a stimulation to greater effort in living'. If then we acknowledge 'a sense of balance and proportion – an aesthetic sense' underlying Winnicott's psychology, we ought also to recognize that the experiences to which Moore's sculptures invite us go beyond the formal to affirm the meanings and values which make life worth living. In saying this, however, we must be cautious, for, as Winnicott once put it, 'Content is of no meaning without form'.[15]

Moore is a profoundly original sculptor; but his originality is rooted in – to use a word which again had a special significance for Winnicott – the ordinary. Moore is living proof of one of the most significant insights of the English school of psychoanalysis; namely that there is no necessary link between artistic creativity and neurosis, nor between genius and psychosis.

I would suggest there is a continuity between the security and happiness of Moore's childhood environment and the particular nature of his adult sculptural vision. Moore himself has spoken about the direct way in which one experience of his mother's body affected his adult work as a sculptor. Mary Moore suffered from bad rheumatism in the back. 'She would often say to me in winter when I came back from school, "Henry, boy, come and rub my back". Then I would massage her back with liniment.' Moore relates this to a seated figure of a mature woman he made in 1957. 'I found', he said, 'that I was unconsciously giving to its back the long-forgotten shape of the one I had so often rubbed as a boy.'[16] This much repeated anecdote has all the over-polished feel of a screen memory; it seems to stand in for a range of early experiences which informed far more of his adult sculptural activity than just this single sculpture. Once a Jungian analyst, Erich Neumann, sent Moore a book he had written about his work. Moore read the first chapter, and then laid the book aside – not because he felt it was nonsense but rather because, as he put it, 'it explained too much about what my motives were'. He shared the understandable – but almost certainly erroneous – fear of many creative people that, as he put it, 'If I was psychoanalysed I might stop being a sculptor ... but ... I don't want to stop being a sculptor.'[17]

A great gulf, of course, divides infantile experience from the creation of major sculptures. As a student, Moore soon discovered that the academic tradition was not going to help him bridge that gap. Much of the sculpture he encountered was based on debased Greek anatomical ideals; or, alternatively, it involved an illusionistic naturalism which veered towards the sentimental. Many sculptors made tiny maquettes which were then simply pointed up for them by craftsmen. He turned towards so-called 'primitive' art which he felt revealed an 'intense vitality' because it was something 'made by people with a direct and immediate response to life', and not an activity 'of calculation or academicism'.

Gaudier Brzeska, who was killed at the age of 24 in the First World War, and Jacob Epstein had both preceded Moore in their celebration of the 'primitive'. Epstein encouraged the young Moore, buying from him a beautiful little study of a baby suckling at the breast, and introducing the exhibition he had at the Leicester Galleries in 1931. This brought down on Moore's head some of the outrage which Epstein himself had endured.

Of one image of a mother and child, *The Evening Post* declared, 'most people will hold it to be revolting as a representation of a woman and child and ignoble as a work of art'. Moore was also accused of allowing 'the cult of ugliness' to flourish. *The Morning Post* announced, 'he shows an utter contempt for the natural beauty of women and children and in so doing deprives even stone of its value as a means of aesthetic and emotional expression'. But *The Times* wrote sympathetically of the special appeal the formal relationship between mother and child had for Moore, and added, perceptively, that the emotional strength of his work flowed out of the way in which he had reworked that formal relationship.

Half a century later Moore himself confirmed this. 'The mother-and-child theme', he said, 'poses for the sculptor the relationship of a large form to a small one, and the dependency of the small form on the larger. Its appeal lies particularly in its expression of two basic human experiences: to be a child and to be a parent.'[18]

Winnicott, you will remember, differentiated between the way in which the infant–mother relationship appeared to an independent observer and the way in which it felt, as it were, from the inside. Moore outraged taste in 1931 because, in a fully sculptural way, he was making that shift. He was moving away from the naturalistic spectacle of an infant suckling at the breast – as offered by so many nineteenth-century salon sculptors – towards work which had greater continuity with the 'subjective objects' of the potential space.

One of the most fundamental ways in which Moore did this concerned not his imagery but his practical affirmation of the doctrine of 'truth to materials'.

You will recall how Winnicott associated 'transitional' phenomena with the notorious arguments surrounding the status of the bread and wine in the eucharist and the degree to which they were, or were not, imbued with the Real Presence to become the actual body and blood of Christ. In recent aesthetics, a parallel concern revolves around the relationship between the image in a work of art and the physical materials used for its realization. Like Gaudier Brzeska, Moore felt the nineteenth-century sculptors had tilted things too far by trying to handle, say, marble as if it really was flesh. The myth of Pygmalion was wrecking sculpture's transitional qualities and turning it into mere mimesis, or an adult version of infantile magic-making. Moore, by contrast, celebrated the conspicuous and undeniable stoniness of Mexican carving. 'I began believing in direct stone carving', he was to say later, 'in being true to the material by not making stone look like flesh.'[19] But by the 1950s Moore himself was saying that as a young man he had exaggerated the argument from 'truth to materials'.[20] If this was taken too far sculpture could – and in the hands of others did – become dominated by the material to such a degree that the image disappeared altogether and the transitional paradox on which good sculpture depended was again lost. The artist must offer a 'moment of illusion' which cannot be challenged, within which a block of stone is at once both a real and unmistakable block of stone and, simultaneously, a mother with her child, or a couple locked in a kiss that is a sculpture.

The first phase of Moore's work came to an end with a monumental mother-and-child group, in green Horton stone, now in the Sainsbury Centre. After 1932 there were no new developments in the figurative mother-and-child theme for over a decade. But if the 1920s had been marked by Moore's revival of a 'traditional' use of materials themselves, the 1930s were a period of novel, and not always entirely convincing, experimentation with new sculptural forms. 'My sculpture is becoming less representational', Moore explained in 1937, 'less an outward visual copy, and so what some people would call more abstract.' But he went on to say this was 'only because I believe that in this way I can present the human psychological content of my work with the greatest directness and intensity'.[21]

Some of Moore's formal experiments in these years were to affect his sculpture for the rest of his working life: others, almost inevitably, proved to be cul-de-sacs. One of the most fruitful was also among the most simple; that is, the hole, or, as Moore describes it, 'the penetration through from the front of the block to the back'. Moore had said that the making of the hole was, for him, a 'revelation'; having the idea to do it involved 'a great mental effort'.[22] Predictably, Moore's holes have been subjected to silly psychoanalytic interpretation. David Sylvester, who really should have known better, once associated them with female sexual organs. But I do not think that, even unconsciously, Moore intended to evoke a mood of genital – or indeed any other – kind of excitation. Nor, of course, do these holes represent a point of entry into the figure.

The hole is a good example of how, in Moore, new content finds its meaning through formal originality. Moore himself has explained that the holes enabled him to make a space and a three-dimensional form within a single object. As he points out, through this device sculpture in air becomes possible; the hole itself can be the 'intended and considered form'. The psychological force of this new formal device may have stemmed from the fact that the hole blurs the boundary between the object and its environment. The punctured figure can no longer be said to be contained by a limiting membrane, or skin, separating inside from outside; rather, this distinction has itself dissolved and disappeared.

This interest in the fusion of interior-exterior forms takes another guise in Moore's work; that is, in his lifelong obsession with the idea of one form enclosing another. As a student, he was fascinated by the suits of armour in the Wallace Collection, which reminded him of 'the shell of a snail which is there to protect the more vulnerable forms inside'.[23] In his sculpture such form ideas have, he says, 'led sometimes to the idea of the Mother and Child where the outer form, the mother, is protecting the inner form, the child, like the mother does protect her child'. But note how in the 'Reclining Figure', 1945-6, the 'armoured' form is in fact the interior one.

Two years after he made the fused 'Mother and Child', with which I began, Moore began to produce a stream of 'Stringed Figures'. I do not feel that they are successful as sculptures, and Moore himself looks back on them somewhat dismissively. He has criticized their repetitiveness, sterile ingenuity, and divorce from what he calls 'fundamental human experience'.[24] He once commented that he could have carried on turning out hundreds of them. Some of you will, I think, recall Winnicott's essay on string, in which he suggested that its joining capacities meant it had a symbolic meaning for everyone. But Winnicott also discussed the case of a small boy who made exaggerated and repetitive use of string as a way of expressing his denial of separation from the mother. The union between the forms in the stringed sculptures has just such a sterile and obsessive feel.

Interestingly, immediately after making the 'Stringed Figures', Moore created another psychologically curious, but sculpturally unsatisfactory, work which he called 'Three Points'. 'This pointing', he explained, 'has an emotional or physical action in it where things are just about to touch, but don't.' He associates this – among other things – with an early French painting, 'where one sister is just about to touch the nipple of the other', but doesn't. 'It is very important that the points do not actually touch', Moore says. 'There has to be a gap.'[25] If the 'Stringed Figures' were obsessive, even perverse, denials of separation, here it seems to me to be equally stultifyingly insisted upon. Those works which are formally more successful involve neither the denial of separation, nor yet the frozen assertion of it, as it were, in perpetuity. Rather, they present us with formal equivalents for a space which exists, yet cannot exist – a potential space.

After 'Three Points' Moore temporarily abandoned sculpture, because of the War. He was appointed an official war artist, and he produced, among other works, his famous 'Shelter Drawings'. Moore's drawing techniques, as much as his use of sculptural materials and forms, reveal the importance of transitional experience to his art. From a very early age, Moore drew, and drew brilliantly, from life. But early on he also developed a method he called 'transformation' drawing – rather like a one-person version of the squiggle game. He described it as working with no preconceived problem to solve, with only the desire to use pencil on paper, and make lines, tones, and shapes. Moore found that, at a certain point, imagery would begin to crystallize, and a sense of meaning and order would arise seemingly from the process of drawing itself. When he came to make his great 'Shelter Drawings' of the sleepers on the platforms of London tube stations during air-raids, Moore made use of both his acute perceptual observation and his powers of intense imaginative transformation.

The imagery of the protective bowels of the earth, the engulfing cloak of the mother, rugs, and blankets, which are at one moment warm covering and, in the next, a shroud – all this was certainly there to be seen in the underground. But it also suggested to Moore his most intimate concerns – his interest in a space between mother and child, free from the terrible impingements of the world.

Will Grohmann has written well about these drawings. He says that it is almost always women that Moore drew, women 'reclining, or more rarely seated women, mothers with their children, and where the women have children, they automatically assume the stature of madonnas through the immensity of their responsibility'. He speaks too of 'countless wrappings, stretching out in endless rows, at bottomless depths'.[26] I feel sure that Neumann was right in his observation that this motif of a blanket, swaddling cloth, or winding sheet – so insistent throughout these drawings – 'has the same formal role of uniting mother and child that the stone once had'.[27] Equally, I am sure I have no need to labour the parallel here between Moore's cloths and blankets, and Winnicott's transitional objects.

The making of the great 'Madonna and Child' for St Matthew's, Northampton, towards the end of the War not only marked Moore's return to sculpture, but signalled a new maturity and confidence in his developing sculptural vision. Even so, it has sometimes been suggested that, despite the serene repose of this great figure, something was lost in the making of it – what Moore learned when he punctured a hole through the block. That may seem to be so if we consider the work in reproduction. In situ, however, it is another matter. As Eric Newton once put it, the mother and child harmonize unexpectedly with their neo-Gothic setting, 'because the statue is so designed in scale that the space it occupies seems to have been waiting for it'. The transept itself provides the enclosing exterior form, and brings into play those emotional connotations of boundary and space upon which Moore's work, in its fullness, depends.

After the Northampton Madonna, an astonishing series of mature works began to flow from him. Intriguingly, the birth of his own child, relatively late in his life, appears to have been one of the factors which encouraged him to realize a theme he had been thinking about for many years – a family group. It was as if he was asking – as even Winnicott finally got round to doing – 'What is the father's role in all this?' But the mothers and children, and also the great reclining figures in stone, elmwood, and bronze, also continued, and I now wish to say something about them.

Moore was very well aware of the way in which his great love of landscape had influenced the making of these figures. He once explained that landscape 'has been for me one of the sources of my energy'. This, of course, is rare among sculptors. Moore's sculptures are usually best seen in the natural landscapes – nowhere better than in the fields round his home at Perry Green in the midst of the Hertfordshire countryside. Very often, Moore relates a piece to the morphology of the landscape where it is situated. You can see this, for example, in the great carved stone reclining memorial figure he cut for the grounds of Dartington Hall where the raised knees echo the hills. But the relationship he proposes between figure and landscape can be more radical than that.

Early on, Moore associated his reclining women with the earth itself. His belief in 'truth to materials' accentuated and drew out the association. A writer in the *Yorkshire Post* perceptively commented about one of the first 'Reclining Women' exhibited in the 1931 exhibition that it was like 'a Grampian landscape'. He referred to its refusal to be separated from the terrestrial rock from which it is hewn. Moore underlined these associations by peaking the breasts and bunching the knees of his reclining women so they appear to us as mountain ranges, or sometimes as more gently rolling lowlands.

In 1959 Moore tried to sum up thirty years of exploration of the reclining female figure as both a nurturing and consoling body, and a landscape. He did this in the great 'Reclining Figure' which he worked at over a five year period. It is a consummate expression of all he knew about the theme at the time he made it; its quiet contrasts with the fact that, during the years he worked on it, his conception of the figure was undergoing cataclysmic changes. Other sculptures he made around this time show how his epic female figures were fragmenting, cleaving into their several parts. The great rocks and cliff faces of breasts, torso, and mountainously raised knees were severing and drifting apart as if some geological convulsion was trembling upwards from the lower strata of Moore's imagination itself.

Moore himself describes the process in a characteristically matter-of-fact way:

> I realised what an advantage a separated two-piece composition could have
> in relating figures to landscape. Knees and breasts are mountains. Once

these two parts become separated you don't expect it to be a naturalistic figure; therefore you can justifiably make it like a landscape or a rock.[28]

Even so, these changes led to some of the strangest of Moore's sculptures based on the female body, sculptures which seem menaced by a constant threat of distintegration, even disappearance. In these works, the illusion seems about to fade into the materials, but is redeemed, only at the last moment, by the cohesive and unifying power of Moore's formal arrangements. Personally, I do not think it was just the accident of a commission which led to the terrifying intensity of 'Atom Piece' of 1964. See how the terrifying 'head' of 'Atom Piece' resembles the interior form within the 'Reclining Figure' of 1945–6 which we looked at earlier. But the great 'Reclining Figure' of 1959 seems to have been an affirmative denial of such disruptive themes; in its mingling of inner and outer into a new kind of unity, in its serenity, authority, and silent equilibrium, it embraces us with all the consoling power of a great secular cathedral in wood. In a single free-standing piece, it offers us the experience, if you will, of the Northampton 'Madonna', and the church which encloses her.

What then are we to make of this extraordinary series of reclining figures? Winnicott, you will remember, once argued that the infant's emotional experience tends to split the mother in two. He distinguished between the 'object mother', who is the specific object of the infant's affections and excited instinctual needs, and the 'environment mother', whose holding, sustaining, and providing provides the ground of the infant's 'going on being' before he becomes a separate person. Elsewhere, I have tried to relate these two poles to the two poles of adult aesthetic experience – that is, to the sort of defined, limited, and formal experiences we describe as 'beautiful', and to the engulfing, suffusing, or oceanic kinds of experience which have traditionally been given the label sublime. The sense of the beautiful has something to do with the object mother, and the sense of the sublime has something to do with the environment mother. The sublime – with its sensations of engulfment – is always tinged with terror, as even Edmund Burke recognized; with a threat of the annihilation of the self, and the subsuming into another. Prior to Henry Moore, the experience of the sublime was possible only in, say, cathedrals, or viewing actual landscapes, or certain kinds of painting. As John Read has put it, 'This blending of human and natural form, this ability to see figures in the landscape, and a landscape in the figures, is Moore's greatest contribution to sculpture.'[29]

But these figures offer more than a new aesthetic experience, or a new view of woman; they speak, by extension, of Moore's vision of the sustaining environment of nature – and indeed of culture itself. If we look back over Moore's work, we cannot help but notice that – with the exception of his unsuccessful 'Stringed Figures', which were partly derived from things seen in the Science Museum – he has eschewed the whole world of mechanical and technological imagery. One of the many meanings of Moore's work seems to me to be that he implies that when we lose sight of our sense of unity with nature, then there is a danger of destroying both ourselves, and, indeed, perhaps nature itself. That is, perhaps, where 'Atom Piece' comes in. Moore presents us with an aesthetic of ecological harmony, which, although unfashionable, can be compared with that of the great cathedrals. He has spoken often enough of his love of organic forms – of 'the growth of branches from the trunk each finding its individual air-space, the texture and variety of grasses, the shape of shells, of pebbles'. But for Moore this organic sense of nature is not something to be set apart from culture, as an alternative to human creativity.[30] As he himself once said, 'Culture, as the word implies, is an organic process. There is no such thing as a synthetic culture, or if there is it is a false and impermanent culture.'[31] I believe that, in his great reclining figures, Moore pointed towards the location of true cultural experience, and he did so in a world in which the 'false and impermanent values' of synthetic substitute for a culture were, of course, elsewhere proliferating.

Before I end I want to offer you a far-flung *excursus*. Moore often spoke about the 'universality' of the mother-and-child theme. And yet, if we look at the art of the past, we find that it is far from ubiquitous. In western art, mother-child imagery only achieves any prominence with the arrival of the Gothic style, and the cult of the Virgin Mary, in the later twelfth century, in France. Indeed, the mother-child theme begins to come into its own with the re-building of Chartres Cathedral, which housed the most famous relic of Our Lady – the actual tunic she was supposed to have worn at the time of the Annunciation. The cult of the Virgin Mary was associated with the architectural and aesthetic efflorescence of European Christendom. Intriguingly, within a hundred years or so, the actual representation of Our Lady had become increasingly intimate, even playful. Truth to materials, and formal novelty, certainly thrived – not just in great cathedrals, but even in details. For example, carvers made ivories of Our Lady and her Child which follow, seemingly naturally, the curve of the elephant's tusk. But gradually, the great Gothic cathedrals ceased; emphasis shifted in representations of the real mother and child towards the image of the *Pieta* – of a woman, old before her time, who weeps over the bleeding face of her increasingly human son.

Now I have written elsewhere of the crisis which secularization and, subsequently, industrialization caused for the arts, and of how their effects were to seal over that playful potential space, where subjective and objective can freely mix. These things led to the domination of human social and productive life by the reality principle. 'The Reality Principle', Winnicott once wrote, 'is the fact of the existence of the world whether the baby creates it or not. It is the arch enemy of spontaneity, creativity, and the sense of Real ... The Reality Principle is an insult.'[32]

Our century has been marked by the intrusion of this reality principle even into art itself, by the destruction of those moments of illusion which art can still offer. At the Hayward Gallery recently you could see Moore's great 'Reclining Figure' of 1959–64, which I was discussing earlier, standing opposite an enormous, volumetric cube of fragments of wood and detritus, put together by one of the most fashionable of the new sculptors, Tony Cragg. Cragg's work is just stuff. Matter. Signifying nothing. In a way, this juxtaposition calls for a decision: a decision between the search for the secular circumstances which can sustain a potential space, in which creativity and culture remain possible; or the continued domination of our lives by the tyranny of the reality principle.

Recently, however, there have been signs that some sculptors, at least, have been prepared to take up the challenge where Moore left off. In particular, I would point you towards the work of Glynn Williams. Here, as in Moore, we can see an interest in the qualities of materials, and a desire to create new sculptural forms. But Williams, too, brings these materials and forms – through 'moments of illusion' – into contact with a world of human values. Roger Scruton has pointed out that in Williams's sculptures, as in Moore's,

> there is an affirmation of the human form which is also a recognition of the spiritual need which speaks through it. The plastic values of these sculptors are not separable from their moral sense: they touch the human form as something sacred, whose meaning transcends the matter that conveys it.[33]

Or, to use Winnicott's terminology, for both Williams and Moore form and matter are transitional.

I have tried to suggest to you strong parallels and continuities in two very different sorts of vision – in Winnicott's psychology and Henry Moore's sculpture and drawings. Both Winnicott and Moore have been concerned with the intimate interaction between the mother and child, and with the significance of those moments of transition, transformation, and illusion, where imagination and reality meet. The prototype of all such moments is surely that in which the mother offers her breast at the moment when the child wants it, thus strengthening, in the child, the feeling that there is an outside world which corresponds to his capacity to create. From these distant beginnings there followed, in both Winnicott and Moore, a vision of culture, indeed of man's relationship to nature itself. But now seems the time to stop unwinding the wool between these two monumental figures, and to let my argument about their maternal imaginations rest. Perhaps there is no better way of tying up the continuities between them than by quoting to you Winnicott's view about artists: 'They do something very valuable for us', he wrote,

> because they are constantly creating new forms and breaking through those forms only to create new ones. Artists enable us to keep alive, when the experiences of real life often threaten to destroy our sense of being alive and real in a living way. Artists best of all people remind us that the struggle between our impulses and a sense of security (both of which are vital to us)

is an eternal struggle and one that goes on inside each one of us as long as our life lasts.[34]

Unfortunately, what Winnicott says is not true of all artists. I hope I've said enough to indicate that it is true of Henry Moore – pre-eminently so.

Notes

1 See D. W. Winnicott, *The Maturational Processes and the Facilitating Environment*, The Hogarth Press and The Institute of Psycho-Analysis, London, 1965, p. 39.
2 D. W. Winnicott, *Playing and Reality*, Penguin, Harmondsworth, 1974, p. 152.
3 *Op. cit.*, p. 45.
4 For D. W. Winnicott's attitude towards Melanie Klein see his paper, 'A personal view of the Kleinian contribution', in *The Maturational Processes and the Facilitating Environment*, The Hogarth Press and The Institute of Psycho-Analysis, London, 1965, pp. 171–8.
5 David Mitchinson (ed.), *Henry Moore Sculpture with Comments by the Artist*, London, Macmillan, 1981, p. 212.
6 *Op. cit.*, p. 50.
7 Philip James (ed.), *Henry Moore on Sculpture*, Macdonald, London, 1966, p. 220.
8 For an introduction to Winnicott's basic ideas – on which these remarks are based – see Peter Fuller, *The Naked Artist*, Writers and Readers, London, 1983.
9 See Winnicott's seminal paper 'Transitional objects and transitional phenomena', in his *Playing and Reality*, Penguin, Harmondsworth, 1974, pp. 1–30.
10 For a full discussion of this 'third area' see the papers gathered in the latter part of Winnicott's *Playing and Reality*, Penguin, Harmondsworth, 1974, especially 'The location of cultural experience', pp. 112–21.
11 *Op. cit.*, p. 128.
12 *Op. cit.*, p. 118.
13 Charles Rycroft, in Peter Fuller (ed.), *Psychoanalysis and Beyond*, Chatto & Windus, London, 1985.
14 Madeleine Davis and David Wallbridge, *Boundary and Space*, Karnac, London, 1981, p. 143.
15 *Op. cit.*, p. 146.
16 Philip James (ed.), *Henry Moore on Sculpture*, Macdonald, London, 1966, p. 146.
17 *Op. cit.*, p. 50.
18 Henry Moore, *Henry Moore at the British Museum*, British Museum Publications, London, 1981, p. 125.
19 For Moore's statements on his changing attitudes to stone carving see Philip James (ed.), *Henry Moore on Sculpture*, Macdonald, London, 1966, p. 135.
20 *Op. cit.*, p. 113.
21 *Op. cit.*, p. 68.
22 David Mitchinson (ed.), *Henry Moore Sculpture with Comments by the Artist*, Macmillan, London, 1981, p. 65.
23 *Op. cit.*, p. 228.
24 *Op. cit.*, p. 81.
25 *Op. cit.*, p. 88.
26 Will Grohmann, *The Art of Henry Moore*, Thames & Hudson, London, 1960, 8 p. 137.
27 Eric Neumann, *The Archetypal World of Henry Moore*, Princetown University Press, Princetown, 1959.

28 Philip James (ed.), *Henry Moore on Sculpture*, Macdonald, London, 1966, p. 266.

29 John Read, *Portrait of an Artist: Henry Moore*, André Deutsch, London, 1979, p. 82.

30 See for example Philip James (ed.) *Henry Moore on Sculpture*, Macdonald, London, 1966, p. 68, for Moore's discussion of the continuing importance of organic form in his work.

31 *Op. cit.*, p. 90.

32 Madeleine Davis and David Wallbridge, *Boundary and Space*, Karnac, London, 1981, p. 57.

33 Roger Scruton, 'Aesthetic atheist', *The Listener*, 20 June 1985, p. 26.

34 Madeleine Davis and David Wallbridge, *Boundary and Space*, Karnac, London, 1981, p. 50.

Chapter Two

Early modern painting in Europe: the psychopathological dimension

Brandon Taylor

What interests me in this chapter is the period of early modern European art in which the word 'expression' became widely used in *avant garde* circles for the first time; the period, roughly, between the turn of the present century and the beginning of the First World War.[1] This period is also the one in which the concept of the 'self' became firmly established within *avant garde* discussions – or re-established, one should say, after its earlier appearance in Romanticism. For I want to argue that during this period *avant garde* artists became able to do through the activity of painting what therapists today do with their patients – namely explore aspects of feeling that are often not accessible by other means. But the way they did so, of course, was very different.

We first of all need to recognize that early modern European art has a psychopathological dimension – a fact all too often neglected by art historians. And, second, we shall need to explain why the stylistic conventions used to embody this art diverge so markedly from paintings produced solely for the sake of their psychopathology at around the same time; such as the celebrated case studies made by Prinzhorn and published some fifteen years later.[2]

Let me take straight away the singular case of Kandinsky, the Russian-born artist who came to dominate at least one corner of early modern art in Germany before 1914. I do not propose to summarize the literary, artistic, and philosophical influences that played upon Kandinsky, either in his native background in Russia, or in Munich itself. The list of important and merely notorious characters who played a part in Kandinsky's intellectual growth is simply too long to elucidate. We have probably all heard something of the Cosmics who gathered around the poet Stephen George and his magazine *Blätter für die Kunst* – a circle which included mystics, spiritualists, vitalists, graphologists, anthropologists, and believers in imminent world-apocalypse, as well as poets and literary men; while close by lay Rudolf Steiner and his evolving theosophical doctrine which later (in 1913) changed itself into anthroposophy.

There is enough even in this short list of fashionable names to explain how it could be that when Kandinsky wrote his influential book *Concerning the Spiritual in Art* before 1912, he could state that painting could contribute to the 'reconstruction, already beginning ... of ... the epoch of great spirituality'.[3] His own time, he argued, was transitional. It sat between an old age of materialism and a new era of the spirit. He saw this transitional time as one of 'jangled nerves', 'storm and tempest ... broken chains ... antithesis and contradiction' – qualities which he believed should be reflected in art in order to awaken people's consciousness of the gradual movement forward into this 'epoch of the great spiritual'. In front of this particular intellectual background we find, indeed, that Kandinsky's paintings are in several ways devoted to the embodiment of the great crisis through which he felt Europe was passing. In his 'thematic' and 'apocalyptic' paintings between 1908 and about 1913 we find that the antithetical forces of the wholly good and the wholly bad are never kept separate, but always intermingled as if the balance between them were never precise. Sometimes bad predominates clearly over good, as when the deluge pitches the whole of life into a watery chaos; and sometimes good predominates over bad, as when All Saints' Day or the Last Judgement announces the final victory of Christ and the beginning of his reign of a thousand years. Certain benign 'deluge' pictures on the other hand seem to invoke the existence of a countervailing good, represented by human figures still safely ensconced in their boats of voyage, or clinging bravely to pieces of driftwood. And some of the 'paradise' pictures of the same period can be seen similarly as announcing the possibility of total good, but remain unable to deny the presence of bad elements which always threaten – a storm, black spots, or distant turbulences in the atmosphere which threaten the establishment of a completely peaceful order in the world.

In explaining the occurrence of these paintings at this particular historical juncture one can obviously point to objective external events such as the rise in tension which preceded the outbreak of war in August 1914. But the psychopathological dimension is equally interesting. (Kandinsky himself tended to play down any connection with the war and to see his work as a representation of the 'terrible struggle ... going on in the spiritual atmosphere'.) Certainly, we can see these paintings as evidence of an emotional struggle taking place within the artist. Jung, you will remember, took a similar view of the significance of the original apocalyptical images received by St John, from which Kandinsky's paintings are derived. Jung says that apocalyptical images only rise up in those who suppress negative feelings and consciously strive for a perfection which is unattainable. He sees psychological apocalypse as a necessary prelude to certain kinds of psychological rebirth – as well as a drama of good and evil on a cosmic scale.[4] Kandinsky's biographer Will Grohmann tells us that Kandinsky suffered a nervous breakdown in the late part of 1907, torn by what Grohmann calls 'psychological and intellectual conflicts'. Historically it was from this point onwards that the apocalyptical themes first appear in Kandinsky's work, to continue for some five or six years in a more or less unrelenting flow. Kandinsky's second wife, Nina, refers to the 'years of internal conflict, search, sometimes of depression' that preceded her husband's discovery of a new kind of painting style around 1908 or 1909.[5] It fits the pattern of Kandinsky's life precisely that apocalypse should have been the theme in the years before 1914.

But it is not only the themes of apocalyptical destruction and rejuvenation that made Kandinsky's modernism interesting from a psychopathological point of view. It is the treatment of the actual surface of the painting where the most powerfully affective interchanges take place. We have Kandinsky's own testimony that in a general way he viewed the activity of painting as both releasing and redemptive – and also extremely difficult. Painting 'alone had the power to lift me beyond time and space' he wrote in an autobiographical essay published in 1913.[6] But the paintings themselves have special qualities. In the first place they are flat, even by comparison with Kandinsky's earlier work. The drawing is incomplete and suggestive. The colour is anti-naturalistic and bright – what in the more usual jargon would be called 'abstract'. Kandinsky had by this time come to believe that a painting should work slowly, and not be graspable all at once. It was for this reason that he adopted the device of 'stripping' (*blosgelegten*) an image of its customary form, principally by giving it a partial outline so that more than one image might be suggested by it. Next, he worked out a method of 'veiling' (*verschlierten*) the image by such means as placing it where it would not necessarily be expected, by blurring its outline and by changing the colour of an object in an intentionally misleading way.

These tactics of 'stripping' and 'veiling' the image did away with exact representation while retaining a bare sense of what the object was. Objects, he convinced himself, were not necessary to art; otherwise they would have been more roundly described by artists like Monet and Wagner – whose work seemed to lack them. (In any case, he argued, they appealed only to possessive and materialistic instincts in the viewer.) More crucially, we read in Kandinsky's writings of a kind of nervous insecurity that beset him about the stability of the physical world. He writes of Rutherford's subdivision of the atom, that it seemed to him 'like the crumbling of the whole world'. This suggested to Kandinsky that the material world was actually unsafe. 'Suddenly the heaviest walls toppled. Everything became uncertain, tottering and weak. I would not have been surprised if a stone had dissolved in the air in front of me and became invisible.'[7]

This very concern with the collapse and disintegration of objects may be read as an anxiety about change, about identity, perhaps even about death. But a concern with the limits and character of personal identity are also obviously present in Kandinsky's famous idea of 'internal necessity' or 'inner necessity' which occurs in most of his writings after about 1908. The vitalist philosophy of a Cosmic like Ludwig Klages would have made good use of the term – but here again Kandinsky puts the idea to use in his own way. Inner necessity, he believes, was the 'unchanging principle' which should underlie every decision the artist makes. In some passages he makes inner necessity widely inclusive, summarizing both subjective, historical, and trans-historical aspects of art. In others, he grounds it in an intuitive, authentic, 'inner' voice of the artist, which he claims is the only true datum by which art can proceed. The artist, as he puts it, 'must watch his own inner life and hearken to the demands of internal necessity'.[8]

Indeed the similarity between Kandinsky's 'inner necessity' and the modern meaning of phrases like 'the subjective', 'the unconscious', 'the intuitive', 'the spontaneous', and 'the irrational' receives support from that other metaphor he uses so often to describe the creative process – the metaphor of the horse and rider. The horse and rider appear literally in his works in numerous guises – as St George, as a traveller, and so on. But the significance of the horse deepens when we find Kandinsky comparing it to the 'creative power' within him that needed harnessing and controlling. 'With the passage of the years' he writes in 1913,

> I have now learnt somewhat to control this creative power. I have trained myself not simply to let myself go, but to bridle the power working within me, to guide it .... The horse bears the rider with strength and speed. But the rider guides his horse. Talent carries the artist to great heights with strength and speed. But the artist guides his talent.[9]

I need hardly spell out the ways in which this image stands metaphorically for the relation between primary and secondary processes, between ego and id. Internal necessity was the id – the horse image – which needed understanding, harnessing, and then putting to use.

Psychopathology is no less interesting in the difficult case of Cubism. Art historians have tended to argue that little more was at issue in Cubism – in the whole of Cubism – than the elaborate working-out of a new way of making pictures which were flat, spatially disjointed, sometimes geometrical, in order to present reality in a new, analytical, and perhaps even 'scientific' way. The emotional, affective content of Cubism has been presented as being zero. Picasso, however, as we know from his later work, was nothing if not an emotional painter, capable of an astonishing range of moods, styles, feelings. It might just have occurred to us before that his Cubist period was unlikely to be an exception to this general rule.[10]

Picasso's aggressions on the female body start with the portrait of Gertrude Stein in 1907, where the face is slightly separated from the head and shoulders. Then, from 1907 to 1910, the female body is subjected to a range of violations which stand uneasily with the seductive poses of many of Picasso's figures. Whatever meanings are assigned to individual figures – the fatal dangers of venereal disease is the latest in a long line of possibilities for the Demoiselles d'Avignon[11] – there is no escaping the fact that the angularization of the female torso represents more than just a sharpening of its literal form. Picasso is endowing the female figure with persecutory attributes, or else inflicting damage on the female form in retaliation, it would seem, for some real or imaginary pain caused to him.

A purely cultural reading of these paintings might accuse them (and here I cite another interpretation) of constituting 'the rock foundation of sexist anti-humanism'; an attempted justification of 'the domination of women by men'[12] at a time when the suffragette movement was making its first stirrings in the European countries, just as it was in Britain. But such readings constitute only a partial account of Picasso's work.

Certainly there is more in these works than meets the sociologist's eyes alone. By 1910, for example, the aggressions perpetrated on the outside form of the body give way to a superficially more abstract phase of work which I think can best be described by saying that the female body is now being rendered – and openly attacked – in terms of its insides. When Picasso returned to Paris from his trip to Cadaques in Catalonia in the autumn of 1910, what had occurred was a breakthrough in his work, not just to a new formal 'solution', as is so often alleged, but to a new level of affective feeling. Firstly, there is the opening up of the closed form of the body. But this penetration of the female body is followed, in 1911 and the beginning of 1912, by what are best called substitutions, in which the explicit form of the female body is all but abandoned in favour of other objects and forms.

One fairly ubiquitous substitution, for example, replaces the form of the head or the body with a violin, a guitar, or a mandolin. Of the several hundred images produced in the brief collage phase of 1911 to 1913, there are many which rely upon an obvious analogy between the form of the guitar and the human head, in which the double-curve of the guitar becomes the cheek and forehead of a male head, echoing a similar double-curve in the ear;[13] or in which it resembles the features of a female head,[14] with the curves of the guitar doubling as her wavy hair to the left or right;[15] or in which the characteristic 'f' holes in the violin have become eyes, and in one case[16] the scroll of the violin has become a curl of hair atop a singing face. A variation on this theme makes the guitar mimic the form of the female body, either standing[17] or recumbent[18] or as an attribute.[19] In these, the double-curve of the musical instrument stands for the breasts or the buttocks, the sound hole for the stomach or the vagina, and the neck and scroll of the violin for the neck and head, sometimes embellished with a pair of keys which repeat the breasts in a manner which Picasso was to pick up again in his Surrealist work. In fact it is extremely unusual for Picasso's *papier collés* not to have some relation to the forms of the body. Even the well-known 'Bottle of Suze', which contains no overt bodily descriptions, is constructed around a basic spine-like structure (sometimes called the 'armature of Cubism') with a bodily mass at centre and internal organs within.

The concealment of the female body within the shapes and textures of the Cubist surface is nowhere more evident than in the well-known series of images which Picasso dedicated, covertly, to his mistress Eva Gouel (actual name Marcelle Humbert). Picasso had met Eva at the Steins back in the autumn of 1911; but since his 'official' woman-friend was still Fernande Olivier, he had at that stage a good reason for keeping the dedications secret. The famous painting known as 'Ma Jolie', painted in the autumn of 1911 and now in New York, is presumed to be the first covert reference to Eva in Picasso's work; the phrase 'ma jolie' is taken from a then popular song. The painting itself appears to contain a woman with a guitar (or possibly a zither) but both she and it are hidden in an impossible system of triangulations and can hardly be seen at all. By the summer of the next year he was to begin to refer to Eva directly in his paintings; announcing to Kahnweiler by letter (12 June) that 'I love her very much and I shall write her name on my pictures'. This he indeed does in the so-called 'Violin: "Jolie Eva"' of that summer, where a guitar lies horizontal with neck to the right; and in the better-known 'Guitar "J'Aime Eva"' of the same period, in which the curvaceous form of the guitar is unmistakeably female. Picasso wrote the words 'j'aime Eva' on a gingerbread heart and stuck it on the picture below the curves, as a kind of pendant. Subsequently, in the main phase of *papier collé* activity of the next two years, the words 'Eva' and 'Ma Jolie' do not appear at all. However, the guitar remains a persistent theme, and explicit references to a single woman are replaced by punning references to sex or to the body. Well-known examples of this are the inclusions of the letters JO or JOU, which pun not only on the French *jouailler*, to play a musical instrument badly, but also on *jouer*, to play, or *jouir*, to reach an orgasm.

It would be wrong however to give the impression that all Picasso's collage constructions involved references either to his lovers, to women in general, or to sex. They do not. Indeed, even when these references can be teased out, it is their very inscrutability which is striking and at the same time perplexing to the viewer. Furthermore, the inscrutability of Picasso's method – the success of his concealments – comes in degrees. Sometimes a sexual reference is virtually explicit, as in the 'Man with a Violin'[20] of autumn 1912, which presents the violin in place of the genitals and makes the double-curve into the testicles; or the 'Still-Life Au Bon Marché'[21] of early 1913 in which the reference is to sex purchased for money; a newspaper clipping at lower centre says 'Trou ici' ('hole here'), while the female figure appears at the top with an underwear advertisement in between. The words 'Facilités de paiement 20 mois' and 'massage' provide a heading above. In other cases the submerged theme is all but invisible, certainly below the level of conscious creation. An example of this is the 'Guitar'[22] of spring 1913, which suggests a couple locked together in lovemaking, but with irony added in the form of an advertisement for a 'Dr Casasas, specialist in genital complaints' which appears on the penetrating male member at lower left. Many another *papier collé* work contains a hint of a figure or two figures in half-formed images of erection or recumbency, replete with bodily organs both internally and externally displayed.

But what do such substitutions mean? Traditionally they have been assigned a place within a system of humorous puns that may have been typical of the studio manners of the artists themselves – their conversations, their jokes. This is all well and good, up to a point. But psychoanalytic thinking has a different proposal to make on this subject which makes human as opposed to merely sociological sense and which throws light on how one type of Surrealism began.

Some years ago Marion Milner wrote a paper on 'The role of illusion in symbol-formation'[23] in which she proposed, I think convincingly, that such substitutions in mental life can either reflect an experience of fusion between the two things concerned, as in pre-logical or 'primitive' thinking, or that (what is surely more likely here) they bring two dissimilar things together in order that one of them might be concealed lest it stimulate emotions which the artist wishes to hide. According to a speculation by Melanie Klein, the identification of one thing with another is 'the foundation of all sublimation and every talent, since it is by way of symbolic equation that things, activities and interests become the subject of libidinal phantasies'.[24] It is a further remark by Mrs Klein, however, that throws such a strong light on the characteristic symbolisms of Picasso's collage phase. She says that the mechanisms of identification are set in motion by anxiety arising in the highly sadistic pre-genital phase, the phase in which the child attempts 'to possess himself of the contents of the mother's body and to destroy her by means of every weapon which sadism can command'. The child conceives a dread of these organs lest they retaliate with equal ferocity, and the resultant anxiety makes him 'equate the organs in question with other things; owing to this equation these in turn become objects of anxiety, and so he is impelled constantly to make other and new equations'.[25]

My brief analysis suggests that for Picasso if not for others, Cubism was an affective rather than a formal style, having a vivid and perhaps near-universal emotional content; that it focused and articulated his conflicts in a visually novel form; and that his status as an important artist can be attributed, in part, to his ability to reach back to infantile modes of thinking in a compelling and authentic way.

I am convinced, in fact, that many of the important artists of Picasso's generation – before 1914, when world events precipitated their own changes – were in some way implicated in a dual pictorial process of destruction and control – 'control at the price of destruction' was the phrase Ernst Kris[26] used in his discussion of caricature.

The phrase also applies to an artist like Matisse, in so far as his technique becomes the subject of our attention. Matisse, of course – and here I refer in extreme brevity to a small phase of his prewar work – is generally thought of as a relaxed, hedonistic, even serene painter who wanted a painting to be 'like a good armchair in which to rest from physical fatigue', to quote his well-known statement from 'Notes of a painter'.[27] But I want to ask whether we really understand this remark in the way we should. To do so, I propose we go back to the divisionist phase of Matisse's work, in the later part of 1904 and the early part of 1905, the date of his 'Luxe, Calme et Volupté'. On the level of content the work is highly problematic. It shows an idealized bathing scene of full light and rich colour; and yet we know from contemporary reports (of Edmund Cross in particular) that Matisse was in a 'madly anxious' mood that summer. Certainly his domestic circumstances were not conducive to relaxed bathing parties by the sea; he was recently married with a young family, and would scarcely have taken part in a nude bathing party himself. But we have Matisse's own judgement on the conflicts within 'Luxe, Calme et Volupté'; for he soon complained to Signac, who by then owned the picture, that the drawing which is linear, and the painting, which is not, are 'absolutely contradictory'. Already it becomes apparent that the technique in which the painting was constructed had become, for Matisse, an important determinant of meaning. His anxiety here was that the technique he had used was internally inconsistent. It is hardly surprising that no clear relationship could and id. Internal necessity was the id – the horse image – which needed understanding, harnessing, and then putting to use.

It was presumably in answer to this impasse that Matisse gave up Neo-Impressionist divisionism in the following year, 1905, when he began again, this time at Collioure, to formulate a style that was in some sense adequate to his ambitions. Here, in the style that became known as 'wild beast' or Fauve, he abandons all tonal contrasts of light against dark. He applies paint thickly, sometimes leaving parts of the canvas untouched, and brightens his colour in ways that are astonishing to see but never easy to describe. In fact I believe these paintings do inaugurate the beginnings of an authentic and gratifying style – but how they do so needs explanation. In the first place, by abandoning tonal relations between the parts of a picture he became free to set up purer relationships between the elements of a picture that had never before been attempted in this particular way. The contrasts between equal-valued hues, particularly, helps create a method of expressing light rather than of describing it; the animating relationship is now within the painting rather than along the axis between the artist and his work.

Later on Matisse was to reflect back on this period of manic intensity and speak about 'the dominating anxiety of Fauvism', which, he explained, was nothing more nor less than the problem of answering the question 'What do I want?' He speaks about the artist who is 'encumbered with all the techniques of the past' before he comes upon this momentous question. 'If he starts within himself, and makes just three spots of colour', Matisse went on, 'he finds the beginning of a release from such constraints.' One needed, he said, to 'recognise the quality of your desire', for only the man who has 'meditated upon himself for a certain length of time ... can act effectively'.[28]

These brief statements should be sufficient to indicate that, for Matisse, style – by which I mean the manner and means of paint application – had become an enormously significant vehicle for statement and counter-statement, by which the painter could somehow find out what his sensibilities were. In fact the Fauve paintings marked the beginning of this process, not its conclusion. After the excitement of Fauvism, Matisse began to seek something more – something more stable, more complex, certainly something more difficult to achieve. Our guide here is again the essay 'Notes of a Painter' that Matisse reluctantly published in 1908 to explain the nature of his work to a still sceptical audience. One of the key ideas in 'Notes of a Painter' is that the impression conveyed by the whole picture is more important than the details: 'I do not insist on all the details of the face, on setting them down with anatomical exactitude' he wrote apropos his Italian model Bevilaqua. 'A work of art must carry within itself its complete significance and impose that upon the beholder even before he recognises the subject.'[29] He speaks of the 'condensation of sensations', by which he means extracting an essence from his sensations of nature which would then stand autonomously for the 'spirit' of the real thing. 'The almost unconscious transcription of the meaning of the model is the initial act of every work of art', he wrote later. Gauguin, like other Symbolists, had spoken of 'dreaming his subject'. Matisse extended the metaphor by saying that he wished to depart from nature 'only to interpret her more fully'.[30]

It is tempting to compare Matisse's processes of condensation, simplification, and elimination to the processes Freud had postulated for the dreamwork only a few years before. Certainly Matisse's technique around 1907 became extraordinarily sketchy, provisional, and incomplete. And on looking at the paintings we can certainly understand the force of Felix Vallaton's perceptive description after the Salon d'Automne of that year. Vallaton, having mentioned the 'hypnotic and broken draughtsmanship' of 'Le Luxe I' in particular, postulates that these 'can record without betrayal the meanderings of his [Matisse's] sensibility'.[31]

Indeed 'meanderings' is precisely the word here. Matisse seemed to know that his informal and broken draughtsmanship, his opaque yet suggestive subject-matter, was somehow essential to the end which he wished his paintings to fulfil. For he wanted this to be the achievement of pleasure of a certain very definite kind. When he made that famous statement that a painting should act upon the beholder 'like an appeasing influence, like a mental soother, something like a good armchair in which to rest from physical fatigue',[32] he was far from advocating the use of appeasing subject-matter for its own sake. In fact, far from proposing a kind of tranquillizing principle for art, he was proposing a profound sense of serenity that he believed was available from painting if it was engaged with and understood in a certain way.

Many people will have noticed a curious but interesting phenomenon in Matisse's later drawings, which is that they divide fairly neatly into those that consist of a single outline, executed in a single movement without erasure;

and those which consist of a quite opposite conglomeration of rubbings out, re-workings and changes of decision which in some cases reduce the paper to a blur of smudged grey charcoal or lead. The first of these tendencies is well exemplified in the paintings of 1907 that were probably about contemporaneous with 'Notes of a painter'. I think it could be said that this radical incompleteness in the finished product offered something like an invitation to the beholder to fill in the remaining detail for himself. 'Serenity' here results from the work the beholder has to do in completing something in phantasy which is offered to him incomplete.

Matisse's second tendency, which is in a way the converse of the first, initially appears on a grand scale in 'Music', the second of the two panels commissioned by Schukine, two years later, for his Moscow house. Here, Matisse takes the novel step of dispensing altogether with a preliminary sketch (such as had been used for the earlier 'Dance' panel), now taking the liberty of simply painting over a previous design in order to bring the picture to a new state of realization. Matisse seemed aware that this process signalled a departure, for he took the trouble to have the painting photographed several times while he was working on it – something he had not done before. So we know from these photographs that the composition was altered radically between the first and second states; and from the second state to its final form, the last transformation of which eliminated a sleeping dog and several bunches of wild flowers that had been there before.

The importance of this new 'layering' technique derives from the visible fact that Matisse actually leaves most of the previous work still dimly visible underneath, whence it shines through the uppermost layer like a fossil record of the pre-history of the picture. What this now signifies is that previous 'errors' have been accommodated by change rather than by banishment or destruction. They are now tolerated, loved, and given a life within the richness of the final surface. Matisse would often describe, later in his life, how he would gradually move forward in the construction of a painting, often through a sequence of failures, until something final and resolved was eventually achieved. At each stage he said 'I reach a balance, a conclusion. At the next sitting, if I find a weakness in the whole, I find my way back into the picture by means of the weakness. I re-enter through the breach – and reconceive the whole.'[33]

'I re-enter through the breach and reconceive the whole': the unintended references here to birth and procreation may tempt us to see the method as a kind of fertility rite which the artist had been conducting with himself, with his paintings as offspring. 'At the final stage', Matisse said elsewhere, 'the painter finds himself freed and his emotion exists complete in his work. He himself, in any case, is relieved of it.' The rules by which nature is thus transformed come 'from me', Matisse asserted, 'and not from my subject . . . it is from the basis of my interpretation that I continually react until my work comes into harmony with me'.[34]

Here then is further evidence that the psychopathology of the early modern painting was centred in its surface; in its method of being marked, drawn upon, inflected, held together, broken. 'Control at the price of destruction' was the formula Kris later used to describe the process of caricature. In fact it seems to summarize most of the surface marking devices of early modern painting, in so far as they have a psychopathological dimension. Matisse was involved in a dual process of destruction and rejuvenation, in so far as he resolved one act of destruction by coming to tolerate the remains of that which had been destroyed. Kandinsky also, as we saw, immersed himself in this process of the destruction of objects – but not beyond the point where a new kind of unity could be perceived, even admits the marks of the fractured object-world. Picasso too, more clearly bent on destruction than most through his fragmented and broken bodies – most of them female – nevertheless retains a minimal sense of unity and coherence in what has been destroyed; a unity which prevented him, if you like, from collapsing into total psychic dissociation in what he was trying to achieve.

But it is now necessary to ask, simply, why this should be so. Why was it that in the *avant garde* of pre-First World War Europe, the emotional power of painting rested not in its illusions or its dramatic qualities, but in its surface – its way of being flat. The answer, I think, lies in the presence of two factors which came into play at this historical moment in European culture but which have nothing intrinsically to do with the psychopathological process. One of these factors concerns the conditions of artistic production in *avant garde* circles at the time: and the other concerns the observer.

Avant garde art had only come into existence in Europe a mere two generations previously, around 1870; or, if you stretch the point, at the beginning of the nineteenth century with the Romantic upheaval in cultural values generally. In signalling a vivid opposition to academic naturalism, it suited this *avant garde* art to become flat, as well as relatively explicit in terms of how it was made. This was the most obvious way in which academicism could be transgressed.

But this tendency of painting in the early twentieth century to become flat and explicit was predicated on a further assumption, namely that of the artist as a worker, as someone who wished to announce his sympathies, not only in dress and behaviour but in the things he made, with the artisan rather than with the middle class or with the aristocratic devotees of the academy. The surface, here, was his place of work, the place where he felt things could be manipulated and manufactured. I believe we can say that the 'flatness' that has so often been noticed as an essential quality of modern art was in fact, in part, nothing more nor less than a display of workmanship in the old-fashioned sense. For men, it was within or alongside this artisanal ethic of flat workmanship that the personal, subjective markings of the early modern picture came to be positioned. Thus, to some extent this also explains the maleness of early modernism, its domination by men and its virtual exclusion of women. Women never adopted this method in anything like the same way.

The observer's condition has something to do with the taste of the urban intellectual, who by 1900 was immersed in the artistic traditions of the west, but who, as Gombrich pointed out, had come by this time to depend upon a certain oral 'crunchiness' in what he consumed in pictures.[35] To put it differently, this observer had become interested by the turn of the present century in taking risks in his perceptual attitudes, in tolerating the discomfort of the aggressive component in perception in return for a new kind of balance with an increasingly pleasurable subject-matter – the naked body in particular. Rather than yield to the obvious seduction of the saccharine or the overly sentimental, he was now prepared to make his own discoveries, to risk his own aggressive identifications in the consumption of the picture. His preference for the 'crunchy' rather than the 'soft' encouraged the very types of surface whose construction and destruction by artists we have been considering in this chapter.

These are some of the reasons why the psychopathology of the modern picture has to be elucidated in terms of its flatness, its surface, its manner of being made. It isn't that flatness is *naturally* a symptom of a psychopathological process. It may have lent itself to psychopathology; but the fact remains that it had come to dominate the early twentieth-century *avant garde* largely for other reasons.

The psychopathological paradigm of 'control at the price of destruction' (or of 'reparation', to use Mrs Klein's metaphor) summarizes the facts and achievements of early modern painting in a way that perhaps no other paradigm can; though its applicability here depends upon historical factors which have nothing to do with psychopathology pure and simple. Prinzhorn's subjects, though also trafficking in subjectivity, were not touched by these factors, and knew nothing of the discourse of 'advanced' art surrounding Kandinsky, Picasso, and Matisse. Though concerned with similar questions, their 'subjectivity' was contained within a different discourse – a split between professions which, regrettably, remains firmly in place today.

Notes

1 M. H. Abrams dates the earliest use of the word 'expression' in literary and poetic criticism to the 1830s; for example John Stuart Mill's characterization of poetry as 'the expression and uttering forth of feeling' of 1833: see M. H. Abrams, *The Mirror and the Lamp*, Oxford University Press, 1953, p. 208.
2 H. Prinzhorn, *Artistry of the Mentally Ill*, Springer Verlag, Berlin, 1922.
3 This and the following quotations are taken from W. Kandinsky, *Concerning the Spiritual in Art*, Wittenborn edition, New York, 1970 (originally published in 1912 by R. Piper & Co., Verlag, Munich).
4 C. G. Jung, 'Answer to Job', in his *Collected Works*, vol. II, Routledge & Kegan Paul, London, 1952, pp. 438ff. For a different but equally illuminating case study

see S. Freud, 'Psychoanalytic notes on an autobiographical account of a case of paranoia (dementia paranoides)', in his *Standard Edition*, vol. XII, The Hogarth Press, London, 1911.

5   N. Kandinsky, Preface to W. Kandinsky, *Concerning the Spiritual in Art*, Wittenborn edition, New York, 1970, p. 10 (originally published in 1912 by R. Piper & Co., Verlag, Munich).

6   W. Kandinsky, 'Ruckblicke', in R. L. Herbert (ed.), *Modern Artists on Art*, Prentice Hall, New Jersey, 1913, p. 25.

7   *Op. cit.*, p. 27.

8   W. Kandinsky, *Concerning the Spiritual in Art*, Wittenborn edition, New York, 1970, p. 63 (originally published in 1912 by R. Piper & Co., Verlag, Munich).

9   W. Kandinsky, 'Ruckblicke', in R. L. Herbert (ed.), *Modern Artists on Art*, Prentice Hall, New Jersey, 1913, pp. 32–3.

10 A version of this and succeeding paragraphs appeared in Chapter 3 of B. Taylor, *Modernism, Post-Modernism, Realism*, Winchester School of Art Press, 1987.

11 M. Leja, 'Le vieux marcheur' and 'Les deux risques: Picasso, prostitution, venereal disease and maternity', *Art History*, vol. 8, no. 1, March, 1985.

12 C. Duncan, 'Virility and domination in early twentieth century vanguard painting', *Art Forum*, December, 1973, pp. 30–9.

13 C. Zervos, *Pablo Picasso*, vol. II, Cahiers d'art, Paris, 1923–78, no. 403; P. Daix and J. Rosselet, *Picasso, The Cubist Years 1907–16*, Thames & Hudson, London, no. 592.

14 Zervos, *op. cit.*, nos 420, 427, 426; Daix and Rosselet, *op. cit.*, nos 588–90.

15 Zervos, *op. cit.*, nos 771–2, 774; Daix and Rosselet, *op. cit.*, nos 517–19.

16 Daix and Rosselet, *op. cit.*, no. 519.

17 Zervos, *op. cit.*, no 409; Daix and Rosselet, *op. cit.*, no 525.

18 Zervos, *op. cit.*, no 413; Daix and Rosselet, *op. cit.*, no 521.

19 Zervos, *op. cit.*, no 330; Daix and Rosselet, *op. cit.*, no 563.

20 Zervos, *op. cit.*, no 399; Daix and Rosselet, *op. cit.*, no 535.

21 Zervos, *op. cit.*, no 378; Daix and Rosselet, *op. cit.*, no 557.

22 Zervos, *op. cit.*, no 348; Daix and Rosselet, *op. cit.*, no 608.

23 M. Milner, 'The role of illusion in symbol-formation', in M. Klein and others (eds), *New Directions in Psychoanalysis*, Tavistock, London, 1955.

24 M. Klein, 'The importance of symbol-formation for the development of the ego', in M. Klein, *Love, Guilt and Reparation and Other Works, 1921–45*, Hogarth Press, London, 1975, p. 237 (originally published in 1930).

25 *Op. cit.*, p. 238.

26 E. Kris, *Psychoanalytic Explorations in Art*, International Universities Press, New York, 1952, p. 201.

27 H. Matisse, 'Notes of a painter', in J. Flam, *Matisse on Art*, Phaidon, Oxford, 1973, p. 38 (originally published in 1908).

28 H. Matisse, 'Matisse speaks', in J. Flam, *op. cit.*, p. 132 (originally published in 1952).

29 H. Matisse, 'Notes of a painter', in J. Flam, *op. cit.*, p. 38 (originally published in 1908).

30 *Op. cit.*, p. 39.

31 F. Vallaton, 'Review of Salon d'Automne', *La Grande Review*, 25 Oct., 1907, p. 920.

32 H. Matisse, 'Notes of a painter', in J. Flam, *Matisse on Art*, Phaidon, Oxford, 1973, p. 38 (originally published in 1908).

33 H. Matisse, 'Statements to Teriade', in J. Flam, *op. cit.*, p. 74 (originally published in 1936).

34 *ibid.*

35 E. H. Gombrich, 'Psychoanalysis and the history of art', in his *Meditations on a Hobby Horse*, Phaidon, London, 1963.

Chapter Three

Fantasy and the figurative

David Maclagan

For things beyond the physical world language can only be employed as a sort of adumbration, but never even with approximate exactitude, since in accordance with the physical world it deals only with possession and its connotations. (Kafka, *Notes on Sin, Suffering and the True Way*)

'Imagination', 'dream', and 'fantasy' are slippery concepts by nature. In the theoretical scaffolding that supports therapy, they are often defined in technical, quasi-scientific terms; as though they were 'mechanisms' or 'functions' that have always been in place, the sources of data to be assimilated into a hypothetical model of the psyche. But they are not 'given'; the great psychoanalytic systems elaborated by Freud and Jung, although they derive much of their evidence from art, literature, and philosophy – all of which have acknowledged histories – make the assumption that the characteristics of imaginary experience have always been the same. But imagination should have a history; indeed, its very constitution (in terms of an interior or subjective domain, for example) is as much a cultural invention as it is the natural basis for a description of psychic phenomena. Significantly, we lack a proper history of the imagination, which might provide answers to such questions as: At what point did fantasy begin to acquire its modern association with unreality and subjectivity? And when do notions of a 'self' with a private and interior hinterland expressed in fantasy begin to emerge?[1]

Oppositions between 'outside' and 'inside', 'real' and 'imaginary', and literal and metaphorical are neither necessary nor inevitable: they are, rather, the consequences of a complex set of assumptions about the nature of imagery, and about how 'figures' should translate the invisible into visible terms. 'Making visible' is what the word 'fantasy' means at root, and most imaginative processes (dreams, reveries, visualizations, etc.) seem to revolve around images or 'pictures'. But the question is not so much what is made visible – the kind of image, or the value assigned to it – as how, in what way, are things 'inside' bodied forth in terms of a space, objects, and scenes that borrow the appearance of things 'outside'? The fictitious, secondhand nature of fantasy that supposedly results from this makes it inherently a suspect form of experience, tinged with unreality. Yet arguably the most powerful images, in psychological terms at least, are just such figurative and fantastic images.[2] The idea that fantasy and imagination speak a language that is not really their own, that their idiom is a re-production of external reality, gets support from philosophy, aesthetics, and psychology; it has also been incorporated in the mainstream of post-Renaissance art and rehearsed in a figurative tradition that still exerts a subliminal influence. That influence is all the more deeply ingrained because psychoanalytic theories about imagination and fantasy do not simply use works of art as supporting material; they secretly depend for their concepts on the very same figurative conventions as the evidence they put forward.

This means that the psychoanalytic interpretation of imagery has much more in common with art than its quasi-scientific posture seems to allow. If, out of the full range of interpretive responses, analysis (or therapy) chooses those most strictly governed by 'responsible' conventions, or if it uses a fixed array of concepts ('the penis', 'the parental couple') as a baseline to which images can similarly be reduced, it risks colluding with a structure of meaning which implicitly refers back to a particular, dominant theme, and which is inclined to make any 'figures' strictly accountable to this 'original' basis. Not only are the aesthetic premises that once justified this privilege obsolete (to deny this would be to ignore the history of Modernism), but the result is to confine therapy to a narrow waveband of meaning, and to render its stance both reductive and conservative. Not every form of fantasy conforms to this template, but the pervasive influence of figurative conventions has subtly skewed our understanding of what fantasy typically consists of, and how the images it gives rise to might be understood.

In the history of art, attempts to subject images to some kind of logic of representation and to establish a vocabulary of symbolism – in effect, to try to make them conform to a linguistic mode of signification – seem, at first sight, to have succeeded. But even the most literal, matter-of-fact image has an aura, a fringe of allusion, that no amount of verbal prescription can eliminate; and there is a powerful countercurrent in the history of art, that seeks to capitalize on the mysterious, evocative power of the visual image.[3] Art therapy, standing as it does between the therapeutic need to connect and to articulate, and a creative involvement with imagery that is immediate and inarticulate, is bound to have to deal with this tension between the programmatic and the unaccountable. In the majority of cases, art therapists (or psychiatrists dealing with pictures) operate from a pragmatic perspective – whether it is one of encouragement or of diagnosis. But the issue is not just a theoretical luxury: structures of meaning that regulate the traffic between 'inside' and 'outside', and that effectively license certain forms of expression whilst disqualifying others, have real human consequences; we have an ethical responsibility to re-examine them.[4]

'Psyche *is* image', said Jung. But what is an image? The difficulty we have in deciding between a scribble or a doodle and something that qualifies as an 'image' points to the fact that we expect an image to have a certain formal coherence, to form a 'figure'. But in the therapeutic context from which Jung was speaking, the figure is more than a mere 'gestalt': the image is assumed to be an image *of* something, it is supposed to refer to something beyond itself. Such a figure is likely to belong to a tradition which we know as the 'figurative'[5] and which, if it happens to be superseded in art, still exercises a considerable imaginative influence.[6] The word 'figurative' itself denotes two apparently separate forms of signification: one 'representing a human figure; pertaining to plastic or pictorial representation'; and the other 'not literally true; metaphorical, symbolic'. But these representational and symbolic functions, which appear to distinguish between an image of the real and visible world and a fictitious or symbolic domain, are, in practice, subtly confused.

One reason for this elision between the real and the imaginary is that the imaginary is depicted in terms of external reality; it is *real*-ized in naturalistic terms. In a nativity scene, for example, angels occupy the same space, have the same appearance, as shepherds or cows; apart from some degree of idealization, the cues that declare their other-worldliness are largely iconographic – haloes, wings (themselves a non-biblical invention), etc. The metaphysical, whether it is religious or philosophical in origin, is translated into physical – specifically visual – terms. What is in-visible can only be alluded to, given a fictitious embodiment. But this fiction, this make-believe, is deceptively naturalistic. Often there is no clear indication of where the boundary between reality, apparition, and fantasy has been crossed.[7] Indeed, we have come to expect the visionary to be *visual*, to be couched in perceptual, almost hallucinatory, terms.[8] And the concept of 'hallucination' itself is indicative of the privilege tacitly assigned to the world of external, perceptible, phenomena; when, in the early nineteenth century, it is defined as a key feature of psychopathology, it is precisely because it is a sense-perception that is uncorroborated and therefore illegitimate.[9]

The notion that 'reality' is somehow the prerogative of experience in contact with a world of sense-data that are external and objective, and that dreams, visions, and fantasies belong to a realm that is less solid and correspondingly interior or 'subjective', is a familiar theme in philosophy and science. But these commonplace assumptions are the result of an historical development, in which, while the idea of an objective science concerned with the quantifiable aspects of phenomena develops, so the more elusive and qualitative aspects of experience come to be assigned to a private and subjective realm.[10] If, in reverie, dream, or some other imaginative mode, images emerge from this realm, they must be derivative and secondhand – supposedly mere reproductions of what was originally an authentic, perceptual experience.

The role of art in confirming this split between inner and outer, reality and fantasy, is crucial, for art does not simply record or express what is already there: it actively creates and serves as a conductor for experience.[11] Here the visual arts have a particular responsibility, for it is easy to believe that images and the pictures derived from them are in some way more fundamental than thoughts, or at least than thoughts articulated in words. There is a central issue here, about what kind of 'thinking' or shaping of experience might precede or underlie the thinking of which we are conscious (and here I am including in this latter thinking the deliberate exercise of visualization or fantasy). The effect of pictorial images in the figurative tradition is to support a model of fantasy; but this 'fantasy' is an elaborate fiction that has eclipsed and overruled the status of a more fundamental and deeply metaphoric fantasy, one whose implications are radical in every sense of the word.

I mentioned the root meaning of 'fantasy' – to make visible. In terms of the traditional frontier between inner and outer worlds, fantasy is, in the history of art, a system of *translation*, from the metaphysical into the physical. Like all translations, this making-visible is subject to restrictions and rules. Just as there are complex conventions governing the representation of the visible appearance of things,[12] so there are rules governing the symbolic or 'figurative' function of those representations – most obviously, those formulated by iconography. The basis of these rules is the idea that the image is accountable; that because metaphor, for example, is the result of a translation, it should not stray too far from its original reference and must be properly 'legible'. We acknowledge the impressive power that the artist has, to create and concert images in a coherent imaginary space and thereby convey or express all sorts of ideas and sentiments. But this power is granted at a price; for the other half of the invisible contract is an obligation to follow these conventional guidelines.[13] If the artist's work is judged, against these criteria, to be improper or excessively subjective, it may be disqualified or ignored.

The problem is compounded by the gradual intensification of interest in the expression of personal, or 'original', sensibility, and by the development of a myth of individualistic creativity incarnated in the artist.[14] Since originality is expressed in departures from the conventional, the artist is under increasing pressure to push up against the conservative boundaries of tradition; and this pressure is aggravated by a cult of artistic invention that is relentlessly progressive. With the emergence of the '*avant garde*' and the appearance of those critical fractures that constitute Modernism,[15] the figurative tradition is effectively challenged or undermined to such an extent that it can no longer be taken for granted in good faith.

Yet, at the turn of the century, when figurative conventions are already being seriously challenged in art, a version of them is built into the foundations of Freud's psychoanalytic model of unconscious processes. When he talks about that crucial stage in the dreamwork – one that is, by implication, the prototype for most forms of imagination or fantasy – the turning of 'unconscious thoughts' into pictures, he makes a comparison with the process of deciphering or translating hieroglyphs or rebuses. Although Freud makes a great show of complaining about the virtual absence of a pictorial syntax and the imprecision of images – of which he clearly disapproves – the translations effected by pictures or images in the dreamwork are actually quite strictly regulated – as they are in the rebus.[16]

In the 'pictorialization of thought' (as opposed to other dream ingredients such as memories or circumstantial details) images may have a strictly analogical role (as in the famous equation between penis and umbrella), or they may have a wider symbolic function (as with those carrying fabulous or mythical associations); very often, they are treated in much the same way as 'switch-words', i.e. the unconscious thought is turned into a pun-like image, the innocent half of which fits into the dream-narrative. The business of interpretation is, of course, a reversal of this chain of causation, but what it amounts to is the imposition of an iconographic scheme that is essentially similar in its operation to the figurative apparatus used in art; it even resorts to the same devices of condensation and metonymy. This apparatus is used as much to interpret images as it was (supposedly) to compose them. The 'conditions of representability' through which unconscious thoughts have to effect a passage are not just technical requirements of translation: they entail a subordination of the image to rules and to a discipline that governs their 'reading' as much as it did their original 'inscription'.

Thus, to the iconography deliberately deployed in the figurative tradition of art, there corresponds a parallel and secret iconography deviously employed by those 'unconscious' processes involved in dreaming, imagining, or fantasizing. And just as there is a sophistication, a cultivated finesse, in the traditional understanding and appreciation of 'figures', so there is a sophistication and privilege in the psychoanalytic interpretation of 'unconscious' images. In both cases this privilege depends upon a conventional notion of fantasy and the ways in which it 'figures', that structures and informs the ways in which imagery is constituted, and justifies discrimination between legitimate and illegitimate forms of signification. The privilege consists, not in asserting that the image means only what the convention allows, but in implying that this meaning is the one preferred. The question of what is a proper or improper use of metaphor, for example, is not just a matter of mere hermeneutics, nor even of rhetorical 'hygiene',[17] but a political question. And in a psychiatric context politics often wears a clinical disguise; the disqualification and pathologizing of certain forms of imagery, or the imposition, with the full weight of diagnostic authority, of what amounts to an interpretive straitjacket, are the authoritarian effects of a model of imagination that is inherently conservative.

One example is the persistent tendency in psychiatry to assume that drawings of the human figure by patients who have no known artistic training must naturally conform to a literal and unsophisticated representation; any deviation from the figurative norm can then be fitted into the diagnostic pattern of 'distortion' or 'disorder'.[18] The assumption seems to be that only trained or 'professional' artists disobey the rules of the figurative in ways that have any deeper significance than the symptomatic or the pathological. Since the exercise of artistic 'skill' is, supposedly, a deliberate and largely intentional affair, the same assumptions apply to any 'symbolic' work that cannot easily be read as some kind of 'expression' or 'communication'; such images allegedly present the shell or 'scaffolding' of significance, without any of the prescribed content.[19] Equally, there is a tendency to see work that is, one way or another, 'non-figurative' as being evidence of a withdrawal from reality or a refusal to signify in the proper way.[20] The majority of pictures reproduced in books on art therapy are either figurative, or are interpreted according to a loosely figurative matrix (e.g. by association of colour or forms with body parts or secretions). There is a difficulty, a sense of indirectness, in talking about non-figurative works in a therapeutic context, with which we are all familiar.

In all these cases, the work is treated as naif, arbitrary, or 'unconscious', whilst the ingenuity and subtlety of diagnostic or analytic interpretation assumes a privileged authority, one that, in the politics of psychiatry, is beyond question by the patient.[21]

But suppose 'fantasy' worked differently. Suppose that there isn't some kind of *a priori* idea or 'thought' that is then to be 'translated', in a suitably codified fashion, into 'figurative' images, which are then interpreted according to essentially similar conventions. Suppose, instead, that metaphor, not the 'figurative', was radical, that it was primary, there from the beginning and not inserted in some secondary way on to a literal (and therefore verbally accountable, ultimately analysable) basis. Suppose that the complication and the ingenuity – even the element of paradox and irony – were implicit at this original level and were not solely the prerogative of subsequent interpretive expertise. Suppose, finally, that 'creativity' was neither an automatic, quasi-neurological 'function', nor a supremely sophisticated and highly cultivated achievement, but something more complex and radically 'in between'.

What we would then have to reconsider would be, not just the effects – the unconventional workings of fantasy, the possibility of non-figurative mental imagery,[22] the problems of non-translatable metaphor – but their fundamental implications, as far as the relation between inner and outer worlds, or between imagination and reality, are concerned. We might have to embark on a new kind of therapy as a result.

Notes

1 We have some clues in etymology. Modern usages of 'self' – as in 'self expression' – first appear in the sixteenth and seventeenth centuries.
2 It was for this reason that *The Art of Memory* focused on images that were

designed to be bizarre and impressive (see F. Yates, *The Art of Memory*, Routledge & Kegan Paul, London, 1966).

3   An obvious example would be the Renaissance cult of talismanic images, under neo-Platonic influence, of which Ficino wrote:

> To signify divine mysteries, the Egyptian priests did not use the detail of individual letters, but whole images of plants, trees and animals, since God's knowledge of things is not through numerous thought-processes, but rather through the firm and simple form of a thing (see F. Yates, *Giordano Bruno and the Hermetic Tradition*, Routledge & Kegan Paul, London, 1964).

4   Lichtenberg's comment 'Maybe a good metaphor is something even the police should keep an eye on' has a psychiatric relevance today.

5   The art-historical brackets for this would be approximately 1450–1850.

6   Think of the way in which the naturalistic idiom of most films has expanded on many of the functions once performed by salon painting.

7   Take, for example, the hordes of demons in Grunewald's 'Temptation of St Anthony', who almost overwhelm the saint in pictorial terms.

8   Even as orthodox an art historian as Panofsky has this to say:

> By performing this curious transfer of artistic objectivity into the domain of the phenomenal, perspectival vision denied to religious art that realm of magic in which the work of art on its own accomplishes miracles ... but it opens to this religious art a completely new realm, that of the 'visionary', where the miracle becomes the spectator's immediately lived experience; supernatural events making, so to speak, an incursion into the visual, apparently natural space of this spectator and strictly speaking 'penetrating' him with their supernaturalness thanks to this very incursion. (Panofsky, *La perspective comme forme symbolique*, Eds de Minuit, Paris, 1975)

9   For further discussion of this pathologizing of the visionary, see J. Hillman, *The Myth of Analysis*, New York University Press, New York, 1972, pp. 131–2.

10 For a clear and sensitive account of how the 'objective' world is the result of a process of externalization, see R. Romanyshyn, *Psychological Life*, Open University Press, Milton Keynes, 1972.

11 One of the clearest examples of this is the role of literature, and specifically of the novel, in elaborating both the notion and the experience of selfhood (see J. Lyons, *The Invention of the Self*, Southern Illinois Press, S. Illinois, 1978).

12 The sophisticated conventions on which 'natural' representation depends are amply illustrated in E. Gombrich, *Art and Illusion*, Pantheon, New York, 1960.

13 The threat of excommunication was once ecclesiastical – for example, in the case of Veronese's 'Marriage-Feast at Cana'. Now it is psychiatric. The consequences are not so different.

14 A key feature of this myth is the post-Renaissance notion of the 'genius' – a word that in classical times had a much less exclusive meaning (see J. Hillman, *The Myth of Analysis*, New York University Press, New York, 1972, pp. 38–9).

15 'Movements' such as Cubism, Futurism, and Dadaism mark the crucial departures, both from traditional representation and from conventional notions of expression.

16 See my 'Freud and the figurative' (*Inscape*, October, 1983, pp. 3–10). It is a nice irony that both Freud and the psychotic artist Adolf Wölfli took off from the 'Bilder-Rätseln' (picture-puzzles) that were as common a feature of magazines and newspapers as crosswords are today. Freud used them as a reductive model, whilst

Wölfli compounded their key with other codes.

17　The most recent of periodic attempts to filter metaphor out of discourse and clarify it might be Robbe-Grillet's *Pour un nouveau roman*, Gallimard, Paris, 1961.

18　For a more detailed argument of this, see my 'Methodical madness' in J. Hillman (ed.) *An Annual of Archtetypal Psychology and Jungian Thought*, Dallas, Texas, Spring 1983. I am not saying that there is no link between states of mind and formal qualities; in calling a drawing 'psychotic', I might be trying to describe a style of sensibility as much as of *facture*. What I am against are the simplistic equations to be found so often in psychiatric literature.

19　In the case of Wölfli, for example, the problem is not that there is no meaning, but that there is a surplus, an excess, of meaning (see my 'Inspiration and madness: the case of Adolf Wölfli', *Art Monthly*, no. 45, 1981).

20　When working as an art therapist I was once asked by a consultant to try and get a patient to draw something recognizable, like a house. The purpose behind this was presumably twofold: to bring him into closer contact with 'reality'; and to give the consultant something to get a better diagnostic grip on.

21　Antonin Artaud's brilliantly vitriolic ripostes against his psychiatric treatment are a rare example of a sustained contradiction of this privilege.

22　The question of images that, under psychic pressure, cannot be translated into representational terms is raised independently by the poet Henri Michaux (see *Les grandes épreuves de l'esprit*, Nouvelles Editions Françaises, Paris, 1966) and the psychopharmacologist Roland Fischer (see 'On creative, psychotic and ecstatic states' in I. Jacab (ed.), *Art Interpretation and Art Therapy*, Karger, Basel, New York, 1969).

Chapter Four

Chagall's erotic imagery

John Birtchnell

Introduction

The reason for presenting an analysis of the paintings of a great artist in a work concerned with the therapeutic use of the arts is that Chagall's capacity to allow his inner fantasies to spill out uncritically on to the canvas makes it so much easier to see the kinds of processes with which the art therapist should be concerned. One of the many skills required of the art therapist is the ability to enter into the fantasies of the patient, get the feel of them, and get some idea of how the world is experienced from the patient's inside. The patient's creations are like a new language which has to be learned before communication with him becomes possible; for it is incumbent upon any good therapist to become able to communicate on the patient's terms rather than compel the patient to communicate on his.

Languages are learned by looking for recurrent words and taking note of the contexts in which they are used. Gradually, by comparing their use in these varying contexts, the linguist is able to get a progressively more precise idea of the meaning of the words. The language of an artist's pictures is learned by looking for recurrent themes, images, symbols, scenes, colours, etc., and observing the contexts in which they are presented. It is particularly important to appreciate that that which is presented may also stand for something else. Thus in attempting to decipher an artist's creations one must take note both of the images themselves and of the additional overtones of meaning which have been incorporated into them. They must be perceived both literally and figuratively.

Artists vary a great deal in the extent to which they incorporate additional layers of meaning into their creations. A great many artists hardly do it at all. Their major preoccupation is with accurate representation of that which inspires them and the aesthetic effect of their creations is due to their skilful use of their selected medium to recreate in another form that which they see in the real world. The viewer is fascinated by the fact that the picture is both a scene from reality and a conglomeration of different coloured paints on a canvas. When Chagall's work is viewed in historical perspective it is clear that much of his earlier work was predominantly of this representational kind. He appeared to derive satisfaction from depicting scenes from rural Russia. As he grew older he came more and more to use certain familiar images in a metaphorical or symbolic way. His pictures acquired a kind of poetic quality, and the aesthetic effect was due largely to the interplay between the image presented and the additional meanings which the image took on.

Why, it may be asked, do artists choose to complicate their pictures by introducing into them ideas over and above the images depicted. The most likely explanation is that they choose apparently innocent pictures as a vehicle for communicating certain ideas, the overt representation of which may meet with disapproval. In Chagall's case such ideas are predominantly to do with the coming together of men and women. I was recently relieved to learn from a television programme about Chagall that he had at one time been described as pornographic. I say this because his pictures have always struck me as being blatantly erotic and I have been surprised that few have ever described them in such terms. I choose the word erotic, rather than sexual, because they tend to be gloriously romantic, and in no way naughty or titillating in the way that truly pornographic pictures are. The use of non-sexual images to represent sexual themes enhances the power of the non-sexual images whilst, at the same time, imparting a certain poetry to the sexual themes which are depicted by them.

Although much of the art produced by patients during art therapy sessions is of the strictly representational variety, it is also very common for patients to use their pictures as a means of alluding to disturbing ideas with which they are preoccupied. Whilst in no way wishing to insinuate that Chagall may have been emotionally disturbed, I would like in this chapter to use his pictures to demonstrate the principle that apparently innocent objects and scenes are sometimes a cover for certain underlying obsessions and preoccupations. There are those who would argue that works of art should be left to speak for themselves, and that though it may be acceptable to dissect out the components of pictures produced during art therapy sessions, it is sacrilegious to do the same thing to pictures produced for purely aesthetic purposes. My counter to this is that Chagall was so good at unquestioningly allowing the outwardly irrational imagery of his psychic interior to flood out on to his canvas that we can learn more from studying his rich output in this way than we can from examining the more limited creations of psychiatric patients. I would also maintain that for me, and I would suspect for others too, the exercise contributes to a fuller appreciation of these exquisite fantasies.

Analysis of his pictures

Picture 4.1, entitled 'Adam and Eve', was painted when Chagall was in his early 20s. It was part of his preparation for his well-known 'Homage to Apollinaire' (1911), though I think it is superior to this later picture. The

4.1 Marc Chagall, 'Adam and Eve' © ADAGP, Paris and DACS, London 1988.

picture is important because it is the forerunner to the vast number of
subsequent studies on the theme of the young lovers. In accordance with the
biblical story, Eve is depicted emerging from Adam's ribs. It is my belief that
Chagall has taken up the story of Adam and Eve because it enables him to
represent the fusion of the bodies of the young man and the young woman as
if they were siamese twins. In his many subsequent representations of young
lovers the bodies are frequently fused in this way. It is a complex piece of
symbolism. It is partly saying that man and woman are one hermaphrodite
mass, that each of us is both male and female. It is also saying that in love this
internal fusion of man and woman is reproduced in the literal fusion of the

45

male and the female body. Finally I think it is proclaiming how central to his whole being is the romantic love of man and woman, and it is impressive that, even in his 90s, he was continuing to paint idyllic scenes of young lovers in fond embrace.

In this particular picture the man and woman share the same legs but separate out at the waist forming a kind of Y shape. At the centre of the Y is the pubic triangle, represented by a thick mass of pubic hair, but no genitalia. I would contend that the pubic triangle and the pubic hair, that point at which lovers actually do fuse in the act of making love, is a major preoccupation of Chagall's, though it assumes a number of different guises. Picture 4.2, which is entitled 'Bella in Green' (1934), is a portrait of his wife. She is holding a large fan roughly in the position of the pubic triangle. Thus, although she is fully clothed, the hidden pubic hair is symbolically represented by the apparently innocent fan. I would go so far as to suggest that the positioning of the fingers of both hands bears some resemblance to the female genitalia. The same motif is repeated in the elaborate neckline of her dress. The fan featured in some of Chagall's earliest paintings but reappeared in symbolic form in 'The Bride with Double Face' (1927), the beautiful 'Equestrienne' (1931), and 'The Bride and Groom of the Eiffel Tower' (1938–9). At times when the fan has been in vogue its significance as a replica of the pubic triangle has doubtless not been overlooked. It has the characteristics of a shield or mask which, while serving to cover this most intimate area, also bears some resemblance to it. It can also be moved back and forth in tantalizing or teasing manner in a sort of once-removed courtship ritual. It may even be that the word fanny, a slang term for the female genitalia, was originally derived from the fan.

In subsequent pictures the fan gave way to the posy or bouquet of flowers which was sometimes held over the pubic area in a similar sort of way, e.g. 'Nude in Ocher' (1949). There were even some pictures in which the woman held a fan in one hand and a bouquet of flowers in the other. The flowers, with their stalks drawn tightly together at the base, formed an excellent substitute for the pubic area and gradually bunches of flowers in various forms and sizes became prominent in most of Chagall's pictures. Not only do flowers bear a resemblance to pubic hair, they also provide poetic overtones. They are larger, more beautiful, and more brightly coloured, and give greater prominence to what in reality is a fairly dull anatomical feature. They are of course the reproductive organs of the plant and their principal function in nature is to attract the insects which are going to bring about the plant's cross-fertilization. At some level we are always aware of this and it is bound to affect the way we view them. The bride carries a posy of flowers at her wedding, partly perhaps as a kind of external representation of her hidden genitalia and partly as a symbol of fertility. This theme occurs occasionally in Chagall's work, e.g. 'Bridal Pair with White Bouquet' (1944). The young man proffers a bunch of flowers as a token of love which may be accepted or

4.2 Marc Chagall, 'Bella in Green' © ADAGP, Paris and DACS, London 1988.

declined. This theme occurs more frequently, e.g. 'The Visitor' (1952–6). More generally the flowers are interposed between the lovers as a representation of the love which joins them, e.g. 'Woman with Blue Face' (1960). In some of Chagall's most romantic pictures the lovers are immersed within an enormous bunch of flowers which takes up the entire picture, e.g. 'Lovers in the Lilacs' (1930). Sometimes the flowers are replaced by a small shrub or sapling. Flowers abound in Chagall's pictures and their prominence and sheer profusion reflect the ecstacy of the love relationship, e.g. 'The Red Flowers' (1950) and 'Bouquet and Red Circus' (1960).

Though it may seem absurd, the symbolism of the fan and the posy of flowers is carried through into the fluffed-up tail feathers of the chicken. Picture 4.3, 'The Red Cock' (1940), a still relatively early picture, shows a large bunch of foliage on the right which is echoed on the left by the tail feathers of a rather stylized cockerel. The other odd thing about this cockerel is the big round eye and the sharply pointed beak. Evidence from a number of pictures suggests that paradoxically the cockerel is strongly linked in Chagall's fantasies with the female genitalia, the tail feathers sometimes doubling as pubic hair and the fierce-looking beak representing the labia. Such an extravagant claim requires some substantiation. Take for example Picture 4.4, 'Night' (1953). Sweeping diagonally across the picture are the ubiquitous lovers. Intermingled with the woman's skirt is the symbolic vase of flowers and a little to one side of this is a basket of fruit, equally symbolic. Suspended in the sky, alongside the woman, is the chicken, greatly modified to accommodate Chagall's erotic needs. The eye and the labial beak are nicely juxtaposed to correspond with the woman's genitalia. The chicken has been inverted so that the tail feathers are superior to the beak and are able to take on the appearance of the pubic hair. In fact there is a hair-like quality to the feathers. The upturned chicken and the vase of flowers have a remarkable

4.3 Marc Chagall, 'The Red Cock' © ADAGP, Paris and DACS, London 1988.

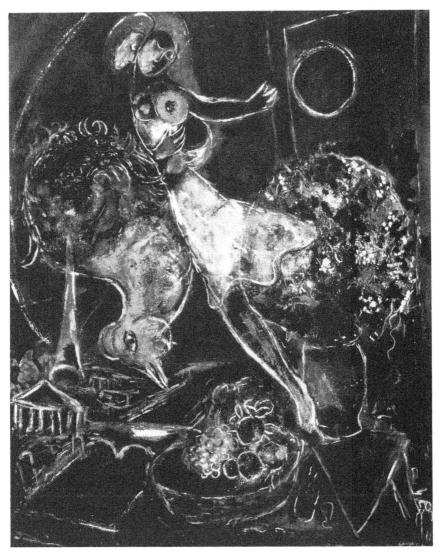

4.4 Marc Chagall, 'Night' © ADAGP, Paris and DACS, London 1988.

structural similarity and balance each other perfectly. This would appear to insinuate that they are two sides of the same image, both are enormous representations of the very much smaller and totally hidden real genitalia of the woman. This is an example of the phenomenon, described by Freud in his book on dreams, called displacement. The totally unrepresented but highly emotive image is displaced on to a totally innocent object as a form of camouflage. In this instance the displacement has occurred in two directions

49

at once. It may well have been displaced in more directions still, for the River Seine with its arched bridges and the Eiffel Tower to one side of it would also seem to have been used by Chagall in a number of pictures as further echoes of the female part. A closely related picture, painted the following year, is 'The Red Nude' (1954). In this picture the chicken and the lovers appear to be interlocked and the tail feathers are also a brightly coloured bouquet of flowers held by the young man. The chicken's head is even more closely apposed to the woman's pubis and its symbolic function is emphasized by its being coloured a bright yellow. The beak has quite blatantly been fashioned into labia. This magical chicken crops up in a variety of guises in a large number of Chagall's pictures, sometimes, like the bunch of flowers, taking over the whole picture, e.g. 'The Cock' (1946) or 'Flowering Feathers' (1943). In 'Village with Dark Sun' (1950) there is actually a cockerel with a woman's head.

Picture 4.5, 'The Cock on the Shore' (1952), was painted one year before Picture 4.4 and is structurally related to it. The weird cockerel is standing in the foreground with its prominent beak characteristically pointing backwards. Suspended in the air corresponding exactly in position to the cockerel of Picture 4.4 is an inverted fish, the head of which is almost identical to that of the cockerel. Symbolically therefore the fish and the cockerel are interchangeable. The sea corresponds in position to the River Seine of Picture 4.4 and the boat is perhaps a forerunner to the Eiffel Tower. The lovers appear to be floating in the sea and there is a suspicion that the young woman is a mermaid. In the late 1940s and early 1950s Chagall did paint a number of mermaid pictures and the scaly fish is a kind of shorthand for this. Besides this, the fish's head, like the cock's head, has been modified to represent the pubic triangle. In the surrealist picture 'Fishes at St Jean' (1949) three beautiful red fish, one lying on a white plate, are in the foreground and the lovers are rising above the horizon in the background. An enormous bunch of flowers held by a mysterious hand is suspended in the sky above.

The male counterpart to the cockerel or the fish is the donkey or the horse, though sometimes it is a goat or a cow. In another early, though quite well known, picture 'I and the Village' (1911) there is a very obvious self-portrait of Chagall on the right which is reflected in a donkey's head looking back at him. Within the donkey's head there is a smaller donkey being milked. The picture suggests that Chagall is identifying with the donkey and it seems likely that in many pictures he depicts himself as a donkey. This is made explicit in a picture called 'Self-portrait with Wall Clock' (1947) which is of a red donkey painting at an easel with the blue face of a woman fused with the donkey's head. Interestingly the picture being painted is Christ on the cross, with Mary's face arching over him in similar fashion. Thus the picture is a self-portrait of Chagall representing himself as Christ. As with the chicken, the eye of the donkey is often strikingly prominent. Sometimes the donkey has a mythological or god-like quality with a kind of reassuring presence. What I

4.5 Marc Chagall, 'The Cock on the Shore' © ADAGP, Paris and DACS, London 1988.

suspect appeals to Chagall about the donkey is its benign innocence. It crops up in various guises performing various functions. Sometimes it pulls a sledge carrying the lovers. Sometimes it bears the lovers on its back. It is at its most dramatic when it replaces the young man as the young woman's partner. Sometimes she rides him, sometimes she flies across the sky on his back. Sometimes the two are fused together, as in Picture 4.6 'For Vava' (1955). Here the donkey, or more probably a horse, is presented in its most phallic

4.6 Marc Chagall, 'For Vava' © ADAGP, Paris and DACS, London 1988.

form, pressing sensuously against the young woman who is holding a love posy. In 'Midsummer Night's Dream' (1939) Chagall draws upon Shakespeare's story about Bottom the weaver who has been given an ass's head to rework the same theme. In this picture the donkey is much more docile and the young woman is holding a blue fan.

The donkey or horse, cockerel, and fish appear in all manner of combinations in various pictures. In 'The Flying Sleigh' (1945) the sleigh is being pulled by a magnificent chimera of chicken and horse. In 'Woman with Blue Face' (1960) there is a creature with a fish's head at one end and a donkey's at the other. In 'Yellow Donkey' (undated) the donkey appears to be giving birth to the chicken but at the same time the chicken could also be the donkey's genitalia. The birth-giving theme is reinforced by the presence of a pregnant woman in the top right-hand corner of the picture.

One further image to which I would like to refer is the violin, or sometimes cello. It is tempting to speculate that Chagall uses the violin in much the same way as Picasso used the guitar, namely as a substitute for the female torso. Certainly in 'The Cellist' (1939) the cello is both the cellist himself and also probably a female torso, *vide* the black pubic triangle at the base. The cellist is therefore playing the woman, and one interpretation of 'playing' would be making love to her. However in the foreground of this picture there is a very small goat playing a very small violin. It is in some way accompanying the cellist. Unlike Picasso's guitar, the violin when it appears in Chagall's pictures is usually being played. In the magnificent picture 'The Dance' (1950) it is being played by a human with a cow's head. In that equally spectacular 'Equestrienne' (1931) the horse, bearing the lovers on its back, has under its chin a violin and a bunch of flowers, and the woman is holding a red fan over its head.

Issues concerning men, women, and sexuality are best kept hidden and disguised. It is their secretness which contributes to their exciting magic. Chagall's voluminous output has added in abundance to the poetic beauty of sexual relations and it is his own conflicts over how explicit to be about them which have been the sand in his particular oyster. My excuse for this exercise of rushing in where angels might otherwise fear to tread is that art therapists need to be aware of such stuff as dreams are made of.

Chapter Five

Symbiosis as a driving force in the creative process

Annie Hershkowitz

The origins of art, religion, and magic are rooted in the symbiotic unity and the experience of separateness that follows the earliest phase of infancy. Symbolic equivalents for parts of the mother's body are the earliest manifestations of play. Play is the precursor of creative acts, of art.

In neolithic cultures, the earliest pictorial representations were of female genitalia (the triangular symbol for the yoni in tantric art still prevails). Convolutions in pyramids and other religious and burial monuments symbolize the female genital tract from which one is born and to which one returns at death – the threshold back to Mother Earth and spiritual rebirth.

Primitive man feels one with nature, and the whole act of living is in harmony with nature as their art. The very act of hunting and killing for food is part of a religious act. The small objects and artifacts they carve or decorate are to them insignificant reflections of their total art of living.

Freud's theory of the urge to create is ultimately to become one with mother, return inside her body, the artist wanting to deny the primal scene and erase the real presence of the father. The artwork thus becomes the child that becomes implanted into the mother, it involves killing the father, and so is rooted in oedipal conflict (Spector 1972). For Jung, the creative act involves the fusion of animus and anima. This notion is further taken up by Marion Milner (1981) and Hanna Segal (1964), who define the creative act as the interaction and interdependence of consciousness and unconsciousness, of control and surrender, of activity and reflectivity, and they describe the creative process itself as 'a genital bisexual activity, necessitating a good identification with the father who gives and the mother who receives and bears the child', a conceptualization which was echoed by Neumann in his thesis that every artist is an essentially bisexual type of person.

Melanie Klein (1975) postulates that the restoration and recreation of the good object externally and internally is the basis of creativity and the characteristic feature of the depressive position, namely the guilt and despair at having omnipotently destroyed the good object/mother. Marion Milner (1981) suggests that the function of art as restoring lost objects is secondary, and that the primary role of art is the creating of objects, in the

psychoanalytic sense, not the recreating of them. (And Adrian St
that 'we are whole in so far as our objects are whole .... The
function of art is the creation of objects (Stokes 1972: 120)). This is
with Winnicott's formulation of the transitional space wherein ....
creates an object to buffer the stress of separation and the growing awareness
of his separateness, so defined:

> The hypothetical area that exists between the baby and the object
> (mother/part mother) ... which is at the interplay between there being
> nothing but me and there being objects and phenomena outside omipotent
> control. (Winnicott 1971: 100)

I should like to try and illustrate the theme of symbiosis and transitional
phenomena between 'Me-Not-Me' and animate *vs* non-animate by referring
to the work of Camus, Genet, Henry Moore and Magritte.

Camus

In *The Myth of Sisyphus*, Camus (1942) claims that art is the path by which
one seeks the primal images which opened the heart. In *The Exile and the
Kingdom* (1957) he describes the libidinal regression of Jonas, a painter, to
the foetal stage, when his creativity dries up. Camus wrote this at the death of
his own mother.

Camus was born in 1913 in Algeria and died in a car crash in 1960. Camus's
father was unknown to him, having died in the First World War when Camus
was an infant. His Spanish-born mother was illiterate and, following an ear
infection, was left partially deaf. She was silent and depressive. These
circumstances, together with his illness at 17 and again in 1937, were to have a
decisive effect upon his imaginative works.

The young Camus's experience, as he lay ill with tuberculosis and was told
he was going to die, must have been a profound emotional shock and also a
first 'revelation of the absurd', the crucial experience which turned him from
an unreflective enjoyment of life to the long, sometimes anguished,
meditation on existence which informs his whole work. The frequency with
which images of breath and breathing recur in much of his prose suggest that
tuberculosis had an influence on his writing, though Camus admitted that the
theme of death and the fleetingness of the world is as much literary as
personal in origin.

Death is never far away for Camus. The imagery of gravestones set beyond
rooftops, amongst trees, overlooking the sea, where 'sun and water compose a
symphony of joy and nothingness'. Most of the sights evoked are littered with
the ruins of an ancient great civilization – could this be a metaphor for the lost
paradise, the breast, the mother? We shall see that Magritte, too, shows this
fascination for the stone and the classical ruins.

Camus speaks of man's purity as the search for the primal paradise of the soul, in which 'the throbbing of the blood becomes one with the violent pulsations of the early afternoon Mediterranean sun' (Camus 1959: 48). His descriptions of the landscape are imbued with the quality of the sublime that Berenson, Fuller, and others have discussed. Gombrich suggests two polarities in taste, the 'soft' and the 'crunchy', which can be correlated with the 'passive' and the 'active', and with the 'sucking' and 'biting' oral modes respectively. Gombrich further equates the 'soft' with the more primitive and infantile, and the 'crunchy' with sophisticated, civilized taste. These polarities are forever present in Camus's scenery; the sensuousness, all the anthropomorphic qualities attributed to the mother, are projected on to the landscape. He even goes so far as to compare the sexual embrace to the ecstasy of the landscape: 'to embrace a woman's body is also to hold this strange joy which merges from the sky into the sea' (Camus 1959: 16). But he also speaks of the sun-drenched Mediterranean landscape as being 'black with sun'.

His mother's enigmatic silence gave rise to ambivalent feelings in the young Camus. He loved her intensely but found difficulty expressing this love. He sought refuge in the theatre, in which he felt 'innocent and freed of superego'. In the theatre Camus was able to resurrect the image of the father. His favourite role, and his earliest, was Dostoevsky's Ivan Karamazov, the oedipal character who kills his father. Camus said that he expressed himself directly through this role and understood Ivan completely. Each performance was a lived psychodrama for Camus. If we remember Jung, Milner, and Segal's definition of the creative process, we have a clue as to the meaning of the theatre for Camus, an experience which for him verged on the hallucination. Camus assumed exhaustively every possible function in the theatre, from director, actor, writer, theorist.

The 1950s were a difficult period for Camus. His creativity dried up. Camus partially compensated for this by staging theatrical productions. He hoped to relive, with an adaptation of *The Possessed*, the entrancement he had experienced with Ivan Karamazov; the project had been with him since his youth. It was on his way to this accomplishment that fate, on the roadside, decided otherwise.

Camus projected the good mother/object on to nature. He was able to experience the transcendental, the symbiosis, through his pantheistic communion with nature. This communion is celebrated in one of his earliest works, *Les Noces*, which translates as *The Nuptial*, from which most of the quotes are taken. However, the enigmatic silence of his mother had already made its mark. It colours Camus's entire work.

Jean Genet

In her studies with bereaved children, Anna Freud (1969) found that transformation of narcissistic libido was carried out inadequately in these children deprived of their mothers. Blunting of libidinal development resulting from these early deprivations leads further to inadequate binding of destructive urges in the child. Therefore these destructive urges, instead of being incorporated into oedipal manifestations, act in isolation and manifest themselves more independently in various ways, as sources of delinquency and criminality.

Jean Genet was born in 1910 and never knew his real mother, having been born an illegitimate child, abandoned at birth, and reared in institutions. He escaped reformatory and took to a life of theft and wandering across Europe, some of it being spent in various prisons. He escaped life-sentence when pardoned by Auriol, the then president of the Republic, who had been petitioned by eminent writers and artists including Cocteau, Picasso, Sartre, and others.

Genet's output can be regarded as a medium in which he created and permutated images of the mother he never knew, and of the mother he did know – the Institution – and, on one important level, his life and work may be regarded as a revenge for this primal act of rejection by his mother. The inherent horror in his writing may be seen as a striving for love and recognition in moments of despair. His writing represents the interface between the label he was given by society, the false self wherein the infant, deprived of the good-enough mothering agent, develops compliance and his life becomes built upon reactions to self-created impingements – and the absence of object (in the psychoanalytic sense) – and the creation of a reality in the becoming, and which included that of his own individuation processes. Genet's writing can be understood in the context of Winnicott's location of play:

> Baby and object are merged in with one another. Baby's view of the object is subjective and the mother is oriented towards the making actual of what the baby is ready to find .... The object is repudiated, re-accepted, and perceived objectively .... This complex process is highly dependent on there being a mother or mother-figure prepared to participate and to give back what is handed out. This means that the mother (or part of mother) is in a 'to and fro' between there being that which the baby has a capacity to find and (alternatively) being herself waiting to be found. (Winnicott 1971: 47)

We recognize here the definition of the therapeutic process itself. It can be considered that Genet, through ten years of writing, achieved something of the equivalent of a psychoanalytic cure, each book representing a crisis in catharsis, each a psychodrama, each theme reproducing the theme of its predecessors – his new love-affairs replay his old loves – each making him a little more master of the demon which possesses him, bringing on his individuation.

Genet's best novel is *Querelle de Brest*, which is an account of homosexual love, mythic twinning, and in which he is able to diagnose his own condition sodomite who phantasizes over the murderously evil Querelle, of whom he says 'through crime he found a world of intense feelings' (Genet 1966: 69). *The Thief's Journal* is the reconstruction of a phantasy autobiography of himself in the years 1932–40, and it embodies a type of chosen, voluntary, masochistic homosexuality. *The Balcony* explores the nature of reality versus phantasy.

When pardoned by Auriol, who invited him to dinner, he earned the respectability, the money for which he always yearned. There was no longer anything for him to write about. He was shocked into silence and has kept out of the public eye ever since. He married, has an adopted child, and apparently leads a somewhat puritanical bourgeois life. Genet has internalized the act of society and of his mother's.

Henry Moore

Henry Moore, the seventh child of a Yorkshire miner, was born in 1898, and is considered England's greatest sculptor, largely responsible for the gradual emergence of British art into the mainstream of modern art. He followed on from Rodin, who defined sculpture as the science of the hump and the hollow.

While studying on the three-year diploma course at the Royal College of Art in 1921, Moore frequently visited the British Museum and studied primitive and Mexican sculpture. He particularly admired Greek sculptors 'who carved their sculptures with vision, understanding and sensitivity, and knew what was beneath the surface, and were able to release the life force which gave strength and vitality to their work' (1986: 102). However, Mexican art was to become the major influence on his work during the 1920s.

In 1922 he visited the Pellerin Collection in Paris, which included Cézanne's 'Bathers'. This was the first Cézanne painting he had ever seen. It was an unforgettable experience with a lasting effect. The impact it had on him was essentially sculptural: 'The nudes in perspective, lying on the ground as if they had been sliced out of mountain rock. For me this was like seeing Chartres Cathedral' (Moore 1986: 190).

Like his contemporaries Modigliani, Gaudier-Brzeska, Brancusi, Epstein, and Hepworth, Moore was interested in direct carving and he believed in the doctrine of 'truth to materials', understanding and being in sympathy with the qualities of wood or stone, letting the material help shape the sculpture and speak its own language, as if to release its hidden essence. This process can be compared to finding a plastic expression for inner psychological truths.

In the early 1930s Moore visited the studios of Picasso, Braque, and Brancusi, which made a profound impact on him. In 1936 he visited the prehistoric caves in the Pyrenees. During that period he did a series of drawings of bones and shells, transforming shapes in nature into human forms. In the multi-part sculpture of 1934, the human body was broken up into fragments and reassembled. With it came the idea of the reclining woman as a metaphor for the landscape ('Reclining Figure', 1929). Breasts and knees are like hills or mountains, and holes like caves in a hillside ('Recumbent Figure', 1938). He always preferred to have his work in a natural setting, such that its rhythm and line became interchangeable with the landscape and the pulse of nature.

From 1940 to 1942 he made exhaustive drawings of underground shelters. His fascination with shelter drawings, which did not detract from the human tragedy, can be seen as a metaphor for the descent into Hades or the Underworld, as in dreams, where caves and quarries are often symbols of psychic transformation, a return to the amorphous state, to the Source or clay.

Carving in stone satisfied him for a time, until he experienced it as limiting and preventing him from including the full three-dimensional world with air around it, so he began to make holes in sculpture, thereby making the back have a connection with the front. Holes could have as much meaning to Moore as a solid mass, holding mystery, as a hole in a cliff or hillside, in its depth and shape. He called it 'a revelation'.

By hollowing out his figures, Moore arrives at a situation approaching inner and outer sculpture, which may be equated with the window theme in many paintings, symbolizing the inner and outer world, or the 'me-not-me'. The interaction of voids and masses gives rise to greater plastic motility, richer contrasts of light and shadow, and a quality lacking in sculptures that deal with surfaces only. These qualities also grip us as they activate very early associations of part objects and aspects of the depressive position, and the tensions it held.

His subject matter is mostly restricted to the female figure, mother and child, family groups. Some configurations suggest embryonic forms, full of the promise of development and the thrust of life. The head and limbs are often reduced to a stump. At times, violent laceration and piercing are inferred. The dismemberment theme in much of Moore's work is an archetypal theme, closely associated with myths and rites of rebirth, of which death is a necessary preliminary, and dismemberment a forerunner of conception.

There is an increasing trend towards the non-figurative, as Moore believed that in this way he could represent the human content of his work with greatest directness and intensity, freed from aesthetic preoccupation with form. With the non-figurative idiom came the notion of asymmetry, which he associated with organic growth, as opposed to the mechanical repetition of the manufactured object.

For Moore, sculpture is akin to poetry, about people trying to express their feelings and responses to the world. For this reason, Cycladic art was a great influence, as Moore felt 'it had the purity of all early art which stemmed from the people who made it feeling something so very strongly, unlike later work which was often to do with copying other influences' (1986: 56). He believed there was so much more to learn from the dawn of art. This quest for the primeval is explicit in Moore's own words and in his work: 'a sculptor wants to know what a thing is like on top, and from beneath – a bird's eye view and a worm's eye view. It's infinite .... Sculpture is a full-time job, a mental obsession' (1986: 79). Does this statement not conjure the earliest perceptual behaviour, the crawling toddler eager to explore the world in all its exciting novelty, a yearning to get back to that primal state of being and apprehending the world, of passionate encounter, characterized by the experience of totality! 'The human form has always been my main concern. It's what we know most about – the softness and slackness of flesh, the hardness of bone, all the energy that is pent up in our own bodies' (1986: 102). The quality Moore admired most in a work of art was that of monumentality, which is irrespective of scale, and is a function of 'the mind behind the work', a deep human understanding and ability to transcend the everyday and commonplace. The striving for power of expression has for Moore a spiritual vitality more moving and deeper than beauty of expression, which aims at pleasing the senses. In common with all great sculptors, he always loved hands; hands, after the face, being the most obvious part of the human anatomy for expressing energy.

Rough versus smooth textures is a contrast Moore uses the most in his sculptures. Touching with the hand is a part of sight, and an essential aspect of the aesthetic dimension of sculpture. The emphasis Moore places on these contrasts, and the transition from soft to hard, in addition to the symbolic implications of transformation and nascence, seem to indicate an increasing preoccupation with kinaesthetic sensations, rather than visual ones:

> To make a shape so strongly significant, without knowing why, or why it is so ... perhaps ability to do so comes about because of the sculptor's intense interest in all forms and shapes ... through empathy and human connections .... It has to do, in a way, with sculpting like a blind man .... Whenever I see this figure ['Seated Female Figure'], I am reminded of a boyhood experience that contributed towards the conception of its form. (1966: 131)

Moore's sense of form can be traced back to those childhood experiences of rubbing his mother's back with liniment: 'When I came to this figure which represents a fully mature woman, I found that I was unconsciously giving to its back the long forgotten shape of the one I had so often rubbed as a boy' (1968: 131). For many sculptors, life becomes subordinated to the search for primordial forms, laws, and primordial experiences.

Magritte

Magritte was meticulous, punctual, had a dislike for familiarity. He suffered from chronic melancholia, which he lived as a metaphysical condition. He

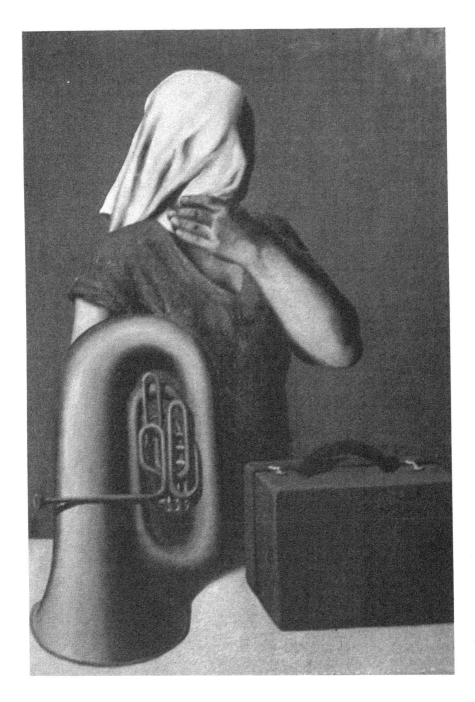

5.1 René Magritte, 'The Heart of the Matter' © ADAGP, Paris and DACS, London 1988.

5.2 René Magritte, 'Collective Invention' © ADAGP, Paris and DACS, London 1989.

was a hypochondriac. Hypochondria can be regarded as a split of self into psyche and soma, the psyche taking on the nurturing function of the soma. Hypochondria is a response to loss. Anna Freud found this syndrome occurring widely amongst deprived children following the death of their mother.

His mother drowned herself under mysterious circumstances when he was a boy of 14. Her head was veiled by her nightgown. It was never established whether she covered her head before jumping in the river, or whether the current draped the gown over her head. The question is raised: What part of him died with her? I quote:

> The sight of my painting is often followed by a feeling of estrangement. This is not my deliberate aim – as any aim I might have would be derisory. Contact with my paintings should make the viewer sick – contact with reality always makes one sick. (Magritte Exhibition Catalogue 1978: 17)

Is Magritte referring to this boyhood experience when he witnessed, either in real life or in phantasy, his mother's body being recovered from the river?

In his painting 'The Human Condition', the tree represented on the paintings hides the tree behind it, outside the room – the tree is therefore both inside the room, on the canvas, and outside, in thought, in the real landscape. This is how we relate to the world. We see it outside ourselves, yet we have a representation of it within ourselves.

The problem of the window also entranced Baudelaire, who speaks of the 'fecundity of the window', particularly if lit by a candle. It is no chance

Magritte was influenced by the poet, whose creativity helped allay the inner, centrifugal sense of the abyss – which may be compared to the dread of separation and what Winnicott has called 'the fear of the interruption in the going on being, which antedates the fear of death itself'.

Like Baudelaire, Magritte believed in the mysterious existence of objects and felt himself in contact with their reality. This may be compared to animism, which is a means of relating to objects in an uncontrollable, unpredictable world, and may be the inspiration for exhaustive explorations of the mental phenomenon of inside *versus* outside – the theme of window and doors occurs widely in Magritte's imagery. Like Baudelaire, he amused himself all alone – and knew how to people his solitude or to be alone in a crowd. He manipulated objects until he became the man who discovered their destiny. In the medium of painting therefore he became omnipotent and godlike.

For him painting was a means of making his thought visible. He made a discovery in painting, that not only a situation, or a group of objects represented became mysterious, but also the gradual transition from one state into another, or one object into another – like the nude whose body becomes woody in patches. Through painting he explored not only the relationship between art and reality, but between ourselves and the world outside, questioning the meaning of meaning. Later he began exploring the relationship between word, image, and reality. He had a passion for hiding one thing behind another, emphasizing that a painting, even a representational one, is but an object and cannot be a substitute for reality. He felt there was little relationship between an object and its representation. This notion was further taken up in the deliberate naming of his paintings, arrived at through discourse with his friends – 'a name neither describes nor interprets he who bears it'. The sign merely points to reality. These philosophical problems preoccupied Wittgenstein as well as Baudelaire and James Joyce.

By juxtaposing incongruous objects he manipulates the viewer's expectations and precipitates a state of shock, of surprise, of laughter, as in theatrical practice, thereby inviting the audience to partake, perhaps in an attempt to replay his experience as a boy before his drowned mother's body, her head veiled over by her nightgown. His irony, and his distance, from the work, makes us realize this is Magritte the man, not the child.

The experience may be the key to Magritte's focusing on the frontiers of animate versus inanimate, the tension between reality and illusion, which he continually formulated and explored in endless permutations.

The work of Magritte appears like a huge question mark on the human predicament, the fragility of it, and of our perceptual concept of the material world. The mystery surrounding the death of his mother may be the heart, the essence, of Magritte's work. Her death may have precipitated for him all the issues of the depressive position.

Conclusion

I have tried to show how the earliest relationship with the mother has coloured the work of the artist, art becoming a means and a medium to replay the relationship in an attempt to understand and negotiate it, and to invite an audience to partake in it.

References

Camus, A. (1942) *Le mythe de Sisyphe*, Gallimard, Paris.

Camus, A. (1957) *L'exil et le royaume*, Gallimard, Paris.

Camus, A. (1959) *Les noces*, Gallimard, Paris.

Cassou, J. (1965) *Chagall*, Thames & Hudson, London.

Fuller, P. (1981) *Art and Psychoanalysis*, Writers and Readers Cooperative, London, p. 169.

Freud, Anna (1969) *Indications for Child Analysis and Other Papers*, Hogarth Press, London.

Gablick, S. (1976) *Magritte*, New York Graphic Society, Boston.

Genet, J. (1966) *Querelle de Brest*, trans. Gregory Streatham, A. Blond, London.

Gordon, Lyndall (1986) *Virginia Woolf, A Writer's Life*, Oxford University Press.

Klein, Melanie (1975) *Love, Guilt and Reparation*, Hogarth Press, London.

Koffman, S. (1970) *L'enfance de l'art*, Payot, Paris.

Laing, R. D. and Cooper, D. (1971) *Reason and Violence*, Tavistock, London, pp. 67–90.

Magritte Retrospective Exhibition Catalogue (1978) Palais des Beaux Arts, Bruxelles.

Milner, M. (1981) *On Not Being Able to Paint*, Heinemann, London.

Moore, Henry (1966) *On Sculpture*, ed. Philip James, Macdonald, London.

Moore, Henry and Hedgecoe, John (1986) *Henry Moore: My Ideas, Inspiration and Life as an Artist*, Ebury Press, London.

Neumann, E. (1972) *The Great Mother*, Princeton University Press, p. 158.

Neumann, E. (1973) *The Origins and History of Consciousness*, Princeton University Press, p. 403.

Neumann, E. (1979) *Creative Man: Five Essays*, Princeton University Press, pp. 204–6, 214–15.

Neumann, E. (1985) *The Archetypal World of Henry Moore*, Princeton University Press.

Segal, Hanna (1964) *Introduction to the Work of Melanie Klein*, Heinemann, London.

Spector, J. J. (1972) *The Aesthetics of Freud*, Allen Lane, London.

Stokes, Adrian (1972) *The Image in Form*, ed. R. Wollheim, Penguin, Harmondsworth, p. 120.

Torczyner, Harry (1978) *Magritte, Le veritable art de peindre*, Draeger, Paris, p. 17.

Winnicott, D. W. (1971) *Playing and Reality*, Tavistock, London.

Chapter Six

'More or less a sorrow': some observations on the work of Edward Lear

Joan Woddis

A keen sense of every kind of beauty, is, I take it, if given in the extreme – always more or less a sorrow to its owner – tho' productive of good to others. (Edward Lear, *Diaries*, 29 January 1862)

Edward Lear remains one of the most curious figures in English literature; a serious landscape painter, one-time drawing master to Queen Victoria, who also wrote an abundance of comic limericks and poems, ostensibly for children, which he characterized as 'pure nonsense'.

Most English readers will have encountered 'The Owl and the Pussycat' who 'sailed away in a beautiful peagreen boat' and will have been amused by his illustrated limericks, for example:

> There was a young person of Bantry,
> Who frequently slept in the pantry;
> When disturbed by the mice
> She appeased them with rice,
> That judicious young person of Bantry.

I should like to begin this brief examination of the nonsense poems and drawings of Edward Lear with a quotation from the work of Peter and Iona Opie, the tireless iconographers of children's games. 'A true game', they record, 'is one that frees the spirit. It allows of no cares but those fictitious ones engendered by the game itself. When the players commit themselves to rhythm and incident they opt out of the ordinary world.'[1]

Edward Lear was, as I hope to illustrate here, a man of great courage, battling throughout his life with both epilepsy and his latent homosexuality, for at that time either of these attributes might render the sufferer a social outcast, and the resultant constraints produce profound isolation and loneliness. I believe his nonsense to be a significant defence, a means by which he could articulate the suffering he had experienced, but in such a way that he was protected from close scrutiny; the very absurdity of the form obscured the meaning and the pain. Perhaps it is this feature of his work that will most interest us as therapists.

Edward Lear was born in Holloway, London, in May 1812, the twentieth of twenty-one children, many of whom had died in infancy. His family were well to do, but during the unsettled economic aftermath of the Napoleonic Wars, Jeremiah Lear, Edward's father, fell a defaulter to the Stock Exchange. The family fortunes reversed and they left their large and comfortable house, Bowmans Lodge, the older children scattering among relatives and friends. Edward was just 4 years old, and to ease the burden on his mother, it is said, he was given into the charge of his sister Ann, who was twenty-one years his senior. From that point his mother's contact with him virtually ceased. Although the family returned to Bowmans Lodge quite soon after, Mrs Lear never again concerned herself with her son who remained bewildered and hurt by her rejection of him throughout his life. He seems to have blamed the house and their possessions for his sudden misery and we see traces of that rationalization in his work, and while it is clear that Ann devoted herself to him and earned his lasting love, Edward's childhood was strange and unhappy. Although the Lears had produced a vast quantity of children, there is apparently little evidence that the marriage was a happy one; the avoidance of noise and argument, and the search for calm and tranquillity, were a lifelong preoccupation for Edward Lear.

When he was about 7 years old his early traumatic rejection and his anxious and bewildered existence manifested themselves into bouts of acute depression which he named the 'Morbids' and he has left us an account of their first occurrence.

> The earliest of all the morbidness I can recollect must have been somewhere about 1819 – when my father took me to a field near Highgate, where was a rural performance of gymnastic clowns, &c. -& a band ... sunset & twilight. ... I can recollect crying half the night after all the small gaiety broke up and also suffering for days at the memory of the past scene.[2]

Even earlier he had experienced his first attacks of epilepsy, 'The Demon' as he called it. Later he wrote of 'a sorrow so inborn and ingrained, that was evidently part of what I have been born to suffer',[3] and it is inescapable that his illness profoundly affected his entire life. It was felt that he should never be alone and in addition to his sister Ann's single-minded attention he became cocooned by protective older sisters. His play, his art, his creativity itself, became his toy, companion, playmate, and his defender.

However, despite this isolated and sheltered childhood, he was able, when his family moved to Kent and he and Ann set up home alone in Clerkenwell, to set about earning his own living at the age of 16. 'Considering all I remember to have passed through from 6 years old to 15, is it not wonderful that I am alive? Far more to be able to feel and write',[4] he wrote fifty years later.

It is not my intention in this chapter to catalogue the major events of Edward Lear's life or to chronicle his considerable career as a landscape painter. Rather my focus is on his childhood, for its reverberating effects can be discerned in his work and in his very existence: hence my concentration on the nonsense verse and drawings which most clearly illustrate this. However, I must not omit the fact that Lear was a life-long traveller, almost an expatriate, who throughout his adult life spent long periods of his time abroad. His letters reveal that his wanderings paralleled a voyage of self-discovery. Surely this can be seen as an avoidance of permanence, of setting up a home and family, his own early experience of such an arrangement having been so disastrous. And yet, in his work, when he travels to the farthest shores of his fantasies, the strange beings there share his sadness and sense of lost happiness; he has not escaped.

But the once-sickly child could abandon caution and risk hardship in unknown and unwelcoming places, and by this means sometimes experience the physical and spiritual freedom he sought. The delight in the discovery of wonders, of marvels unimagined, however tinged with regret, is a recurring theme in his nonsense songs and is a fervent expression of his restlessness. 'Nonsense is the breath in my nostrils'[5] wrote Edward Lear, and the use of nonsense was an integral part of his life.

Boris Sidis, in *The Psychology of Laughter* writes, 'In the ludicrous and the comic we let go the earnestness, the seriousness of life, we become free agents. We soar in the air of spiritual freedom with ease, grace and the power of a superabundance of energy.'[6] (Sidis 1913: 77) Lear's use of nonsense, of word-plays, puns, and limericks, and the apparent humour and merriment of his personality masked, indeed strongly defended, his inner emotional conflicts, though we shall see how these deeper feelings still found a voice in his seemingly amusing work, and how often wit and humour are combined with sadness. To soar in the air of spiritual freedom was his lasting ambition and his so-called nonsense was the psychic agency of this need, as travel was the physical instrument.

When Lear first began to write there was no literary school or style of nonsense. Lear and Lewis Carroll established the genre. It differs from fantasy itself in that rigid and recognizable elements combine with impossible, fantastic, and dreamlike features; the overriding expression is of a logical order in an absurd setting, nonsense thus has a methodical feeling, a sense of rationalizing and taming wild irrationality. Perhaps the essence of nonsense is detachment; neither author nor reader becomes involved with the characters, so that their vicissitudes, even torments, do not distress us and need not be taken seriously. Their feelings are not part of the game and, like Lear's, remain hidden and secret.

One can divide Lear's nonsense into three groups, each somewhat infringing on the others. The limericks, parodies, comic botany, alphabets, and recipes fall into the sphere of the happy and inconsequential, the totally detached, as do the nonsense letters he wrote to his friends and their children. The purest humour is present in this group. The stories, both in prose and verse, form another section. 'The Owl and the Pussycat', perhaps his best-known poem, is here, and is typical in that it concerns travel and wandering, less so as it has a happy ending. For there are sad endings in this group, but as they often appear as pure nonsense and do not disturb us, we can still view them with unconcern.

The third group of nonsense songs contains Lear's most moving work, written for himself alone, the dreams of a happiness that, like the clowns of his childhood, had left and never returned. There is a sense of loneliness and isolation that roots these poems strongly in reality. His professed belief was in the acceptance of truth, of tolerance, affection, and the wide horizons of total understanding – a paradox in a man who concealed both his epilepsy and his homosexuality throughout his life.

Lear's nonsense verse and drawings act as an extension of his childhood play, constituting a remedy that allows for both the recreation of his early conflicts and their illusory resolution in fantasy. The moral standards of Victorian society, with all its attendant hypocrisies, forced many constraints upon Edward Lear. He longed for a world of honesty, simplicity, and merriment – the lost world of the loving mother, which for him had hardly existed.

'I have come to the conclusion', he wrote 'that nobody ought to marry at all, and that no more people ought ever to be born, and the world left to triumphant chimpanzees, gorillas and cockroaches.'[7] Of course he could not marry, could never risk that another woman might abandon him as his mother had once done. 'There is a fearful gnawing sensation which chills and destroys one, on leaving scenes or persons for which there are no substitutes',[8] he wrote, and he attempted to prevent such feelings by resolving not to 'like everyone else ... any new persons, scenes or places all the rest of my short, foolish life'.[9] He could not adhere to this childlike prescription, naturally; Lear's need to be loved was overwhelming and he fell violently in love several times with both men and women. He proclaimed that he was not free to marry, the barrier of his epilepsy was insuperable. Because of that foreknowledge of the attacks, shared by many sufferers, known as the aura epileptica, he was able to conceal and keep secret his illness and it was known only to his family and to his servant. Poignant little crosses are marked in his diary for each fit, sometimes twenty a month. He told himself he was not free, he could not bestow such an inheritance on his children. He must forswear married love. In reality, it is likely that Lear's wish to marry, recorded long after the event in his diaries, was more imagined than real, and his deepest feeling was that the love of women was shallow and transient, basically untrustworthy.

He probably only partly realized his own homosexuality, and although he certainly had a deep emotional craving for the love of at least two men that we know of, at different times in his life, it seems unlikely that this was ever consummated in a physical act of love. It is likely that the conflict engendered by the stifling of these impulses greatly contributed to his constant state of restlessness and depression. Perhaps his great need was simply for someone to want him as his mother had never done; anything less than that could not cure his loneliness, or calm his turbulent inner feelings.

Can we discern the important themes of Lear's life and his emotional inheritance in his poems? Surely, in 'The Courtship of the Yongy Bongy Bo', the hero who was rejected by his lady and sailed away on a turtle had as his only possessions '2 old chairs and half a candle, one old jug without a handle'. We remember that Lear blamed or rationalized his mother's rejection on his parents' dependence on their wealth and property, and was terrified of burdening himself in the same way. Mr and Mrs Discobollos, in another poem, share his feelings.

> We want no knives nor forks nor chairs,
> No tables nor carpets nor household cares,
> From the worry of life we've fled,
> There is no more trouble ahead,
> Sorrow or any such thing!

In the second part of that poem, Lear's horror of large families, and the memory of their disorder and insensitivity, appears, and he has a remedy. Mr Discobollos climbs down from the 'runcible' wall, their home, and simply blows the whole family into tiny pieces.

> And all the Discobollos family flew,
> In thousands of bits to the sky so blue.

So Lear's fury is just allowed to break the surface.

In 'The Daddylonglegs and the Fly', both creatures are social outcasts; one's legs are too long the other's too short to admit them to society. They escape, sail away, as Lear's creations so often do.

> 'And off they sailed among the waves, far, far away,
> They sailed across the silent main
> And reached the great Gromboolian plain,
> And there they play for evermore
> At battlecock and shuttledore.

So the game is the life-saver, and the courage to risk the unknown. 'The Jumblies', who went to sea in a sieve, found excitement, happiness, and success, and stayed away for twenty years. When they returned.

> Everyone said 'If we only live,
> We too will go to sea in a sieve.'

But they will not, for they cannot; escape is not really possible, for the golden shores also contain loneliness. He wrote,

> Like a sudden spark
> Struck vainly in the night

6.1 The dong with the luminous nose.

> Back returns the dark
> With no more hope of light.[10]

And this is the overriding contention within his work; happiness has slipped irretrievably into the past. You may search, but it is lost forever, it was but a dream, and the sense of a disquieting dream pervades his work.

'The Dong with the Luminous Nose' loses the jumbly girl that he loves and is forced forever to search for her, wandering plaintively over the plain with the strange woven nose.

> Of vast proportions painted red,
> And tied with cords to the back of his head
> In a hollow rounded space it ended
> With a luminous lamp within suspended.

But even with such wild measures, and we can only guess at their symbolism for Lear, he is inevitably left 'on the cruel shore, gazing, gazing for evermore'.

In 'Calico Pie' all manner of creatures dance, hop, and play, but they are observed with the hopeless longing of the outsider, and the chorus repeated over and over tells us,

> They never came back, they never came back,
> They never came back to me.

The memory of the lost clowns still haunts him. And in 'The Pelican Chorus' we actually hear him mourn his rejection and loss.

> Often since, in the nights of June,
> We sit on the sand and watch the moon,
> She has gone to the great Gromboolian plain
> And we probably never shall meet again.
> Oft, in the long still night of June,

> We sit on the rocks and watch the moon,
> She dwells by the stream of the Chankly Bore
> And we probably never shall see her more.

Of course we can find within the nonsense verse many themes that illustrate Lear's defences against his melancholy and sense of isolation. But the most touching are those that speak of the tolerance and acceptance that this man, who considered himself such an oddity, believed to be society's salvation. The world of the unlikely, the ridiculous, and impossible, was a haven, where a marriage between an owl and a pussycat would be a happy one, and the ill-assorted group who came together on the Quangle Wangle's hat would live together in perfect harmony.

> And the Quangle Wangle said
> To himself on the Crumpetty Tree.
> When all these creatures move
> What a wonderful noise there'll be!
> And all were as happy as happy could be.

Edward Lear's nonsense verse is honeycombed with his deepest needs, beliefs, and hopes, as well as with his pain.

When we observe the drawings we are confronted by a vast tapestry of symbols. I have isolated here one feature, that which Lear himself repeatedly complained of, his nose. He felt it was too large, it prevented him from being handsome, and rendered him ridiculous. In selecting humour as the vehicle for his feelings, he was somehow living up to his nose. One can see from the drawings that illustrate the limericks how often his creations are plagued with

6.2   There was an Old Man, on whose nose,/Most birds of the air could repose;/ But they all flew away,/at the closing of the day,/Which relieved that Old Man and his nose.

extraordinary noses that dominate their lives. Lear's dissatisfaction with the shape of his nose was almost obsessional, as the numberless references to it in his letters and diaries reveal.

It is tempting to make a sexual interpretation of such a symbol. In Lear's day there was a widespread belief that masturbation brought on epileptic attacks, and Lear certainly believed there was a connection between the two. In his diaries he blames his attacks on 'his lack of will power'.[11]

In 'The Pobble Who Has No Toes' all is well as long as the pobble keeps his nose well covered. When he loses his scarlet flannel wrapper, his toes disappear, rather like the little boys who were told that their penises would drop off if they continued the forbidden practice. 'The Dong with the Luminous Nose' has to weave himself a more effective nose, although it still does not help him to find his lost love. Lear's perception of his own sexuality seems to have been clouded by guilt and anxiety, and he must sometimes have felt as burdened as the characters in his limericks with their problematical noses. Certainly his relentless discontent with his own articulates a deeper feeling of self-doubt.

'The Pobble Who Has No Toes' was pronounced happier without them, but there was no such simple way to the impediment of inhibition and repression for his creator. Towards the end of his life, Lear fell quite hopelessly in love with a young man, half believing he was seeing the boy as an adored son, but in reality tortured by desperate longings. He failed to come to terms with his impossible desires. The creatures in these drawings accommodate their nonconformity with ease: Lear never did.

'Accept a lonely destiny'[12] – Lear's phrase for his own inability to make lasting relationships, and his sense that his state was somehow ordained – points to a well-defined personality. He believed he was not entitled to happiness, it had been stolen from him, and because of this he felt himself set apart. He idealized his friends' children, but could not bring himself to risk the power of parenthood, which he had experienced as such a destructive force.

6.3 The pobble who has no toes.

Today we should call his a damaged personality, and can only speculate on the effect his pathology had upon his art. One fact remains certain, however. The once-rejected child left the world's children a lasting bequest, which delighted them at the time and still fascinates and enchants.

W. H. Auden ends his beautiful poem on Edward Lear with these lines:

> Children swarmed to him like settlers.
> He became a land.[13]

Perhaps thus was the circle broken.

References

1 Opie, P. and Opie, I., *Children's Games in Street and Playground*, Oxford University Press, Oxford, 1969, p. 1.
2 Diary entry, 24 March 1877, quoted in Noakes, V., *Edward Lear*, Collins, London, 1968, p. 15. (The original diaries are at Harvard University.)
3 Diary entry, 15 August 1866, ibid., p. 16.
4 Diary entry, 29 March 1868, ibid., p. 21.
5 Letter, Edward Lear to Mrs Bruce, 24 December 1870, Ms Robert Manner Strocier Library, Florida State University.
6 Sidis, B., *The Psychology of Laughter*, D. Appleton, New York 1913, p. 77.
7 Letter, Edward Lear to Emily Tennyson, 10 May 1865, Noakes op. cit.
8 Letter, Edward Lear to Chichester Fortescue, 26 August 1851, quoted in Lady Strachey (ed.) *Letters of Edward Lear*, T. Fisher Unwin, London 1907.
9 Ibid.
10 Diary entry, 1 June 1866, Noakes op. cit., p. 171.
11 Diary entry, 17 February 1887, ibid., p. 16.
12 Diary entry, 5 November 1867, ibid., p. 180.
13 Auden, W. H., 'Edward Lear 1812–1888' Catalogue to Exhibition, Royal Academy of Arts, London 1985.

The poems quoted are from Lear, E., *A Book of Nonsense* (1846 and 1855); and *Nonsense Songs, Stories, Botany and Alphabets* (1871).

The author gratefully acknowledges her debt to the work of Vivien Noakes, the leading authority on the life and work of Edward Lear.

Chapter Seven

Art, therapy, and Romanticism

Michael Edwards

There is a passage in Charlotte Brontë's 1847 novel where Jane Eyre shows some of her own amateur paintings to Mr Rochester, her new employer. It is worth quoting in full.

> He spread the pictures before him, and again surveyed them alternately.
>
> While he is so occupied I will tell you, reader, what they are: and first, I must premise that they are nothing wonderful. The subjects had, indeed, risen vividly on my mind. And as I saw them with the spiritual eye before I attempted to embody them, they were striking; but my hand would not second my fancy, and in each case it had wrought out but a pale portrait of the thing I had conceived.
>
> These pictures were in water-colours. The first represented clouds low and livid, rolling over a swollen sea: all the distance was in eclipse; so, too, was the foreground: or rather, the nearest billows, for there was no land. One gleam of light lifted into relief a half-submerged mast, on which sat a cormorant, dark and large, with wings flecked with foam: its beak held a gold bracelet, set with gems, that I had touched with as brilliant tints as my palette could yield, and as glittering distinctness as my pencil could impart. Sinking below the bird and mast, a drowned corpse glanced through the green water; a fair arm was the only limb clearly visible, whence the bracelet had been washed or torn.
>
> The second picture contained for foreground only the dim peak of a hill, with some grass and leaves slanting as if by a breeze. Beyond and above an expanse of sky, dark blue as at twilight: rising into the sky was a woman's shape to the bust, portrayed in tint as dusk and soft as I could combine. The dim forehead was crowned with a star; the lineaments below were seen as through the suffusion of vapour; the eyes shone dark and wild; the hair streamed shadowy, like a beamless cloud torn by storm or electric travail. On the neck lay a pale reflection like moonlight; the same faint lustre touched the train of thin clouds from which rose and bowed this vision of the Evening Star.
>
> The third showed the pinnacle of an iceberg piercing a polar winter sky: a

muster of northern lights reared their dim lances, close serried along the horizon. Throwing these into distance, rose, in the foreground, a head, – a colossal head, inclined towards the iceberg, and resting against it. Two thin hands, joined under the forehead, and supporting it, drew up before the features a sable veil; a brow quite bloodless, white as a bone, and an eye hollow and fixed, blank of meaning but for the glassiness of despair, alone were visible. Above the temples, amidst wreathed turban folds of black drapery, vague in its character and consistency as a cloud, gleamed a ring of white flame, gemmed with sparkles of a more lurid tinge. This pale crescent was 'The likeness of a Kingly Crown': what it diademed was 'the shape which had none'.

'Were you happy when you painted these pictures?' asked Mr Rochester, presently. (Brontë 1966: 156–7)

This passage illustrates, I believe, that some present-day assumptions about the nature of unconscious imagery are echoing ways of thinking which were to be found in earlier times – in this case in nineteenth-century Romanticism. There are several relevant clues to this. The pictures are acknowledged as arising spontaneously from inside the psyche – 'I saw them with *the spiritual eye*, before I attempted to embody them'. This doubtless reflects Charlotte Brontë's own capacity for eidetic vision, a gift which she shared with her sister. Second, it may be noted that Mr Rochester doesn't seem to find this inner and personal source of pictorial inspiration unusual, a situation which is harder to imagine in an earlier period. This point is emphasized by the fact that he asks about her *state of mind* when she made the pictures. There is an implication that she was probably *not* happy at the time; this comment therefore assumes an interpretation of the paintings – something quite remarkable for 1847, and which clearly shows that the Romantic Movement was definitely able to accommodate the idea of interpreting pictures, in a psychological sense, long before the advent of psychoanalysis. Finally, and perhaps less surprisingly in view of the above, the pictures, as described, are symbolic in a way that would be immediately familiar to most art therapists, and even can be imagined as examples of artwork produced in the course of analysis or therapy at the present time. I would say that the described images have something of an archetypal quality about them, in a Jungian sense.

The language used in describing the pictures is strongly evocative, like fragments of a story which the paintings illustrate. All three pictures are ambiguous in feeling. Thus in the first the situation of shipwreck and death is contrasted with the strange and highly focused image of the cormorant holding the precious bracelet, the contrast heightened by words like 'brilliant' and 'glittering' in the context of 'low and livid', 'swollen sea', and 'drowned corpse'. In the third picture there is a somewhat similar kind of imagery, where the 'bloodless, white as a bone', 'colossal head', which rests against an iceberg, wears an enigmatic 'ring of white flame, gemmed with sparkles'. The second painting, unlike the other two, has no apparent sinister implications, conveying rather a sense of awe in the presence of a giant archetypal figure; but here too there is a subtle sense of contrast in the 'dusk and soft', moonlit, feminine image, with her 'dark and wild' eyes, and hair 'like a beamless cloud torn by storm or electric travail'.

The images are not explained; it is assumed that the reader will understand enough of what they mean, in a direct and largely subjective way. There is no obvious iconography or social message; the story indicates that the pictures were influenced by certain of Bewick's illustrations to his *History of British Birds* (1797–1804). At the very beginning of the novel Jane describes her fascination with certain of Bewick's surprisingly bleak themes of shipwreck and Arctic wastes, and her fear of others even more remote from ornithology:

> The fiend pinning down the thief's pack behind him, I passed over quickly: it was an object of terror.
>
> So was the black, horned thing seated aloof on a rock, surveying a distant crowd surrounding a gallows. (Brontë 1966: 40)

Clearly, the themes do not derive from Jane's everyday experience, and yet some meaning in the pictures is ascribed to her personally. Both Jane and Mr Rochester seem to recognize that the pictures have significance mainly for the artist herself. The reader is not persuaded beyond the enquiry about Jane's happiness to confront squarely the depression that seems to be implied. There is subtlety in her reply: 'I was *absorbed*, sir: yes, and I was happy. To paint them, in short, was to enjoy one of keenest pleasures I have ever known' (Brontë 1966: 157, emphasis mine). Jane appears to hesitate on the brink of confirming his interpretive hint of unhappiness, but then she changes her mind nimbly in mid-sentence and offers instead a rather defensive pretence that he was asking simply if she enjoyed making the pictures, another matter entirely. As the reader is well aware, the pictures were painted at a time when Jane was far from happy, but when she was able to escape into imagery as a release from chronic loneliness. This is a substantial acknowledgement of a subjective aspect in the making of art. This assumption is an historically significant change of attitude, for by linking the image to the state of mind of the person who made it, while largely ignoring, in this instance, its artistic pretensions, new importance is assigned to non-professional art and the imagination.

I have drawn attention to the sense of familiarity about the images described in *Jane Eyre* because it seems to me that, with few exceptions, some important historical influences upon, and precedents for, approaching healing through artistic imagery have been largely ignored by the helping professions, including art therapists themselves. The years since 1916 when Jung first encouraged his patients to follow their fantasies through pictorial imagery (Edwards 1987), and the fifty years or so since the professional appearance of art therapists, have to be seen in a much longer time scale and in the context of a more elaborated and enduring scheme of ideas, if the concept of art in the service of healing is to receive proper and sufficient recognition. An outline of such a perspective can be summarized as follows.

1 In *religious* beliefs leading to the production of artifacts representing deities, or as images of spiritual or visionary experience in teaching, worship, and meditation. Conversely, in ascribing *negative* power to images by banning them from sacred situations.

2 In spiritual *healing* practices throughout various cultures, where these include the use of ritual artifacts, designs, mandalas, and other images.

3 In *philosophical* inquiry, addressing questions about possible relationships between creative inspiration and unusual states of mind, including madness. Such questions were discussed by Plato, who detected a 'divine madness', and Aristotle, who described a typical artistic 'temperament'. The Greeks also diagnosed phobias in dance rituals, and understood the cathartic importance of drama (Dodds 1951). Lombroso's cruder and more extreme view in the last century was that creative genius and insanity are but two sides of the same coin (Henzell 1978). On the other hand, the early nineteenth-century Romantic philosophers more sensitively focused attention on the value of subjective experience in the arts and in psychology (Ellenberger 1970).

4 In *artistic* traditions which evolved languages of imagery with their own syntax and values, leading back inevitably to words again, through the discourse that images provoke, and hence to various forms of iconographic and iconological interpretation (Panofsky 1939).

5 In *anthropological* research which records and authenticates the embodiment of custom and belief systems in artistic forms (Joplin 1971).

6 In the *medical* discovery soon after 1800 that institutionalized psychiatric patients, like prisoners before them, sometimes engage in spontaneous art-making, leading to the collection and study of such material, and thence to attempts to *diagnose* a mental patient's condition from his or her pictures.

7 In *educational* assumptions that the arts have a civilizing influence upon human behaviour and, within this, the art educational thesis that intellectual and emotional development is promoted through art activities and art appreciation.

8 In *psychological* theories of the unconscious, and particularly the introduction by Freud and Jung of methods of recognizing unconscious processes in dreams, fantasies, and pictorial imagery.

The relative importance given to different traditions in this wide archaeological survey of the prehistory of art in therapy may be arguable, but I believe that it is crucial that as far as possible they are apprehended comprehensively. In the past, attitudes about imagery and healing have, for the most part, been expressed independently rather than interdependently.

The point has been made that the components 'art' and 'therapy', within the concept 'art therapy', are each subject to very different historically-based assumptions which presage, in their conjunction, potential for both conflict and insight (Champernowne 1971).

In general terms, art has received two broadly different treatments from a therapeutic point of view; both can be discerned in contemporary practice (Edwards 1980). First, the notion that unsolicited spontaneous images can be indicative of a person's mental state; second, the belief that the actual making of images can put a person in touch with natural healing processes in the psyche. In terms of more recent history, I would say that the former attitude coalesced in eighteenth-century Neoclassicism and the latter in nineteenth-century Romanticism.

At the beginning of the eighteenth century the ethos favouring rationality (in 'the Age of Reason') gave low status to the disorderly side of human nature; Foucault tells us that it was the culmination of an age of confinement as well as of 'reason', in which those who fell into vagrancy, criminality, and madness were condemned as threats to the social order, which thus could only be defended by confining the 'irrational' transgressor, in a workhouse, a prison, or an asylum (Foucault 1965). Accordingly, we have come to think of the art of the period as setting a high priority on form and structural composition, expressing emotion only vicariously and distantly; for example, by borrowing from Classical Greek and Roman mythology. Nature was organized according to principles of order and balance. Contemporary society came to be represented, eventually, in satirical cartoons, but the emphasis in early eighteenth-century art was not upon the immediate environment.

In his time, Hogarth was, in part, an exception. Some oil paintings, and especially the portraits, have a freshness about them which anticipates Romanticism, and he was not interested in Classical themes; the works for which Hogath is most famous portray dramatizations of everyday life, in a spirit of moralizing satire. He consciously aimed at stage-like presentation. It is in these theatrically-distanced satirical commentaries that Hogarth comes closest to the spirit of Neoclassicism.

The final scene in the 'Rake's Progress' series of paintings and subsequent engravings (1732–3 and 1735) depicts 'Bedlam', a ward in the Bethlehem Hospital in London. It pictures the dreadful consequences of a dissolute life. In terms of the Age of Reason, madness represents total alienation from society. The hospital staff attending the Rake are grim and matter-of-fact. The two women visitors are not obviously satirized; they are probably there to be diverted by the shocking spectacle of lunacy – an acceptable form of recreation at the time. The Rake's former mistress, Sarah Young, weeps over him. All the other figures are unambiguously patients, in the grip of their hallucinations and fantasies. One poses as a king, naked, except for a crown; one as a bishop, while another plays crazily on a violin. Squeezed behind an open cell door, a man is drawing on the wall. His images include a depiction of the globe, a ship, some kind of cylindrical object, a moon, and a geometrical construction, suggesting navigation. The drawings appear random and inconsequential and could hardly be called expressive in any usual sense of the term.

Everything about the patients as portrayed by Hogarth exemplifies futility in madness, not a plea for asylum reform. It is a parody and travesty of the world outside. One could say that music, art, religion, government, the imagination, and human relationship are all represented, but each is invalidated by madness. The two women visitors are there to be thrilled by a bizarre situation; we might describe this as an anxious celebration of their own precarious sanity. They are the identifiable observers within the picture plane and thus are Hogarth's audience too, witnessing a horror play with real people playing themselves; yet their status as real people in a real world has been withdrawn. Here madness is a divisive projection of irrationality, and in this split between the sane and the insane there is little possibility of empathy with the mentally ill. (Curiously, and somewhat paradoxically, Hogarth happened to be particularly interested in 'empathy' in a different and mainly aesthetic sense, believing, for example, that viewers identify themselves empathically with columns supporting the weight of a building.)

Another significant historical inference that may be drawn from Hogarth's picture is that henceforth certain kinds of imaginative expression might be regarded as typical of insanity. In other words, more concretely than ever before, a person's art has been added to the list of human behaviours to be scrutinized for evidence of madness. A somewhat later engraving, probably derived from Hogarth's, shows a patient drawing a face on an asylum wall. These may be the first illustrations of graphic expression by psychiatric patients.

From this incorporation, however peripherally, of art into symptomatology, there were at least two later developments. First, that a mentally ill patient's artwork might have medically diagnostic implications, a view that was taken by the French psychiatrists Tardieu (1872) and Simon (1876). And second, the more extreme view (a caricature of Plato's belief that creative inspiration derived from 'divine madness') promoted by Lombroso (1882), that artistic inclinations in an individual were likely to be *indicative* of a predisposition to mental instability (Henzell 1978). The Victorian painter Richard Dadd could have been cited by Lombroso as an example of the latter; his descent into madness and violence, including murdering his father, was never 'cured', yet it is generally agreed that the best work was produced during the last forty years of his life, while he was incarcerated (Greysmith 1973). (It need hardly be added that there is no case for generalization here.) The case of James Tilley Matthews was perhaps the first clear example of the former attitude, in that he was judged mad partly on the evidence of his artwork (Henzell 1978).

Matthews was a psychiatric patient between 1793 and 1813 in the same Bethlehem hospital that was the subject of Hogarth's painting and engraving. He was an architect, confined against his wishes and those of his family. This gave rise to lengthy legal proceedings which were subsequently published, in 1810, by John Haslam, the hospital doctor who won the case that Matthews was in fact 'a mischievous lunatic'. The book comes 'with a curious plate', an engraving by Matthews, while he was a patient in the hospital. He described it as an 'Air Loom' which he believed, according to Haslam, depicted the machine used by his enemies to torture him by remote control, causing his acute symptoms of distress. In other words, it seems that Matthews saw his engraving as an explanation of his sanity, while Haslam, perhaps not unreasonably, saw it as proof of his deluded state. Haslam's published evidence about Matthews is simply concerned with proving his insanity, not with the nature of his illness, or the meaning of the 'Air Loom' (Henzell 1978).

A severely rationalistic view of mental illness and its manifestations certainly survived throughout the nineteenth century and accordingly non-professional artwork by the mentally ill tended to be of interest for its curiosity value – hospitals assembled little museums for fee-paying visitors – and as a possible source of diagnostic information. Furthermore, a professional artist who went mad, like Richard Dadd, could scarcely regain an artistic reputation, since he was regarded as tragically 'lost' once he entered hospital (Greysmith 1973).

The noble-sounding eighteenth-century ideals of 'Reason' and 'Enlighten-ment' and the cool formalism of Neoclassical art could only lead to viewing the expression of inner turmoil as an unforgiveable breaking of the rules. As a standpoint it has a place and value; it is not difficult to see why, for example, psychiatrists, following medical doctors, looked for norms in human behaviour. Once patients' imagery came to be included fashionably in nineteenth-century symptomatology, the pathological could be sought and even categorized in its image forms. Inevitably, this idea was liable to extension in perceptions of fantasy and the imagination as worthless or dangerous, or both. In our own time this dominates the (largely unfounded) lay view of art therapy as coldly diagnostic and anti-art.

There is, as I have already suggested through the passage in *Jane Eyre*, a very different historical perspective which allows for a much more sympathetic approach to imagery in the context of healing. This, the other essential voice in the development of art as therapy, was first articulated by the German Romantic philosophers, was listened to, if only for a short time, by the medical profession in Europe (Ellenberger 1970), and was embodied through the rest of the nineteenth century (and up to the present time) in Romanticism in the arts.

The philosophic, psychological, and artistic ideas associated with subjectivity found significant expression in the Romantic movement. As Neoclassicism had cultivated detachment and equilibrium, Romanticism depicted emotional involvement and the sense of restless dynamic change that this implies. The Movement embraced a positive conception of the imagination, gave to dreaming and fantasies the status of creative source-material, and to artistic representation of inner experience a new validity. In the visual arts one has only to think most obviously of Blake, Fuseli, Goya, and Delacroix, to get a sense of this different attitude. Another Romantic painter, Theódore Géricault, is something of a special case.

In the course of a period of depression, Géricault became friendly with a Dr Georget who treated him. This led to the painter becoming a hospital artist for a time; thus a project was devised to portray certain typical psychiatric illnesses, as they were then understood. The project itself, as far as is known, was inconclusive as research, but the portraits Géricault made of psychiatric patients are remarkable in that they show an empathic identification with the subjects. It might be said that Géricault seems to have allowed his own experience of emotional disturbance to influence his approach to the portraits.

For the Romantic, irrationality was accepted as an inevitable and even vital component in life. I do not mean to 'romanticize' Romanticism, which frequently blundered into emotional excesses, or to deny that its revolutionary spirit was sometimes political rather than psychological in intent. What does seem compellingly clear is that a new momentum was generated by the Romantics, without which the conscious idea of art as a vehicle for individual personal expression is difficult to conceive. The Romantic ideal was not about truth to external reality so much as authentic and comprehensive psychophysical rapport with the natural world, a 'philosophy of nature'.

Given that Romanticism flourished in the arts, it is important to remember also that Romantic philosophers like von Schelling, von Schubert, and C. G. Carus (who was also a painter) had a short-lived but extremely important influence upon medicine and psychiatry in the first thirty years of the nineteenth century. In Romantic medicine, to be healthy was to be in complete harmony with nature, an ideal which has far more credibility now than it did when Romantic medicine succumbed to more technologically based treatment strategies. Ellenberger (1970) mentions a number of German doctors who, inspired by Romanticism and *Naturphilosophie*, were prominent in the early part of the century.

The most important of these, from the point of view of the arts in therapy, was Johann Christian Reil (1759–1813) who has been discussed at length by Ernest Harms (1960). Reil's ideas were remarkably in advance of their time. In *The Unconscious Before Freud*, Whyte (1962) quotes Reil's modern sense of psychodynamics in 1790: 'The passions act powerfully on the organism, can make it sick, and kill it. But, by the same powers they have also the capacity under certain circumstances to cure it.' Reil, like some other German Romantic psychiatrists, worked with his patients in what we should now call a therapeutic community. He is perhaps most well known (apart perhaps from giving his name to a small part of the brain) for his conception of a kind of psychodrama in which hospital staff participated in acting out patients' fantasies in specially staged plays, as a part of treatment. Sometimes the patients took part too, but the really crucial innovatory idea was that the plays were based upon individual fantasies, not upon a generalized treatment method. According to Harms, Reil also proposed that mentally ill patients should be housed in pleasant surroundings, that treatment should commence with physical work, then progress to handicrafts, to singing and other music groups, to art activities, and finally to verbal psychotherapy, when appropriate.

This progression certainly implies that Reil had in mind for art activities something more sophisticated and imaginatively involving than simple diversion. In conjunction with the importance that Reil attached to engaging 'the passions', one might say that a model for art therapy was theoretically in an advanced stage of development almost 200 years ago. What is all the more remarkable is that Reil's ideas about art for psychiatric patients predate Ruskin by fifty years. The amateur artist had little place in western society before 1857, when John Ruskin proposed schools of instruction in art, and even then with the intention of promoting artistic talent, not better adjusted individuals. Reil was ahead of the pioneer art educators Ebenezer Cooke, Arthur Wesley Dow, and Franz Cizek by almost a century (Read 1943). Unlike Ruskin and some more recent skill-directed advocates of art education (Edwards 1976; Efland 1976), Reil seems to have seen value in art activity as an emotional engagement of the whole conscious and unconscious personality.

The treatment methods proposed by Reil and other doctors influenced by Romanticism fell out of fashion soon after his death and had all but disappeared by 1850. Psychiatry, unlike the arts, swung in a new and more mechanistic direction. This caused Romantic concepts to be seen as unscientific and therefore tinged with charlatanism. Painters, poets, and composers continued to embody the Romantic preoccupation with subjective experience which suffered half a century of eclipse in psychological circles. However, Freud and Jung were well read in German Romantic philosophy, and greatly influenced by it. As Whyte reminds us, Freud's theories brought earlier concepts of the unconscious into a new and more structured synthesis. Jung, without substantially contradicting Freud, elaborated differently emphasized views of the unconscious and 'subjective reality'. He also showed some early talent for drawing and painting (Jaffé 1979) and later became deeply involved in making images of his own inner experiences; from 1916 onwards, he encouraged his patients to do the same, as an essential part of their psychological work with him.

I rather doubt if Jung (or Freud either) would have approved of being described as Romantic; but the shift of methodological emphasis from therapist to patient, from earlier attempts at treating fantasy as a problem, to allowing fantasy itself a central role in healing through spontaneous image-making or other forms of active imagination, like Romanticism, allows subjectivity its due place. In giving images of 'the passions' symbolic value, we work within this tradition.

References

Brontë, C. (1966) *Jane Eyre*, Penguin, Harmondsworth.

Champernowne, I. (1971) 'Art and therapy – an uneasy partnership', *Inscape*, pp. 2–14.

Dodds, E. R. (1951) *The Greeks and the Irrational*, University of California Press.

Edwards, M. (1976) 'Art therapy and art education: towards a reconciliation', *Studies in Art Education*, vol. 17, no. 2, pp. 63–6.

Edwards, M. (1980) 'Art therapy now', *Inscape*, vol. 5, no. 1, pp. 18–21.

Edwards, M. (1987) 'Jungian analytic art therapy', in Rubin, J. (ed.) *Approaches to Art Therapy*, Bruner/Mazel, New York, pp. 92–113.

Efland, A. (1976) 'Books on art therapy: a personal comment', *Studies in Art Education*, vol. 16, no. 2.

Ellenberger, H. F. (1970) *The Discovery of the Unconscious*, Basic Books, New York.

Foucault, M. (1965) *Madness and Civilisation*, Random House, New York.

Greysmith, D. (1973) *Richard Dadd*, Macmillan, London.

Harms, E. (1957) 'Modern psychiatry – 150 years ago', *Journal of Medical Science*, CIII.

Harms, E. (1960) 'Johann Christian Reil', *American Journal of Psychiatry*, CXVI.

Haslam, J. (1810) *Illustrations of Madness*.

Henzell, J. (1978) 'Art and psychopathology: a history of its study and applications', in *The Inner Eye*, Museum of Modern Art, Oxford, pp. 27–34.

Henzell, J. (1979) unpublished manuscript.

Jaffé, A. (ed.) (1979) *C. G. Jung: Word and Image*, Princeton University Press.

Joplin, C. (ed.) (1971) *Art and Aesthetics in Primitive Societies*, Dutton, New York.

Lombroso, C. (1882) *Genio e follia*.

Lombroso, C. (1891) *Man of Genius*.

Panofsky, E. (1939) *Studies in Iconology*, Oxford University Press.

Read, H. (1943) *Education Through Art*, Faber & Faber, London.

Reil, J. C. (1815) *Entweckelung einer allgemeinen Pathologie*, III.

Ruskin, J. (1857) *The Elements of Drawing*.

Simon, M. (1876) L'imagination dans la folie', in *Annales Medico-psychologiques*, 16, 358–90.

Tardieu, A. (1872) *Etude Medico-legale sur la Folie*, Paris.

Whyte, L. L. (1962) *The Unconscious Before Freud.* Tavistock, London.

Chapter Eight

The imitation of madness: the influence of psychopathology upon culture

Roland Littlewood

We have, I think, reason to believe that the person who has attained perfection of balance in the control of his instinctive tendencies, in whom the processes of suppression and sublimation have become wholly effective, may thereby become completely adapted to his environment and attain a highly peaceful and stable existence. Such existence is not, however, the condition of exceptional accomplishment, for which there would seem to be necessary a certain degree of instability. I believe that we may look to this instability as the source of energy from which we may expect great accomplishments in art and science. It may be also that, through this instability, new strength will be given to those movements which under the most varied guise express the deep craving for religion which seems to be universal among Mankind. (W. H. Rivers (1920) *Instinct and the Unconscious*, Cambridge University Press, p. 158.)

Introduction

Innovators and leaders of new political and religious movements are frequently dismissed as mad, particularly when their innovations are unacceptable or based on premises at odds with those of their critics. To denigrate them as mad is to deny them rationality. It is to mock their followers, for only the credulous and simple-minded could take madmen seriously.

The use of 'mad' or 'crazy' or their equivalents to imply unrestrained or unreasonable actions is of course common to most, perhaps all, societies. For a journalist to describe a community torn between two options as 'schizophrenic' may be a metaphor more currently fashionable than 'the horns of a dilemma'. The journalist may permit himself further licence: for the Caribbean to seek identity with the Third World is 'madness'; whilst the former prime minister of Grenada (who was famed for his speeches to the United Nations on the subject of flying saucers) may be characterized as 'a street-corner eccentric, a mystical maniac'.[1] To explain the origins of war as the conspiracy of a mad dictator may be a commonplace conceit but how seriously are we to take the ethnographer who suggests that Hitler had a 'hysterical phobia, conversion symptoms and classical paranoia' and that St Paul, 'another vatic with inchoate ego boundaries', was epileptic, or the psychologist who confidently asserts that Tiberius and Calvin were schizophrenics, and Stalin 'a paranoic'.[2]

The idiom of disease is a powerful political metaphor[3] and we take it as such when the journalist tells us that the doctrine of the People's Temple in Guyana (Jonestown) was 'infected with disease'.[4] It is perhaps a metaphor when Kroeber calls magic 'the pathology of culture' or La Barre dismisses snake-handling sects as 'zany' or 'crazy'.[5] But when ethnographers explain shamanism as the very specific consequence of 'epilepsy, hysteria, fear neurosis [and] veritable idiocy'[6] or the psychoanalyst characterizes the shaman as psychotic and his religion as 'organized schizophrenia'[7] one may be permitted to wonder as to the explanatory value of such designifications. The Hebrews attempted to discredit their more embarrassing prophets by suggesting they were insane[8] and the anthropologist who talks of the 'authentic schizoid component' of the members of the cult he is studying is clearly not a potential recruit.[9]

Since the aftermath of the French Revolution (which was regarded by some doctors as a veritable epidemic, whilst others dwelt on the psychopathology of the hereditary monarchs,[10] the medical profession has not scrupled to use diagnosis to interpret history. The Professor of Medicine at Makarere University, fleeing Idi Amin, offered this diagnosis of his former president: 'grandiose paranoia, hypomania, probably schizophrenia, hypomanic paranoia, possibly GPI and the Jekyll and Hyde syndrome'.[11] American psychiatrists in a well-publicized report suggested that Senator Barry Goldwater, then a candidate for the presidency, was mentally unstable, and as a consequence were very nearly sued.[12] In their attempt to understand society and social change, psychiatry and psychoanalysis have formulated interpretations couched primarily in psychopathology; Freud suggested that religion is essentially a codification of individual neuroses, particularly when it took the form of innovation.[13] Whilst sociologists following Durkheim's dictum have (at times) been able to dispense with purely psychological or psychopathological interpretations of existing institutions, they appear to have near universal recourse to them when describing social change, particularly when it takes a dramatic or chiliastic form. It may be that functionalist steady-state theorists of society always have difficulty with the problem of innovation and rely on a psychological idiom which lies outside the social domain and which can initiate the necessary changes.[14] Certainly, when faced with millennial movements, particularly those Linton has characterized as 'nativist',[15] not merely do social scientists frequently describe them in psychological terms, but they appear to regard them as somehow *more psychological* in nature than the social institutions of quieter times; millennial movements are more 'affectively laden' and they operate at 'high intensity'.[16] Bryan Wilson, conceptually far removed from the psychoanalytic anthropologists of the United States, nevertheless describes 'affected members ... uttering gibberish [in] outbursts of frenzy' and suggests the social organization of millennial groups is hampered by their 'affectivity'.[17] Similarly, the 'dancing mania' of Madagascar and the 'Vaihala madness' of Papua are described as 'spontaneous and stimulated frenzy',[18] i.e. they are either pathology or passive manipulation, in either case outside normal psychological and social functioning. The contemporary use of 'charisma' unites the two – the disordered prophet with his suggestible flock.

The visions of millennial leaders have been described by scholars as schizophrenic even when normative for their contemporaries: Hung Hsiu-Chu'an, the leader of the Taiping rebellion; Te Ua, the founder of the Maori Hau Hau.[19] Theory aside, colonial and national authorities have frequently interned chiliastic sectarians in psychiatric hospitals: Ne Loiag, the leader of the 1943 Jonfrum movement in the New Hebrides; Rice Kamanga, founder of the Barotse Twelve Society; Alexander Bedward, the Jamaican revivalist; Leonard Howell, the Rastafarian.[20] In Canada participants in a Doukhobor nude protest were put in the local asylum, as were Jehovah's Witnesses in Germany in the 1930s, and Baptists and Pentecostalists in contemporary Russia.[21]

Popular perception of madness leads to official denigration: 'The wider [Jamaican] society associated Rastafarianism with madness' and leaders were

> taken to gaol on sedition or to the asylum for lunacy .... The process of becoming a Rastafarian is still regarded by the wider society as one of mental deterioration and the more modern embrace of the creed by young educated high school and university graduates is seen as an urgent matter for the psychiatrist.[22]

To employ the idiom of insanity in order to discredit implies the prior recognition of a distinct sphere of psychopathology, one that is characterized by a defect, either a disorder of the individual mind analogous to physical disease or a physical disturbance of the brain itself. The small-scale non-industrialized societies with whom anthropologists have been largely concerned may have such a separate domain of psychopathology, or they may regard what the psychiatrist terms mental illness as the secondary and unnamed consequence of unsuccessful interaction with mystical forces.[23]

The legitimacy of madness

There has, of course, been an alternative tradition in the west which, while accepting the existence of a separate domain of psychopathology, nevertheless refuses to denigrate it or divorce it from the possibility of active meaning. This tradition asserts that psychopathology can be both creative and innovative. In any period it seems likely that both positions – the denial of meaning in madness and the affirmation of meaning – are held by some individuals. The first attempt to assert meaning in psychopathology appears to be that of Plato. Whilst he agrees that madness is a 'disease of the body caused by bodily conditions', he is concerned with meaning, not aetiology, and meaning can only be ascribed by reason, coming after the illness or from others:

> We only achieve [prophecy] when the power of our understanding is inhibited by sleep or when we are in an abnormal condition owing to disease or divine inspiration .... It is not the business of any man so long as he is in an irrational state to interpret his own visions and say what good or ill they portend.[24]

In medieval Europe insanity was perceived as a punishment or test, sent by God or the Devil; although in itself it was meaningless as a communication, by rational meditation on it by the healthy part of the mind it could become 'a healing agent of penitence'.[25] At the same time there existed a Christian tradition which placed a positive value on the state of 'folly' itself (including foolishness and insanity) for its intimations of child-like innocence; if the world was rational and thus compromised, then the Incarnation could only have been an act of folly.[26]

The shift in authority from clergy to medicine in the early modern period deprived psychopathology (now totally shorn from its supernatural origins) of any possibility of conventional meaning; it was merely symptomatic of bodily disease. Scot and Bright daringly asserted that the practice of witchcraft was the consequence of brain disease. In the eighteenth century Swift and Pope used the presumed physical origin of mental states as the basis for satire; in *The Mechanical Operation of the Spirit* Swift says eloquence is no more than an orgasm without stimulation, and that when the vapours in Louis XIV's head went up he engaged in war, whilst if they descended Europe was at peace. Like Plato, the Romantics accepted the separate existence of psychopathology but divorced its origin from its potential values as a communication; it was natural and elementary and hence a source of creativity. Madness was akin to genius as it was to the thought of the child or primitive. 'The greater the genius the greater the unsoundness.'[27] So far from the biological aetiology of madness devaluing its products, abnormal mental states, and hence genius, were artificially cultivated; the mentally ill were regarded as additionally advantaged through being placed outside social contraints, and thus resistant to cultural indoctrination.[28] Whilst a few writers like Lamb (in *The Sanity of True Genius*) deplored the necessary equation of madness and genius, the thesis was to grip the poetic and popular imagination into the twentieth century. Nietzsche wrote that 'it seems impossible to be an artist without being diseased' and suggested that in ecstatic madness man gave reign to underlying emotions and participated 'in a higher community ... a collective release of all the symbolic powers'.[29]

In *The Varieties of Religious Experience* William James suggested that the essence of religion lay in the 'pattern setters ... for whom religion exists not as a dull habit but as an acute fever .... [They] frequently have nervous instability'.[30] He quoted with approval the English psychiatrist Henry Maudsley: 'What right have we to believe Nature under any obligation to do her work by means of complete minds only? She may find an incomplete mind a more suitable instrument for a particular purpose'.[31] Whilst James says that religious experience should be measured 'by its fruits' rather than its origin, he clearly prefers pathological religion as more authentic. It is probably Lombroso who is still most closely associated with the equation of madness and genius – 'a system of hereditary degeneration of the epileptoid variety'.[32] If human nature was naturally conservative then change could only be initiated through abnormality, and he distinguished between 'true genius' (of the epileptoid type) aligned with 'the general course of evolution', and 'pseudogenius' associated with unsuccessful rebellions.[33] Francis Galton, too, postulated a link between madness and eminence but Havelock Ellis's subsequent report that there was little evidence for the hypothesis has been confirmed generally. A recent suggestion is that it is the relatives of schizophrenics who are more creative than the general population[34] and the common contemporary conclusion by writers on creativity is that whilst creative people may have more 'psychological conflicts', they are unlikely to be insane because they possess 'greater ego strength'.[35]

The two Romantic axioms, the equation of mad, childlike, primitive, and archaic, and the idea of the artist-genius as an unbalanced prophet without honour, formed the European *avant garde*'s image of itself; Van Gogh, who experienced epileptic fits and periodic depression regarded himself as insane:

> For a madman is also a man to whom society did not want to listen and whom it wanted to prevent from uttering unbearable truths .... It is a man who has preferred to go mad in the sense in which society understands the term, rather than be false to a certain idea of human behaviour.[36]

What George Lukács has called 'modernism's obsession with pathological and extreme states' was most clearly seen in Surrealism; Breton's dictum that the surrealist endeavour was 'Dictée de la pensée en l'absence de toute controle'[37] returned the artist or poet to the untrammelled primitive core of creativity; the models were the mad, the eccentric, the mediums, the cranks, inventors, and self-publicists. Antonin Artaud observed that 'Delirium is as legitimate, as logical, as any other succession of human ideas or acts'.[38]

The 'anti-psychiatry' movement in Europe and the United States in the 1960s and 1970s similarly decided that 'the boundary between sanity and madness is a false one'.[39] In the writing of R. D. Laing we can note a movement from victimology (the psychotic is formed by a process of social labelling) to one in which he is a hero, the artist who can offer a privileged critique of social reason. The counter-culture however failed to establish a situation in which psychopathology could be perceived as a meaningful everyday communication. Mark Vonnegut's autobiography *The Eden Express* describes how the hippie commune in which he lived proved unable to cope with his episode of schizophrenia.[40] After a good deal of debate they took him to the local mental hospital for treatment.

The major anthropological contribution to the question of whether psychopathology can offer a meaningful communication has come from those anthropologists who were influenced by psychoanalysis. For Freud culture was a product of instinctual strivings and social demands, a dynamic conflict whose resolution could include social integration in the form of instinctual sublimation or individual psychopathology. Health was a balance between instinctual strivings and social restraints; if culture was a product of individual conflicts writ large, cultural innovation was only possible through such an individual conflict. As Roheim, the ethnographer who most closely adhered to an unmodified Freudian position, put it '[Social] change is only the discharge of suppressed emotion'.[41] It is not my intention to review here the vast literature, principally American, which seeks to demonstrate the social role of psychopathology by employing psychodynamic theories. Suffice to say that when Devereux and La Barre[42] suggest that culture may originate in individual psychopathology, their use of terms like 'schizophrenia' is unrecognizable to descriptive psychiatrists who would find little to add to Ackernecht's critique in 1943:

> The custom of covering moral judgements with a pseudoscientific psychopathological nomenclature is no advance at all and is equally bad for both morals and science .... When religion is but 'organised schizophrenia' [Devereux' expression] then there is no room or necessity for history, sociology, etc. God's earth was, and is, but a gigantic state hospital and pathography becomes the unique and universal science.[43]

Ackernecht suggested that the only possible instances for religious roles being routinely preceded by mental disturbance were the classical Siberian shamans described by Sieroszerski and Bogoras.

The social institution of shamanism thus might include the mentally ill, those recovered from mental illness, and those incipiently ill.[44] Where medical anthropology has been concerned with the major psychoses it has regarded them as 'natural symbols' upon which social meanings are imposed, not as potentially active social forces in their own right. Is there anything which can be saved from a debate now confined to studies of the history of ethnographic theory?

The influence of psychopathology upon culture

If we accept the existence of an autonomous domain of psychopathology, closely allied to the popular western concept of 'insanity', can it actively influence society? If it does, under what conditions may the statements of the madman be taken by his contemporaries as valid? As there is no biological marker of psychopathology independent of social action, and observers (as we have seen) ascribe psychopathology to normative situations on rather slender grounds, it would be appropriate initially to restrict our search to situations where we find evidence of a biological component in psychopathology, or at least to psychopathology defined on descriptive rather than dynamic grounds. There appear to be five situations under which such 'imitation of madness' is possible.

1 An individual who is already influential becomes psychotic but is validated for a time by the inertia of the political structure. A limited example of this is *folie à deux* where, in a close but socially isolated family, a dominant member develops delusions which dependent family members then accept; the 'passive' delusions of the dependants rapidly disappear when they are isolated from the dominant originator.[45] Something like this is the idea behind the popular perception of Hitler or Amin as charismatic madmen. Whilst it is probably rare for an influential individual to maintain his influence if actually insane, there are frequent instances of absolute rulers becoming increasingly isolated and suspicious as a result of their situation. If leaders become seriously psychotic they are probably soon eliminated, as Suetonius suggested in the case of Caligula. Mad rulers are unlikely in the general run of things, for their predisposition is likely to have manifested itself earlier and to have eliminated them from the power struggle: Idi Amin, for instance, had been head of the Ugandan armed forces for some years before he sought absolute power.

2 Alternatively the individual may be only periodically insane and in between episodes live in the shared social reality where he can validate his delusions as acceptable communications by explaining them in conventional terms. He may find his previous psychopathological ideas strange and the quest for their meaning may then be identical with external validation. In his *Journals* George Fox describes an episode when, passing near Lichfield, he felt impelled to take off his shoes in a field and run through the town shouting 'Woe unto the bloody city of Lichfield'; returning later to his shoes he was puzzled as to the meaning of his act and appears relieved on discovering later that the town had been the site of Christian martyrdom under Diocletian.[46] Psychopathology, like schizophrenia, which includes widespread personality changes and a lowering of social competence, is unlikely to be subsequently integrated in this way. Early psychosis, isolated psychotic episodes, or phasic reactions like manic-depressive psychosis, are more amenable to re-entry into the shared world, and thus to imitation – what Devos has termed 'pathomimesis':[47] the episode itself may be less a spontaneous transformation of existing themes than the signal that legitimates a change which is previously or subsequently conceived of in a normative state. If epileptic fits

are believed to be of divine origin then the presence of divinity will be ushered in by fits, whether spontaneous, sought, or simulated.

The isolated psychotic episode, whether truly innovative or merely a signal for mystical imputation, may resemble the shamanic employment of altered states of consciousness where the visions are culturally standardized and their import agreed by consensual validation. Among the Trinidadian Shouters, fasting and sensory deprivation are used to attain visions but the pattern and authenticity of these are validated by the church as a whole. In fact, members of the group I am going to describe were expelled from the Shouters for their idiosyncratic visions. The psychopathology of the psychotic is likely to be more idiosyncratic than everyday shared beliefs. However, as in the case of Sabbatai Sevi, the innovation involved may be merely tapping certain generally available but latent beliefs, or reversing the everyday themes. The innovative power in these cases comes from the conviction with which psychosis imbues the novelty, or the performance of it in action, as opposed to the more casual mention others may make of its possibility.

3 Nietzsche, Strindberg, and Artaud are not automatically discredited by the western intellectual because they developed, respectively, general paralysis of the insane, paranoia, and schizophrenia, even though it is impossible to separate the later work of each from their psychopathology. Delusions may be isolated from the recognition of pathology: 'He's mad but ...' There is a recognition that there is something valid in psychotic statements without denying the primary illness. In early eighteenth-century North America it was quite acceptable for all whites, including members of the Society of Friends, to own slaves. Two insane inmates of a Friends' asylum independently declared that slave-owning was no longer acceptable for Quakers; the idea spread beyond the asylum walls; and within a few years the practice of slavery was incompatible with membership of the Society. The two innovators, however, appeared to have remained within their asylum.[48]

4 It is the meaning for the community which determines whether psychotic delusions result in the originator becoming a prophet. In his study of 'charisma'[49] Bryan Wilson points out that:

If a man runs naked down the street proclaiming that he alone can save others from impending doom, and if he immediately wins a following, then he is a charismatic leader: a social relationship has come into being. If he does not win a following, then he is simply a lunatic .... The very content of 'plausibility' is culturally determined. It may be a more than average endowment of energy, determination, fanaticism, and perhaps intelligence. Or it may be an altogether different set of attributes, epilepsy, strangeness, what we should regard as mental disorder, or particularly when children are regarded as prophets, even sheer innocence.

If innovation is meaningful it has to respond to certain themes in the audience. At times of crisis, solutions are likely to be accepted or sought from those who at other times would be stigmatized as mad: 'desperate times need desperate remedies'. In the 1660s, Solomon Eccles wandered about London with a brazier of fire on his head, naked apart from a loincloth, proclaiming the imminent destruction of the city; he was largely ignored until the Plague, and then the Fire, made him a fashionable prophet. London was rebuilt whilst Solomon continued to preach the identical doctrine, and he lapsed back into his former obscurity.[50] If we accept, with Laing, that the girl who says she is dangerous because she has an atomic bomb inside her is 'less crazy' than a government prepared to use nuclear weapons, this is because we are so concerned about the possibility of atomic war that we are prepared to modify our conceptions of reason.[51] Murphy has taken this further:

> Delusions may occur in times of increased stress as if, in reaction to changing conditions, the culture does call on individual members to sacrifice their mental health by the development of individual delusions which relieve communal anxieties.[52]

Like La Barre (but without La Barre's pessimism) he offers an active innovative role for psychopathology.

5 To say a mad individual would have been 'accepted' at another time or in another place is a biographical commonplace; the audience has failed the author. Artaud's biographer suggests that 'in other epochs he might have been a shaman, a prophet, an alchemist, an oracle, a saint, a gnostic teacher or indeed the founder of a new religion'.[53] If we accept that both the individual and psychopathology are located in a particular society then this is meaningless, but it is likely that some societies, particularly small-scale preliterate ones, are always open to a greater variety of idiosyncratic communications than is our own. In other words there may be societies which do not share our rigorous exclusion of all psychopathology from the possibility of meaning. This is true of the Quakers and the 1960s 'counter-culture', both open to 'the workings of the spirit'. It may occur when societies have a more restricted concept of psychopathology than our own. While a majority of tribal societies appear to recognize a state akin to 'insanity', this may be restricted to *chronic* mental illness; the early stages of what psychiatrists regard as schizophrenia may be conceived of as a potentially meaningful experience. As Kroeber pointed out, 'In general the psychopathologies that are rewarded among primitives are only the mild or transient ones. A markedly deteriorated psychosis ... would be rated and deplored by them as much as by us'. Murphy suggests that there is a cost: 'Societies which encourage greater contact with unconscious feelings can freely accept the idiosyncratic behaviour and delusions of the mentally ill but they pay a price in economic and social inferiority.'[54] We do not have to accept Murphy's idea of the unconscious to agree that societies which take madness seriously are probably not the most appropriate ones for developing and operating advanced technology. I shall now examine two specific

instances and attempt to see how psychopathology may provide a model for the experiences of others and provide a charter for a common set of beliefs.

Sabbatai Sevi[55]

The exile of the Jews from Palestine at the beginning of the Christian era dispersed a single self-contained community from its own land into a series of complementary relationships with Christian and, later, Islamic communities. The rabbinical tradition preserved the original culture, elaborated into the Law which defined the boundaries between Jew and non-Jew and explained the separation from the historic land as a temporary interlude until the messianic redemption. The traditional Messiah was a conquering king who would re-establish the historical kingdom. Alternatively he was pictured as the suffering and rejected servant who held a message for the gentiles. For others the exile was a metaphor for personal alienation from God and the promised redemption was purely spiritual. One tradition suggested that the Messiah would come when the existence of the community was threatened by internal disharmony and external violence, and another, only when Man had deliberately entered into the sinful world to release the divine sparks hidden there.

With the development of the modern nation state, the traditional Jewish accommodation in eastern Europe began to fail. The physical identity of east European Jewry was threatened by assimilation and attrition; massacre and forced conversion accounted for perhaps half a million Polish Jews in the 1640s. Sabbatai Sevi, a devout young rabbi in the Ottoman Empire, began to engage in frequent fasts, ritual purifications, and all-night prayer. After two successive marriages were annulled for non-consummation he commenced increasingly antinomian behaviour – breaking the Law for the value inherent in this act. A kabbalistic tradition had asserted that as the Messiah had to redeem evil he was in some measure evil himself and Sabbatai offered a new prayer: 'Praised be Thee O Lord who permits the forbidden'.

Expelled by the local rabbis, Sabbatai was proclaimed Messiah by a follower and the movement spread rapidly. Sabbatianism was characterized by miracles, prophecies, mass visions, states of possession, and ecstatic confession and penance, fasts to death, and self-burials. Sabbatai invented new ceremonies and fantastic titles; days of ritual mourning became days of rejoicing. He married a prostitute and encouraged free love, nudity, and incest; if the messianic age could only be ushered in by sin the people must sin. Within a year Sabbatai was arrested by the Sultan for sedition, had converted to Islam under pain of death, and was pensioned off under house arrest. Most followers abandoned him in this ultimate rejection of Judaism and returned to traditional rabbinical teachings, but for others his apostasy was the ultimate messianic sacrifice: 'The Lord was but veiled and waiting.' A few followed him to Islam and some converted to Christianity. Many continued as apparently orthodox Jews but conducted Sabbatian rites in secret. As an organized body of belief the movement soon died away, but in the eighteenth century a Sabbatian, Jacob Frank, proclaimed himself Messiah. The relation of Sabbatian messianism to the subsequent Hasidic movement remains controversial. It has been described as a 'neutralisation of messianic elements into mainsteam Judaism' and as a 'dialectical synthesis of the two'.[56]

There is a certain amount of evidence that Sabbatai Sevi was manic-depressive. He was constantly depressed 'without his being able to say what is the nature of this pain'. Extreme apathy and withdrawal, known to his followers as 'The Hiding of the Face', alternated with periods of 'illumination'; infectious elation and enthusiasm, restlessness, and a refusal to eat or sleep, practical jokes, and flights of apparent nonsense. Jewish mystics already used high/low (*aliyah*/*yorinda*) to refer to nearness to/absence from God, and Sabbatai employed this spatial metaphor to explain his moods as religious experience: 'high' was associated with religious ecstasy; 'low' with self-doubt. His followers accepted his explanation of his mood swings and followed them, themselves experiencing episodes of religious exultation and despair which became normative experiences for many. His psychosis thus provided a natural symbol of the Kabbalistic doctrine, together with a firm conviction on Sabbatai's part (when 'high') of his messiahship and also a model for explaining the fluctuating relations between God and man, and thus the waxing and waning of the movement. It is likely that the jokes and tricks and inversions of normal behaviour make an individual with periodic manic-depressive psychosis a particularly well-placed person to modify traditional modes of belief and behaviour through antinomian acts.

To what extent does Sabbatianism meet our five possible conditions? Sabbatai was certainly respected as a promising scholar before his antinomian actions and it is not easy to see how he could have been taken seriously otherwise; he was not, however, so influential that his community would accept any ideas immediately (situation 1). His reputation did establish his acts as antinomian – controlled and motivated contraventions of the Law rather than a simple failure to follow it. His episodes of madness were periodic, enabling him to explain their meaning within the common shared assumptions (2). The audience did not have a restricted concept of psychopathology and they did not recognize Sabbatai as 'mad but . . .'[57] (3, 5). Certainly eastern European Jews were living in desperate times (4) but the movement was most significant under Ottoman rule, where Jews were more secure than in Christian countries. Sabbatian adherents were as likely to come from the affluent and assimilated sections of the Jewish community as from the pauperized and insecure peasantry. Our example is limited by the usual problem of conjectural psychohistory – 'diagnosis' across time based on secondary sources. Our assumption of Sabbatai Sevi's manic-depression is based on sources compiled by his followers. The fact that his 'highs' and 'lows' were so neatly coded in Kabbalistic terms may lead us to wonder whether the 'coding' was not prior to the experiences, and merely shaped everyday mood changes.

Mother Earth

Trinidad, the most southerly of the Caribbean islands, lies in the Orinoco delta, eight miles away from the South American mainland. A Spanish possession until its capture by the British in 1797, it was largely ignored after the extermination of the Amerindians, although a few French planters from other West Indian islands settled with their slaves who grew sugar in the lower areas in the west. Trinidad's history has been typical of the British Caribbean: the development of sugar plantations; the emancipation of the slaves in 1838, followed by indentured immigration from India in the latter part of the nineteenth century; the collapse of the price of cane sugar, economic stagnation, and imperial neglect; increasing local political participation progressing to internal self-government in the 1950s and independence in 1962. The governing party since 1956 is pro-western and social democratic, committed to a mixed economy and a welfare state, derives its support predominantly from the African[58] population, and has comfortably maintained power through patronage and regular elections, apart from a brief hiccup in 1971 when an army mutiny sparked a shortlived Black Power rebellion.

The oil industry has been exploited since independence and the standard of living is high, reputedly the third highest in the Americas after the United States and Canada; certain rural areas excepted, concrete houses, electricity, piped water, and metalled roads are standard. Secondary education is compulsory and the oil revenues have allowed the establishment of a steelworks, and large construction and other industries. The labour intensive agricultural cultivation of sugar, coffee, cocoa, and ground provisions has been effectively abandoned, and the bulk of 'local' food is brought in from the smaller and poorer islands to the north.

In the north-east the mountains of the Northern range, the geographical continuation of the South America Cordillera, rise from the sea to 3,000 feet. They were only occupied in the late nineteenth century by isolated families who established a peasantry of small estates of coffee and cocoa in the lower reaches, growing coconuts and provision in the narrow littoral.

Few Trinidadian people have not heard of the Earth People, a small community established on this coast. In a country familiar with the millennial religious response of the Shouter Baptists, and with the Rastafari movement, a recent import from Jamaica, the Earth People remain an enigma. Their appearance, from the villages to the capital Port of Spain, causes public outrage to all, for their most outstanding characteristic is that they are naked. Public opinion favours the view that these young men, carrying cutlasses, and with the long matted dreadlocks of the Rastas, are probably crazy; if not the whole group, then Mother Earth, whose visions gave birth to the movement and who leads their marches to 'Town'. Every year the group comes from the coast to Port of Spain to pass on their message and gather new recruits from the poorer working-class areas around the capital, areas which appear to have missed out on Trinidad's oil wealth. Communication is hampered by the Earth People's characteristic language, their deliberate and frequent use of obscenities, and Mother Earth's striking doctrines. She announces to Trinidadians, a largely devout if not church-going population, that God does not exist but that she is the Biblical Devil, the Mother of Africa and India, Nature Herself.

In 1973 when she was 39 she left Port of Spain together with her children and husband, to settle in one of the deserted hamlets overlooking a rocky bay and a long curving beach bisected by a river which, laden with mangroves, slowly enters the sea as a modest delta between the overgrown coconut groves.

The family had been Shouter Baptists[59] and they continued to 'pick along in the Bible', fasting in Lent and interpreting the visionary impact of their dreams. After the birth of twins in their wooden hut in 1975, Jeanette experienced a series of revelations. She became aware that the Christian doctrine of God the Father as Creator was untrue and that the world was the work of a primordial Mother which she identified with Nature and the Earth. The Mother had created a race of black people, originally hermaphrodite, the Race of Africa and India, but her rebellious Son re-entered His Mother's womb to gain the power of creation and succeeded in modifying part of her creation to produce the white people, the Race of the Son, who are the Race of Death. The whites, acting as the Son's agents, enslaved the blacks and have continued to exploit them. The Way of the Son is the Way of technology, cities, clothes, schools, factories, and wage labour. The Way of the Mother is the Way of Nature; a return to the simplicity of the Beginning, a simplicity of nakedness, cultivation of the land by hand and with respect, of gentle and non-exploiting human relationships.

The Son, in his continued quest for the power of generation, has recently entered into a new phase. He has succeeded in establishing himself in black people and is also on the point of creating non-human people, robots, and computers. The Mother, who has borne all His behaviour out of Her Love for Him, has finally lost patience. She is about to end the current order of the Son in a catastrophic drought and famine, a destruction of the Son's work, after which the original state of Nature will once again prevail.

Jeanette herself is a partial incarnation of the Mother who will only fully enter into her at the End. Her role is to facilitate the return to Nature by organizing a community on the coast, called Hell Valley, the Valley of Decision, to prepare for the return to the Beginning and to 'put out' the truth to her people, the black nation, the Mother's Children. She has to combat the false doctrines of existing religions which place the Son over the Mother and to correct the distorted teaching of the Bible. For She is the Devil and represents Life and Nature, in opposition to the Christian God who is her Son, the principle of Death and Science. As the Devil she is opposed to churches and prisons, education and money, contemporary morals and fashionable opinions.

As God is 'right' she teaches the Left and the Earth People interchange various common oppositions: 'left' for 'right'; 'evil' or 'bad' for 'good'. Conventional obscenities are Natural words and should be used, for She Herself is The Cunt, the source of all life. The exact timing of the End is uncertain but it will come in Jeanette's physical lifetime. Then Time will cease, disease will be healed, and the Nation will speak one language. The Son will return to His Planet, The Planet Sun, which is currently hidden by Fire placed there by the Mother.

Since her revelations which mark the Beginning of the End in 1975 Mother Earth's family have been joined by numbers of black Trinidadians, usually young men who sometimes bring their girlfriends and children to come and 'Plant for the Nation'. The community has a high turnover and, whilst over fifty people have been associated with the Earth People, when I stayed with them[60] there were twenty-three living in the Valley of Decision with perhaps twenty close sympathizers in town.

Some of the younger village men in the villages along the coast demonstrate an allegiance to Rastafari and say they remain in the country to pursue a 'natural' life. They express sympathy for the Earth People and would actually join the group if it were not for the nudity, Mother Earth's repudiation of Haile Selassie, and her reputation for making everyone in Hell Valley work so hard. Some of them meet the Earth People in the bush, smoke a little ganja, and exchange fish for provision. Through them and other friends in the village who knew Mother Earth before she went naked, the Earth People are kept well informed of village activities and any gossip about them. The older Creole-speaking villagers regret the passing of traditional rural life and the depopulation of the coast. Whilst valuing the benefits of piped water, state pensions, and a higher standard of living, they criticize the young men's expectations of an easy life: 'It come so all they want is fêting. They can't take hard work again.' They accord grudging respect to the return to the old life in the Valley, all the more so as the Earth People themselves come from the town. Their own opinions about Trinidad's future parallel those of the Earth People: the oil is a natural part of the earth, the blood of the soil; and its removal is slowly turning the land into a 'cripsy', an unproductive arid desert; they too are suspicious of the newer farming techniques advocated by the government agricultural officers and, refusing pesticides or fertilizers, they continue to plant and harvest according to the phases of the moon; the oil wealth is transitory and will eventually cease, to leave Trinidadians starving in a once fertile land.

Their disagreement is less with Mother Earth's eschatological doctrines than with her practice of nudity, for no Trinidadian has gone naked since slavery. Trinidadians who have met her when 'putting out', regarded her less as insane than as eccentric: 'she come half-way mad then'. She has, however, twice been taken by the police to the mental hospital in Port of Spain; there she was diagnosed as psychotic and given psychotropic drugs. Interviewing her with the Present State Examination suggested that she had periodic episodes of hypomania associated with the puerperium; she is also clinically thyrotoxic. In between episodes she is frequently despondent if not depressed. The explanation accepted by the group is that the Mother is only partially incarnated in her and withdraws at intervals (this withdrawal corresponds to depression, a different physical metaphor to Sabbatai's). The practical organization of the group at these times is left to her husband.

With regard to our five conditions, Mother Earth was not initially an important person (1), but her episodes of psychopathology, like those of Sabbatai, have been temporary (2). The local concept of *folie* (madness) is more restricted (5) than the popular British one and emphasizes chronic mental deterioration, although it is also used in a consciously figurative sense as in *tabanka* (love sickness). Sympathizers who are not members may accept that she is mentally ill whilst accepting the validity of her ideas (3), although her followers say 'If she mad, then we mad'. Trinidad can hardly be described as living in desperate times (4) but for the rural migrants to the towns and the remaining country people, the disappearance of an agricultural economy and its associated way of life has certainly been traumatic, particularly for the young male proletariat of the slums, unemployed and non-unionized.

A universal dispensation?

To conclude, I shall say a little about the mode of intellectual innovation we can expect in situations such as those of Sabbatai Sevi and Mother Earth. Firstly it is dramatic – when we have a tradition of linear intellectual development and open dialogue with the dominant culture it is perhaps unnecessary. It seems particularly relevant to those small-scale conservative societies which principally interest ethnographers. It is not limited to them – indeed neither Sabbatai nor Mother Earth come from a tribal society. They are, however, members of a group dominated by another culture. It is dramatic then – often an overturning of the accepted patterns – an inversion of them.[61] As Scholem says 'Sabbatai took over items of Jewish tradition and stood them on their heads'.

Whatever may be the merits of the current anthropological debate on systems of dual classification[62] there appear to be particular situations where two opposed sets of binary oppositions play an important social role: those societies which have been politically dominated for a considerable period of time by outsiders. We may include here colonies and ex-colonies, including much of the Third World, blacks and whites in the Americas, and Jewish communities in Europe. Caribbean society, like Jewish society, has been described as dualistic – 'us' and 'them', in this case black and white (for Jews, Jew and gentile). For the black person there are two contrasted modes of social behaviour, exemplified by 'black' and 'white' and usually glossed as 'respectability' (the white mode) and 'reputation' (the black mode).[63] The black mode is characterized by sexual prowess, cohabitation, seduction, the rumshop, home produce, and egalitarian society, and is typically represented in men. The white mode is characterized by chastity, legal marriage, education, the church, imported goods, and hierarchy, and is represented most typically in women.

The individual has to attain an identity by personally articulating the various elements of the two contrasted sets of values; the minority culture itself is defined by its difference to the dominant set of values (Figure 8.1). Some groups in society, particularly women, are already in an 'inverted' symbolic position relative to men. If West Indian 'respectability/reputation' are articulated by 'white/black' values, then the black middle-class man is, in some sense, white. If the relation Jew/non-Jew parallels that of observance of the Law to ignorance of it, it thus parallels that of male/female so that the Jewish woman, to a certain extent, takes on gentile qualities[64] and the black woman is in the same way 'white'.[65] Trinidadian Rastas accept this dichotomy but change its value; in contradistinction to the majority who (as Fanon showed) are trying to become 'white', they take the black mode as the ideal. The symbolic position of whites is either as evil or they are somehow supposed to exist in harmony with blacks – both black and white accepting each other's values. In other words, there is no major symbolic change. Mother Earth's teaching transcends this dualistic position by asserting that blacks have become corrupted by the Son and their mind is white: only the Flesh, itself part of the Earth, is truly the Mother's.

I am suggesting that certain patterns of psychopathology can, as it were, hot up these latent contradictions, by overt statements and actions, inverting the normal schema in certain areas (represented by a chiasmus in the

SHEYN/PROST

$$\frac{Jew}{Gentile} = \frac{Observance\ of\ Law}{Violation\ of\ Law} = \frac{Ascetic}{Desire} = \frac{Adult}{Child} = \frac{Male}{Female} = \frac{Sacred}{Profane}$$

$$= \frac{Sin\ for\ its\ own\ sake}{Observance\ of\ Law}$$

SABBATAI SEVI

REPUTATION/RESPECTABILITY

$$\frac{Black}{White} = \frac{Democracy}{Hierarchy} = \frac{Home\ Produce}{Imported\ Goods} = \frac{Cohabitation}{Marriage} = \frac{Rum\ Shop}{Church} = \frac{Sex}{Chastity} = \frac{Seduction}{Education} = \frac{Male}{Female} = \frac{Devilish}{Godly}$$

$$= \frac{Good}{Bad}$$

MOTHER EARTH

8.1 Antinomianism and symbolic inversion.

99

polythetic classifications of Figure 8.1). Symbolic inversions can be regarded as intellectual tools which have the potential to enlarge the conceptual repertoire.[66] Although oppositions may be a dominant mode of symbolic ordering, their inversion provides the basis for change. The apparent paradox is resolved at a 'higher' implicit level; simple oppositions thus may become the means by which a more sophisticated, radical and universal conceptualization may be attained.[67] As the original symbolic schema was closely related to the social order, the weakening of this schema in some particular is likely to lead to a greater autonomy of ideology from specific environmental and political determinants and thus perhaps to more 'internalized' values. Thus, when Jesus denied that plucking corn on the Sabbath was work, he implied a new dispensation in which 'the Law was broken in Form to be fulfilled in Spirit'. Scholem suggests that Judaism always contained a 'dialectic' between the rabbinical and apocalyptic traditions, what I have termed the Law and its inversion. Sabbatai Sevi confused the dual classification, called women to read the Torah, ridiculing the learned, encouraging gentiles to join the movement, and maintaining evil could be transformed into good. To follow the traditional Law in the Last Days was, he said, like working on the Sabbath. It has been suggested that the attack on the traditional Law by the Sabbatians both reflected and precipitated the development of modern secular Judaism;[68] freed from traditional constraints, the method of criticism and argument perfected in the ghetto was harnessed to the development of modern rationalism.

It is perhaps too early to characterize any universalist influence for Mother Earth. Certainly her overturning of the dual classification in certain areas allows the Earth People, like the Rastas, to escape from an externally imposed system of values. Her rejection of binarism, her interpenetration of black and white, and of male and female, appear to offer us all a more universal dispensation than the limited 'ethnic redefinition' of Rastafari.

Notes

I am indebted to Julie Moore for her typing of the paper.

1 Naipaul, S. (1980) *Black and White*, Sphere Edition, Hamish Hamilton, London, p. 17.
2 La Barre, W. (1970) *The Ghost Dance*, Allen & Unwin, London, pp. 348, 603, 607; Wolman, B. (ed.) (1973) 'Sense and nonsense in history', in *The Psychoanalytic Interpretation of History*, Harper, London, p. 95.
3 Susan Sontag in *Illness as Metaphor* (Allen Lane, London, 1979) discusses the political use of the medical metaphor at length but restricts it to the metaphors of physical disease – 'infection' and 'cancer'.
4 Naipaul (1980) *op. cit.*, p. 134.
5 Kroeber cited in Lifton, R. J. (1974) *Exploration in Psychohistory*, Simon & Schuster, New York; La Barre, W. (1969) *They Shall Take Up Serpents*, Schocken, New York, pp. viii, 109.

6 Cited by Ackernecht, E. (1943) 'Psychopathology, primitive medicine and primitive culture', *Bull. Hist. Med.*, 14, pp. 30–68.
7 Devereux, G. (1956) 'Normal and abnormal: the key problem in psychiatric anthropology', in *Some Uses of Psychopathology, Theoretical and Applied* (eds Gladwin, J. and Gladwin, T.), Anthropological Society of Washington.
8 Rosen, G. (1968) *Madness in Society*, Routledge & Kegan Paul, London, pp. 21–70.
9 La Barre (1969) *op. cit.*
10 Rosen (1968) *op. cit.*; Ackernecht (1943) *op. cit.*
11 Association of Psychiatrists in Training (1977) *Newsletter*, September, p. 1.
12 Ballard, R. (1973) 'An interview with Thomas Szasz', *Penthouse*, October, pp. 69–74. The poll was published in *Fact* magazine, September, 1964.
13 Freud, S. (1928) *The Future of an Illusion*, Hogarth, London.
14 Kenniston, K. (1974) 'Psychological development and historical change', in *Exploration in Psychohistory* (ed. Lifton, R. J.), Simon & Schuster, New York; Bourdieu, P. (1977) *Outline of a Theory of Practice*, Cambridge University Press, Chapter 1.
15 Linton, R. (1943) 'Nativist movements', *Am. Anthrop.*, 45, pp. 230–40.
16 Beckford, J. A. (1975) *The Trumpet of Prophecy: A Sociological Study of Jehovah's Witnesses*, Blackwell, Oxford.
17 Wilson, B. (1973) *Magic and the Millenium*, Heinemann, London, pp. 317–19.
18 Williams, F. M. (1934) 'The Vaihala madness in retrospect', in *Essays Presented to C. G. Seligman* (ed. Evans-Pritchard, E. E.), Kegan Paul, London. He describes the movement as 'an epidemic', 'antics' which 'originated in delusions'.
19 La Barre (1969) *op. cit.*, pp. 233, 294, 197; Wilson (1973) *op. cit.*, p. 135; Yap, P. M. (1954) 'The mental illness of Hung Hsiu Chu'an, leader of the Taiping Rebellion', *Far East Q.*, 13, pp. 287–304; Williams (1934) *op. cit.*, p. 372.
20 Armytage, W. H. G. (1961) *Heavens Below: Utopian Experiments in England 1560–1960*, Routledge & Kegan Paul, London, p. 282; Worsley, P. (1970) *The Trumpet Shall Sound*, Paladin, London, pp. 168–9; Wilson (1973) *op. cit.*, p. 42; Simpson, G. (1956). 'Jamaican revivalist cults', *Soc. Econ. Stud.*, December; Nettleford, R. (1970) *Mirror, Mirror: Identity, Race and Protest in Jamaica*, Collins, Kingston. Chapter 2.
21 Woodcock, G. and Avakumaic, I. (1968) *The Doukhobors*, Faber, London, p. 59; Beckford (1975) *op. cit.*, p. 34: Bloch, S. and Reddaway, P. (1977) *Russia's Political Hospitals*, Gollancz, London, *passim*.
22 Nettleford (1970) *op. cit.*, pp. 56–7.
23 Compare the Yoruba and Temba (Littlewood, R. and Lipsedge, M. (1982) *Aliens and Alienists*, Penguin, Harmondsworth, Chapter 9).
24 Plato (1965) *Timaeus*, Penguin, Harmondsworth.
25 Feder, L. (1980) *Madness and Literature*, Princeton University Press, pp. 106–7.
26 For instance in Erasmus' *In Praise of Folly* or Savanarola's iconoclastic Feast of the Higher Folly.
27 Cited by James, W. (1958) *The Varieties of Religious Experience*, Mentor, New York.
28 Hayter, A. (1968) *Opium and the Romantic Imagination*, Faber, London, *passim*.
29 Nietzsche, F. *The Will to Power*, cited by Harrison, M. (1922) 'Mental instability as a factor in progress', *The Monist*, 32, p. 19.
30 James (1958) *op. cit.*, p. 24.
31 James (1958) *op. cit.*, p. 36.
32 Cited by Kurella, H. (1911) *Cesare Lombroso*, Rebman, London.
33 Kurella (1911) *op. cit.*, p. 72.

34 Karlsson, L. (1974) 'Schizophrenia and creativity', *Acta psychiat. Scand.*, 247, Suppl. 76.
35 Storr, A. (1972) *The Dynamics of Creation*, Secker & Warburg, London.
36 Translated from Cabanne, P. (1961) *Van Gogh*, Aimery Somogy, Paris.
37 Breton, A. (1969) *Manifestes de Surrealism*, Gallimard, Paris, p. 37.
38 Esslin, M. (1976) *Artaud*, Fontana, London, p. 52.
39 Feder (1980) *op. cit.*, p. 242.
40 Vonnegut, M. (1976) *The Eden Express*, Cape, London.
41 Roheim, G. (1950) *Psychoanalysis and Anthropology*, International Universities Press, New York.
42 Devereux (1956) *op. cit*; La Barre (1969, 1970) *op. cit.*
43 Ackernecht (1943) *op. cit.*, pp. 31, 35. This criticism is not taken to include the 'new psychohistorians' (Lifton, Erikson, Kenniston) for they have largely restricted themselves to a consideration of normative psychodynamics and have developed a considerably more sophisticated conceptualization of the relationship between individual personality and the social order. Erikson's 'great man of history' is not the charismatic psychotic of Devereux and La Barre but one who articulates the 'dirty work of his age' (Erikson, E. (1958) *Young Man Luther*, Norton, New York).
44 Following Eliade, no contemporary students of shamanism have claimed that the shaman is invariably psychopathological. What Eliade (*Shamanism: Archaic Techniques of Ecstasy*, Princeton University Press, 1964) terms 'signs of election' have been recognized as including acute psychosis, along with physical disease or misfortune, but the pattern of shamanism is a conventional pattern superimposed on the psychotic individual and not derived from him. With acculturation, however, increasingly deviant individuals may come to occupy the shamanic role (Murphy, J. (1964) 'Psychotherapeutic aspects of shamanism on St Lawrence Island', in *Magic, Faith and Healing* (ed. Kiev, A.), Free Press, New York).
45 Gruenberg, E. (1957) 'Socially shared psychopathology', in *Explorations in Social Psychiatry* (ed. Leighton, A. H.), Basic Books, New York.
46 Fox, G. (1952) *Journals*, Cambridge University Press, pp. 71–2.
47 Devos, G. A. (1972) 'The inter-relationship of social and psychological structures in transcultural psychiatry' in *Transcultural Research in Mental Health* (ed. Lebra, W. P.), Hawaii University Press, derives the term from an unpublished paper by T. Schwartz and restricts himself to the mimesis of epilepsy, which, if believed to be of mystical origin, authenticates religious experience. The imitation of epilepsy is cited by Eliade (1964) in numerous cases, and Williams (1934) describes a Melanesian millennial leader who spread a stylized epilepsy in his group modelled on his own pre-existing illness (pp. 371–2). 'Psychotomimesis' would perhaps be more appropriate in our context.
48 Davis, B. D. (1966) *The Problem of Slavery in Western Culture*, Cornell University Press, Ithaca.
49 Wilson, B. (1975) *Noble Savages: The Primitive Origins of Charisma*, California University Press, Berkeley.
50 Hunter, A. (1959) *The Last Days*, Blond, London.
51 Laing, R. D. (1959) *The Divided Self*, Tavistock, London, p. 12.
Murphy, H. B. M. (1967) 'Cultural aspects of the delusion', *Studium Generale*, 2, pp. 684–92. How radical we take this to be depends on our interpretation of 'as if'.
53 Esslin (1976) *op. cit.*, p. 116.
54 Murphy (1967) *op. cit.*
55 My argument in this section is derived from a previous paper on contemporary Hasidism (1983) 'The Antinomian Hasid', *Br. J. Med. Psychol.*, 56, pp. 67–78,

which contains more detailed citations. For the history of Sabbatianism I am completely indebted to the work of Gershom Scholem, particularly his (1973) *Sabbatai Sevi*, Routledge & Kegan Paul, London.

56 Scholem, G. (1954) *Major Trends in Jewish Mysticism*, Schocken, New York; Bakan, D. (1958) *Sigmund Freud and the Jewish Mystical Tradition*, Princeton University Press.

57 Gradik, M. (1976) 'Le concept de fou et ses implications dans la littérature Talmudique', *Annal. Med-Psychol.*, 134, pp. 17–36; Scholem (1973) *op. cit.*, p. 54.

58 The customary term for the Trinidadian population of African origin.

59 A loosely organized evangelical church of largely working-class origin whose members practise glossolalia. Akin to the Southern African 'Zionist' churches, it is regarded by some commentators as containing distinctive African elements (Simpson, G. E. (ed.) (1980) 'The Shouters' Church', in *Religious Cults of the Caribbean*, University of Puerto Rico). It does not, however, contain any doctrines incompatible with other Christian denominations.

60 In 1981–2 on a Social Science Research Council post-doctoral conversion fellowship.

61 See Littlewood, R. 'The individual articulation of shared symbols', *J. Op. Psychiat.* vol. 15 1984, pp. 17–24. I am not suggesting that inversion is the only, or indeed the major, mode of the imitation of madness, but it is the one which appears relevant for our two examples, both characterized by 'gratuitious' obscenities and contravention of norms. It appears the more likely mode in bipolar affective psychosis. I have continued to use the term inversion in spite of recent suggestions (Needham, R. (1980) *Reversals*, Henry Myers Lecture, Royal Anthropological Institute) that opposition might be more appropriate; inversion does not describe the latent possibilities of the system so much as convey the physical sense of overturning institutions so characteristic of the participants' experience. In brief, explanations of symbolic inversion have been offered by observers and participants from diverse perspectives, which we can gloss according to three broad western modes of characterization.

1 *Psychological*: the return of the repressed, as elaborated in psychoanalytical and literary theory (Scheff, T. (1979) *Catharsis in Healing, Ritual and Drama*, California University Press, Berkeley). The inversion may be regarded alternatively as a 'reaction formation' of the socialized individual to the recognition of his physiological drives (Freud, A. (1937) *The Ego and the Mechanisms of Defence*, Hogarth, London). There may be a conscious cultural elaboration of some type of catharsis or discharge of tension to restore equilibrium, usually associated with a quantifiable conception of sin or emotion which can penetrate boundaries: we find it in the Jewish rituals of the scapegoat, excretion before prayer, the treatment of illness by enema, or the 'purging' of the house at Passover. Theories of catharsis in drama, following Aristotle, stress the resonance (mimesis) of the dramatic role with the personal experiences of actor and audience; in extreme situations both may run amok together in the deviant role (Geertz, C. (1966) 'Religion as a cultural system', in *Anthropological Approaches to the Study of Religion* (ed. Banton, M.), Tavistock, London). A tentative psychophysiological basis for this type of experience has been elaborated in Smith and Apter's reversal theory (Apter, M. J. (1982) *The Experience of Motivation: The Theory of Psychological Reversals*, Academic Press, London).

2 *Sociological*: inversion is presented by a culture as the only alternative to the established order and as it is both temporary and allowed only in certain specific ritual contexts (or limited to a powerless minority) it reaffirms the boundaries of

control and thus cements the existing system (Gluckman, M. (1962) *Rituals of Rebellion in South-East Africa*, Manchester University Press). While orthodox Jews are usually forbidden to play cards or get drunk, these two activities are tolerated and even encouraged on two specific days in the year; similarly the blood of humans or animals is scrupulously avoided at all times except at circumcisions, when it may actually be sucked. In communities where the ideal of cannibalism is totally repugnant, the homicide may be purified by ritual ingestion of the deceased's liver (Goody, J. (1982) *Cooking, Cuisine and Class*, Cambridge University Press). Inversion thus marks a principle by constrained contravention of it.

3 *Cognitive*: both the psychological and sociological approaches are functional and static; they emphasize the homeostasis of a given system; inversion is either the catharsis of undesirable elements or the passage between two equivalent and coexisting systems. Similarly the antinomian individual who contravenes the norm gives unity to a simple bipolar system (Peacock, J. (1968) *Rites and Modernisation: Symbolic Aspects of Indonesian Proletarian Drama*, Chicago University Press). Inversion may however be innovative – see text below.

62 Particularly the structuralist debate on the universality of dual systems of thought (see Littlewood 1984 *op. cit.*).
63 Fanon, F. (1952) *Peau Noir, Masques Blancs*, Seuil, Paris; Wilson, P. J. (1973) *Crab Antics*, Yale University Press, New Haven.
64 e.g. Zborowski, M. and Herzog, E. (1962) *Life is with People: The Culture of the Stetl*, Schocken, New York; for an analysis of the dual classification of diaspora Judaism see Littlewood (1983) *op. cit.*
65 Fanon (1952) *op. cit.*
66 Turner, V. (1974) *Dramas, Fields and Metaphors*, Cornell University Press, Ithaca.
67 Babcock, B. (ed.) (1978) *The Reversible World: Symbolic Inversion in Art and Society*, Cornell University Press, Ithaca.
68 Scholem (1954) *op. cit.*

Note

This chapter was originally published in 1984. Since then the Trinidadian governing party has been finally displaced in an election by the opposition. Mother Earth died in 1984; the Earth people have fragmented into three groups, one led by her son, another by her husband. Their beliefs and life style have, however, remained unchanged. A longer account of Mother Earth's life and of her community may be found in Roland Littlewood (1987) *Pathology and Identity: The Genesis of a Millennial Community in North East Trinidad*, D. Phil. thesis, Oxford University.

'The imitation of madness: the influence of psychopathology upon culture' by Roland Littlewood was first published as an article in *Social Science and Medicine*, vol. 19, no. 7 in 1984 and is reproduced by permission of Pergamon Press.

Part two

From theory into practice

Commentary

The chapters in the second section consider various ways of working with imagery, beginning with drawings from prehistory and ending with a case history of a young boy's work in art therapy. The authors come from a variety of disciplines and employ differing theoretical structures to assist their understanding of art and art therapy.

Roger Cardinal's chapter, 'The primitive scratch' (Chapter 9), has several connections with ideas expressed elsewhere in this collection. Roger describes the prehistoric Camunian rock incisions as 'picture-making at its most basic' and uses the methodologies of anthropology, ethnography, and semiotics to explore their possible meanings. Like Roland Littlewood, Roger argues that the circumstances and references of the community in which the drawings (in this case) were made have a direct bearing on their meaning. However, Roger believes that although we may have a sense of these images in historical and cultural terms, the lack of a 'code' which may assist the understanding of the symbols does not lessen their impact but can increase it.

His argument is that it is the first-hand experience of seeing and absorbing pictures which creates their impact and meaning – the mark has its own significance, as well as that of the time, place, and original reason for its creation. The important point is that images can hold many meanings at different levels; those of the artist, of the culture within which it was made and in which it is viewed, as well as that which resonates with each of us as individuals. The message to art therapists seems to be that not only should we remain open to the many levels of communication in a picture and to the varying theoretical systems within which imagery may be understood, but that we are also able to work with the imagery in our own counter-transference.

It is interesting to compare Roger's chapter with the difficulties Diane Waller describes in 'Musing cross culturally' (Chapter 15). Her experience of working with art therapists from the United States of America and as an art therapist in eastern Europe illustrate the basic assumptions we have about the use of art materials in art therapy, and about the nature of therapy itself. The constraints of cross-cultural and language difficulties when working in a country other than one's own are all too apparent, but it is interesting to see how the influence of art education and art history permeates each country's expectations of and practice in art therapy.

Diane also considers the problems that arise when trying to work without words, relying exclusively on the communication contained within the artwork, which entails a further set of assumptions about the 'language' of art and the nature of silent communication. The art therapist is left with a visual enigma. The focus then is on the relationship the patient has with their artwork and such understanding as is possible may arise principally from the therapist's work as an artist.

The viewer's response is a constant theme in these papers, whether he or she is a therapist, a gallery goer, or part of a theatre audience. Rosemary Gordon describes such resonance as archetypal, i.e. as evoking powerful feelings across time, language, and culture. In 'The psychic roots of drama' (Chapter 16) Rosemary draws parallels, between the drama of intrapsychic life, the drama that occurs in the therapeutic relationship, psychodrama – where the action is between and within a group – and the contained event of a play in a theatre. She describes how the 'self' embodies many different selves in an individual's inner world, drawing attention to the role of imagination and symbolization in man's ability to translate immaterial thoughts and affects into something material, and shows how a dramatic incident in the day-to-day life of a young artist enabled him to make progress both in his analysis and in his art – the extrapsychic event enabled him to change his intrapsychic world. She thus demonstrates how drama is everywhere, in the microcosm of the individual and in the wider world of everyday experience, as well as in the world of archetypes and universals.

It is particularly interesting to see how two authors from different professions have used the metaphor of theatre to consider the nature of the therapeutic transaction. Joy Schaverien (Chapter 12) also equates psychotherapy with theatre, and extends the metaphor to liken art therapy to an art gallery; both places she suggests are 'framed' like a therapeutic session in time and space, and are 'set apart', requiring suspension of disbelief to allow fully the effects of emotional and aesthetic experience. Both authors examine 'acting out'. Rosemary considers that the acting out of feelings outside the therapeutic hour may not be altogether a bad thing; it can be part of a 'personal drama', and therefore another way in which awareness can be heightened without the use of words. Joy relates the breaking of visual boundaries, i.e. the extension of the picture plane, as being acceptable within the aesthetic terms of reference in an art gallery, and questions whether or not a similar understanding would be accorded to the breaking of pictorial boundaries in a picture produced in therapy.

There is a sense in which Joy's chapter is central to many of the ideas outlined in this collection, and to an appreciation of the disparity of views that were expressed at the conference. Her intention is to clarify the boundaries between art, art therapy, and therapy where art is 'employed' or used as an 'aid' to verbal psychotherapy. Joy's argument is that the primary difference lies in the frame of reference of the spectator, and, as far as therapists are concerned, in the initial training of the therapist. An art therapist will usually have had an extensive art education which calls for self reliance, originality, self expression and exploration. By contrast a medical or scientific education requires the acquisition of prescribed knowledge and observation of others' behaviours; she suggests that a therapist from a scientific background will have to relinquish the primacy of the outer world to allow space for the acceptance of inner experience.

It is the art therapists' knowledge of and formative experiences in art and art history, and their familiarity with how it feels to engage with the process of making images that provide them with a firm base from which to empathize with their patients' picture-making. However, the very background which enables art therapists to have a substantially different approach to imagery and to their clinical work from that of their colleagues in a multidisciplinary team is sometimes in danger of being overwhelmed in the clinical environment. This point is studied in detail by David Edwards.

David's chapter (Chapter 14) gives a clear account of the difficulties art therapists encounter when working in a large institution. The reader is left with no illusions – institutional realities can militate against change and innovation. David warns that the current pressure to validate art therapy as an effective treatment may involve too great an adaptation to the dominant culture of orthodox psychiatry. He urges art therapists to find research methods which do not risk devaluing the particular kind of knowledge and experience that is unique to art therapists.

With this in mind, it is possible to draw comparisons between the chapters of John Matthews (Chapter 10), Roger Cardinal (Chapter 9), and Mary Levens (Chapter 11). All three address analagous images and use different frames of reference to structure their interpretations. Roger considers the rudimentary drawings of prehistory and endeavours to find meaning in these 'signs' in the language of anthropology and semiotics; John's interest is in the early development of children's drawing, which he observes in great detail in a longitudinal study of both individuals and groups of very young children; and Mary Levens uses the theoretical framework of psychoanalysis to explore the nature of scribbling as a defence mechanism.

Children's scribbles have hitherto been regarded as the meaningless residue of sensorimotor activity, or as a means of assembling marks which can later be used to draw figuratively. John Matthews' observations have led him to think that the child records action and movement when drawing, and can perceive many symbolic and representational possibilities in the scribble. He shows how the same type of image can have quite different meanings for the child which are not apparent in the final picture, and would have remained unknown had the process not been closely observed. This chapter is based on the careful recording of material and the conclusions are not within the remit of therapy, but nevertheless the methodology and results are of interest to art therapists.

Mary Levens suggests that scribbling, the smearing of paint, and other pre-representational styles may be indicative of regression and other defence mechanisms when they occur in art therapy. She speaks of regression as a return to earlier stages of functioning, and stresses the importance of appropriate interpretation when the more able verbal defences are circumvented via a therapeutic medium less amenable to conscious control. She proposes that scribbling may represent feelings that may either be too insufficiently formed to be communicable, or may indicate resistance. Placed alongside John Matthews' proposition that scribbling may represent for children a particular kind of ordering or construction of internal reality, scribbling in adults can take on yet another perspective, akin to the positive aspects of the expression of chaos and confusion prior to change.

John Matthews' paper has the artmaking process in the foreground, and his approach is to analyse the way pictures are made rather than interpret the final product. Another approach to art therapy, which has the production of images in the background, is that described by Gerry McNeilly (Chapter 13). He believes that 'art therapy is not art therapy unless language becomes a part of it', his contention being that this places less pressure on the art therapist to explain the pictures (although it must be remembered that this philosophy and way of working is not appropriate for all patient groups). Gerry parallels the dynamics of group analytic art therapy groups with the theoretical constructs of verbal group analysis. He outlines his perceptions of, for example, a copied picture, and speculates about possible meanings it may have for an individual and for the group within which it was produced.

Many art therapists continue their professional development by training as group analysts, family therapists, child psychotherapists, and so on, and it is plain to see how their work as art therapists is influenced. As in Gerry McNeilly's chapter, the application of the theoretical constructs of psychotherapy and family therapy to art therapy can be traced in the last three chapters. Michael Donnelly (Chapter 17) describes his structuralist approach to family art therapy, which uses 'picturing' as a means of communication, and, in a similar way to Gerry McNeilly, perhaps sacrifices some of the art process in art therapy. Michael states that he invites his patients to 'represent with materials' rather than arouse the fears and inadequacies that the word 'art' seems to encourage. Here art therapy becomes a particular kind of intervention – a task-oriented approach in which a family may encounter itself.

Paola Luzzatto (Chapter 18) also considers particular types of images. She relates them to specific analytic concepts regarding the nature of alcohol abuse, and shows how these images were relevant to the present lives of the two patients she describes and also served to illuminate their early relationships. Both Paola and Michael describe short-term art therapy, and choose to focus on particular issues and are active in the therapeutic relationships they have with their clients. It is interesting to see how a comparable time in art therapy was used by the young boy described in the last chapter by Muriel Greenway (Chapter 19), who used a less directive, non-interventionist approach.

This chapter shows how family therapy and individual art therapy may work alongside each other, and reiterates finally the crucial role that observation of the artmaking process played in enabling the art therapist to understand what the child was endeavouring to communicate in his pictures. The images are graphic descriptions which, once created, could be verbalized and consciously understood.

Much is to be learnt from these casework-based papers about the way in which feelings are contained by the artwork and within the boundaries of the therapeutic relationship. It is interesting to see, in practice, the emphasis importance different art therapists place on the art process itself and on the interpretation of the images.

Chapter Nine

The Primitive Scratch

Roger Cardinal

It is signs that have no exact meaning that provoke the sense of magic.
(Miró)

For some while I have been attracted to forms of creativity which convention classifies as marginal or primitive – outsider art, naive art, folk art, tribal art. I have also been drawn to the question of clarifying the phenomenon of Primitivism in twentieth-century art, an impulse, largely inspired by the art of so-called primitive peoples, which may be explained in terms of an essentially modernist yearning for things primal, unspoiled, authentic. It occurred to me that a useful way of highlighting the Primitive and my relation to it might be to examine a single case of an extreme primitive style and to focus upon the act of picture-making at its most basic. To investigate some of the ways in which minimal traces – seemingly mute, indigent, even paltry – can achieve eloquence may be good groundwork for the construction of a model of the Primitive and, indeed, of our reception of human signals at large.

What I shall call the Primitive Scratch is that rudimentary yet expressive mark incised by a human hand upon a surface. Of the many instances of expressive scratchmarks, the most obvious is the urban graffito, commonplace, usually anonymous, and supremely marginal in relation to the fine art aesthetic. Plainly, a vast majority of graffiti are of little artistic resource, and in their futile duplication of stupid or obscene stereotypes have little more import than a motor reflex, like scratching one's skin. At best they may be said to express mindless boredom. However, at a higher level of interest, there occur those rare graffiti which have genuine aesthetic impact. In the late 1940s the photographer Brassai was able to scan the scarred walls of post-Occupation Paris and record a series of graffiti made by people in extreme states of anxiety and deprivation, sometimes in the last moments before deportation. The gouged faces and stark figurines which Brassai captions with emotive titles like 'Death' or 'Love', are evidence of an unusual conjuncture of the crudest means and the greatest expressive density.

Indigent markings occur in all cultures and all parts of the world. A piece of aurochs bone found at Rymarksgaard in Denmark and dating back to the mesolithic period catches our attention through its tactile evidence of primeval scratchings, scorings, and scrapings. A stone age painting made from crayons of mixed animal fat and ochre pigment and scrawled on a rock face at Kolo in Tanzania presents a sequence of stick-men whose physical attitudes bear witness to their creator's intention to celebrate a human occasion (an elephant hunt, a frolic by a river), the reality of the moment being communicated through the visual rhythms that arise out of the interrelationships of separate marks. In the remote spaces of central Australia, a woman of the Waibiri people tells a story to a group of children, poking with her finger in the sand all the while she speaks, to create little pictures which complement the oral tale. As she proceeds she brushes away each image, pursuing her narrative thread and abandoning at each moment these ephemeral yet no less 'telling' markings. At a clinic near Vienna a psychotic patient known as Max will pencil a geometricized human figure on paper and afterwards, in a second phase of the expressive impulse, scribble over it with great vehemence, to the point of obliterating the original, if not of tearing the paper. The result is a page invested with a man's queerly desperate energy, an ensemble of traces that direct us to no known figural code, yet which none the less never lapse into the non-human, never cease to embody human meaning. For no human sign, even at the extreme of minimalism, can entirely relinquish its character as a signature, a mark that signals its originator, and proposes that originator's presence as that of an intentional being. Even the most facile graffiti tell us that 'Kilroy was here' and mean us to know it.

It was while gathering such examples of inherently primitive signs that I came across a group of enigmatic and tantalizing scratches, the prehistoric rock-incisions of the Val Camonica in northern Italy. The Camunian petroglyphs will be my principal example in the following discussion, chosen because of their rudimentary character and our relative ignorance of their meaning.

Now in theoretical terms, a mark made by a human hand might be expected to arise within a context in which several circumstances have a bearing. A scratch is necessarily the result of the hand's physical effort: it can register an intellectual or an emotional impulse; it may be accompanied by vocal utterance, or by gestures made by other parts of the body; finally, it may be expected to constitute an act of communication. Granted, communication can never be totally unproblematic, as has been amply demonstrated in our time by researchers in linguistics, semiotics, and communication theory. Even the simplest reduction of Roman Jakobson's classic account of the speech event – a transmitter, immersed in the codes of a culture, shapes a message in relation to those codes, a message which is decoded by a recipient alert to that same network of reference – at once involves us in questions of scope, clarity, and reliability. As regards the corpus I am proposing here, the questions to ask are: What exactly are the marks I am looking at? And what sorts of meaning ought I to expect of them?

The first question can be reasonably answered by the statement that the Camunian petroglyphs are marks scratched, hammered, pecked (chiselled), or otherwise incised into the glacier-smoothed granite and sandstone rocks of the Val Camonica in Lombardy. The marks are scattered across the high valley above Lake Iseo and are concentrated at such sites as Naquane, Cemmo, Seradina, Bedolina, and Paspardo.

Various strategies can be invoked so as to address the second question. As a seeker after meaning, I might be advised at once to consult the writings of those archeologists and ethnologists who have already wrestled with this material. Their findings will help me to assign approximate dates to the marks, to make reference to the climate of the period, and gradually to reconstruct the conditions of social and cultural life – the contemporary technology, the working arrangements, the economy, the mythic beliefs and religious practices, the relation to wild or domesticated animals, and so forth. The fine work of Emmanuel Anati provides the most obvious introduction to Camunian culture and proposes some persuasive readings of the marks. But is this the best way to start my enquiry?

A different strategy might be to approach the scratched images in a direct fashion which does not immediately seek the support of past research. Can I in fact derive meaning from a sign in ignorance of the circumstances of its making? Is it possible to order my perceptions without reference to prevalidated cultural and historical data? One resource on which I might draw is that of semiotics, and specifically the trichotomy proposed by C. S. Peirce, the sign being seen as:

1   iconic,
2   indexical, or
3   symbolic.

Envisaged as an iconic image, the scratched figure will owe its meaning to an acknowledged visual resemblance to its referent, according to a mimetic principle which, willy nilly, we tend to assume is 'natural' and indisputable. Thus I recognize a stag incised on the rock at Cemmo (see Figure 9.1) because the outline is indeed shaped like that of a deer and there are insistently drawn antlers to confirm the association.

As an indexical image, the scratched figure functions as a carrier of meaning in so far as its literal substantiality is intimately linked with its signified. Thus a figure of a stag might have been chiselled in soft stone with a sharpened antler; similarly the blood of an animal recently killed might have been used to colour in the incised outline of that animal. In such cases, a tangible (metonymic) link would be the guarantee of the efficacy of the image. Principles of sympathetic magic might also be supposed to operate. (That is, a picture made in the blood of an animal might, for a certain mentality, be perceived as conducive to its maker's power over other like animals. Again, in

9.1 Stags and other animals (bronze age) on first rock at Cemmo, near Capo di Ponte, Val Camonica.

a variant example, it might be possible for the image of a hunter's quarry, precisely cut with an arrowhead or spearhead, to be perceived as imparting the power to aim straight and thus literalize the possession of such a quarry. The Abbé Breuil's celebrated thesis that prehistoric art is a form of hunting magic would seem confirmed here.)

The symbolic function posits no evident link between sign and signified; that is, no physical connection, whether of shape or substance, is made available to the viewer. The figure then has to be perceived as, in effect, concealing 'something else' – an idea, a feeling, an attitude, a social or religious value, or whatever. The link in this case rests upon a code of equivalence which is nowhere recorded and the unwritten knowledge of which died out with the Camunians.

I want to suggest that the dominant modes which concern us in the Val Camonica are those of the iconic and the symbolic. On the one hand, I can usually construe the Camunian image as a record of the visual appearance of a given object. On the other, the object depicted may articulate metaphoric meaning, standing for something other than itself. I would suggest that it is quite normal for an image to function in both modes, and indeed that it is frequently the case that an iconic intention releases a symbolic echo as a direct consequence of the fact that the maker is concerned to impart intense significance to what is being drawn. I am tempted to think that the iconic representation of a stag, for instance, could become the locus of symbolic suggestion just as soon as literal designation is accomplished; metaphoric connotation may be a surplus of significatory energy which spontaneously accretes around a sign once it has fulfilled its initial referential task. Let me examine some examples of Camunian imagery in relation to this hypothesis.

A fairly straightforward expectation of prehistoric marks would be that they record exploits or happenings in the experience of individuals or the social group. Among the earliest remnants of human prehistory are animal bones bearing repeated notches; it seems logical to read these as tallies built up across time to document a serial process, such as killing certain animals. The incisions on the great rock at Cemmo depict rows of deer and other animals, and may plausibly be read as the diary of a hunting season or seasons (see Figure 9.1). Each individual figure thereby takes its place as a component of a chronology.

Multiple events are sometimes portrayed in elaborate petroglyphic compositions such as a battle scene in which several warriors brandish shields and spears. It might be supposed that a single historical event occasioned such an image. But is this all the image means? Or, to put the point differently, would the representation of a single event always remain the same for later generations? It is important to remember that scratched marks are a most durable form of imprint; we might well expect that the representation of a single historical event would in due course take on other connotations, for the more a historical precedent recedes in time, the more its depiction functions trans-historically, as the tracing of a narrative outside time – a myth.

A similar development might be imagined in another sphere. There are other marks which depict such seasonal events as the growth of crops. A picture of a single successful corn harvest might, year by year, come to function as the representation of a cyclical event, and indeed as an implicit guarantee of its reliable annual recurrence. The permanence of the rock image would ground this certainty. Whereupon it is possible to conjecture that the making (and the later re-incising) of such important inscriptions might itself constitute a ritual of confirmation and stabilization. Each scratching of a corn plant image ensures agricultural prosperity, just as each rendering of a deer consolidates man's power over the wild creature on which he relies for survival.

Having now sketched a basic model of a mentality open to what might roughly be termed 'superstitious' association (I don't mean this to sound deprecatory), I want to put forward the generalization that the scratches I am considering are typically painstaking and intensely motivated. My hunch is that the process of cutting a figure into granite is sufficiently lengthy and demands such concentration as automatically to marshal concomitant psychic resources; that is, to incise a figure into hard stone is necessarily also to invest emotion in that figure. Indeed such a proposition may be a tautological truism, for who would invest so much time and effort in shaping a sign if there were not emotion invested in its referent already?

This speaks for an intensity of meaning in the Primitive Scratch, even its obsessional nature. And there are plenty of examples of what must surely have been obsessional subjects for any prehistoric artist. Themes like hunting, warfare, sexuality, and death are sufficiently potent as almost entirely to overwhelm the primitive imagination. Thus, even without recourse to comparisons with the practices of tribal groups in more recent times, we can feel confident in the supposition that Camunian rock art constitutes (in many, if not all, its manifestations) a mode of expression indissociable from certain primary preoccupations. The growth of clan solidarity and of religious feeling, and the development of ritual practices, are, I take it, synonymous with the evolution of the metaphysical imagination. The immutability of the scratched designs might be a reflection of their makers' yearning to impart permanence to a desperate intuition of hidden harmony, to carve myth out of accident, and thus to accede to a vision of regularity by way of portentous acts of duplication and possession, comforting to those in fact exposed to an unpredictable reality. The symbolic register of the Primitive Scratch functions precisely as an appeal to forces extending beyond the superficial referent, giving access to deeper levels of signification. The symbolic order would constitute precisely that – a domain sealed against disorder.

In developing an argument through allusive hints rather than strict evidence, I concede that my case must be more intuitive than scientific. Nevertheless, I believe that some such general shift as I have sketched may provide part of the answer to one of the great puzzles of prehistoric art; namely, the paradoxical fact that the early art of the paleolithic appears artistically far more competent than the later art of the neolithic. When, in *Abstraction and Empathy*, Wilhelm Worringer addressed the issue of Naturalism *versus* Abstraction, he offered a theory which links formal tendencies in art to emotional or spiritual preoccupations. He would see the lively naturalism of the early cave painters at Lascaux and Altamira as evidence of a pantheistic involvement in natural life, an unquestioning affinity for the wild. Conversely, the schematic or abstractive tendency of the neolithic would reflect a neurotic spiritualism, and thus be seen as a symptom of alienation from the substantial and the graspable. Unfortunately the Worringer thesis founders once one realizes that, on the whole, neolithic and post-neolithic man must have become progressively less alienated from his surroundings – and consequently more secure and 'in touch' – by virtue of his superior understanding of seasonal cycles and his triumphant grasp of the basics of controlled agriculture and herding.

A more attractive interpretation of the shift towards schematic representation is advanced in Claude Roy's essay on the petroglyphs at Naquane. It is an interpretation which squares neatly with my suggestion that mimesis 'hankers' to acquire symbolic resonance. I feel that Roy takes accurate measure of the Val Camonica style in proposing that we see it not as a lapse from a 'healthy' naturalism to a 'sickly' schematization, but a logical movement from longwinded mimetic explicitness to a shorthand repertoire of simplified signs. The advantage of this shorthand is that it is a lot more manageable than naturalism; its efficacy rests upon the existence of an implicit system. Signs are henceforth identifiable in that they correspond to a cultural code rather than to an averred continuum of actual perceptions of the real.

Where Roy draws a line is at a point just before this idiom slips into outright abstraction. He contends that the scratches of the Val Camonica remain figural while at the same time quivering on the brink of becoming purely symbolic tokens, pictograms modulating into ideograms. I am not sure whether to remain with Roy on this brink, or to contemplate the Primitive Scratch as part of a hieroglyphic system or pictorial alphabet. If a given sign – a deer, dagger, hut on stilts, etc. – were to be a shape related to a conceptual meaning (and presumably an uttered sound) in a purely arbitrary and symbolic manner, it follows that a composition containing several such elements would represent a complex message in coded form. It is a seductive thought that figural ensembles at sites like Seradina and Cemmo might be examples of a rebus, a set of pictograms secreting a hidden message. (These speculations are encouraged by the example of the so-called Bedolina Map above Capo di Ponte, where iconic images of huts are juxtaposed with diagrammatic outlines of fields, streams, and paths, as though to delineate a village in map form. If this is a defensible reading, the coexistence of icons and abstracted diagrams must constitute a case of a transitional idiom built both on perceptual recognition and on intellectual cognition.)

What seems more important to address at this juncture is the question of the resonance which schematized forms might be held to have offered to the Camunian viewer. A schema is a more mental than sensory medium, gesturing towards a shared idea rather than a literal external form; it invokes rather than points. And its power as sign may even be increased to the extent that in signalling the idea of an object, one may be gesturing not only towards a symbolic but also a mythic or sacred register. And once one starts to appeal to universals and archetypes, one accedes to the magic power of generalization.

Given that schematized form and visual codes based on abstract or semi-abstract signs became familiar features of much twentieth-century art, I wish to propose some analogues in the modern field which may help to ratify the above hypotheses. Of course analogies drawn between the neo-primitives of our own age and the original primitives of prehistory can only be tentative, and are qualified by innumerable considerations of differentness. None the less, I trust that the positing of a resemblance may open up one or two valid avenues of discussion. I shall refer briefly to three artists whose work has primitivistic qualities – Jean Dubuffet, Joan Miró, and Henri Michaux.

Dubuffet it was who, in the postwar years in Paris to which allusion has already been made, initiated a series of painterly experiments in primitivism. Works such as the 'Portraits plus beaux qu'ils croient' (1946–7) exemplify a concern for the least sophisticated modes of handling pigment; these representations of Dubuffet's friends are constructed as thick impastos into which are gouged bold black outlines. These last reflect the artist's provocative search for a drawing style least reconcilable with academic tradition; the 'portraits' end up as graffiti, and their deliberate lack of deftness and mimetic fidelity (even though each portrait bears a name, it hardly ever approaches a likeness) make of these paintings experiments in primitivistic unlearning, botched and derisive. At various points in his career, Dubuffet was to emphasize a correlation between the desire to be expressive in a non-academic style (for Dubuffet this tended to mean above all an anti-realistic style) and the impulse to create forms which are drastically simplified, caricatural, and often downright ugly. Dubuffet's outrageous portraits and grotesque cows (see the 1954 'Vaches' series) may be likened to the monsters depicted in certain archaic petroglyphs of North America, as for instance the chimerical beast from the Petrified Forest whose fantasticated shape distances it at once from nearby representations of known creatures, thereby making it an emblem of the monstrous and the unreal (see Fig. 9.2). Such a chimera points to a trend made explicit in the work of Dubuffet, namely the progression from caricature through fantastical depiction to eventual derealization. This is to see caricature as creating a momentum that slides smoothly in a direction opposite to perceptual realism, effecting an escape from sensory referentiality into the dreamworld of the Fantastic.

The pictorial style of Miró presents several points of comparison with that of the artists of the Val Camonica. In his mature work, Miró drew upon a highly personal lexicon of droll stylizations and ciphers. In paintings such as

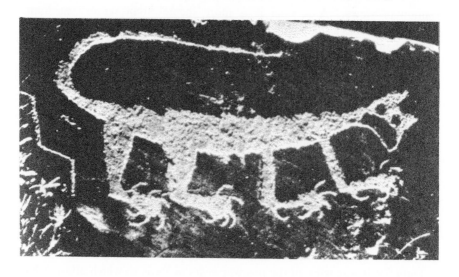

9.2 Chimerical beast, Petrified Forest, Arizona.

9.3 Male figure (neolithic period), rock number 35, Naquane, Val Camonica.

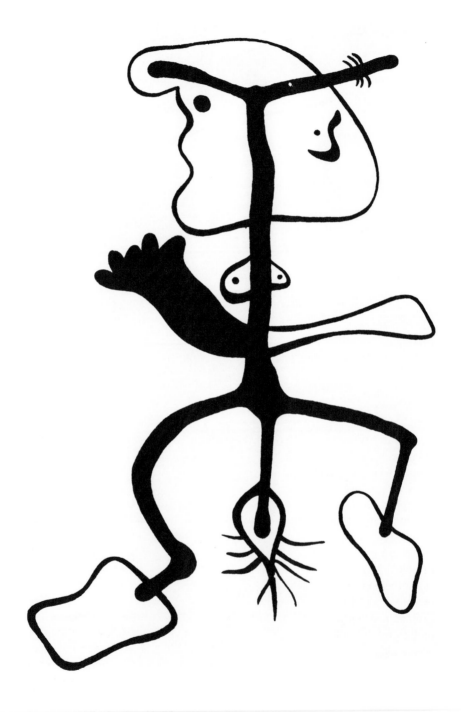

9.4 Joan Miró, ink drawing © ADAGP, Paris and DACS, London 1988.

'The Hunter (Catalan Landscape)' (1923–4), one can read off the central figure by identifying the stick-man which stands for the basic body of the hunter, and then the various attributes which confirm or characterize that figure – moustache, ear, eye, pipe, flaming heart, rampant sex. But whereas these straightforward schemas are decipherable without difficulty, the Miró system is far from being uniformly clear. In many works – and most notably in the crowded album of gouaches done in the 1940s under the title 'Constellations' – the artist indulges in an orgy of doodlings that create the effect of a much-scrawled wall of graffiti. At a certain point, the complexity of the signs and the lack of an authoritative 'dictionary' of meanings provided by the artist mean that Miró's constellations float before the eye in a proliferation of ribbons of possible signification. Of such enigmatic yet playful paintings, the poet Jacques Dupin has written that they derive from 'a system of signs which are elaborated but not fixed, signs in motion, open, available for new combinations whence they derive their capacity for novelty, their freshness, strength and glorious impact'.

A similarly fertile yet even less legible sign-system is to be found in the ink-drawings of Michaux. Whether working under the influence of mescalin or simply drawing fluently and with a serene unconcern for motive or design, Michaux produces black shapes and lines which are the ideographic equivalent not so much of figures, living or imaginary, as of lines of force, emotional knots, psychic vistas. The calligraphic flourishes characteristic of his idiom are the record of nameless impulses, nervous reflexes which vibrate within a space of indeterminate reference. At times, as in the 1950 cycle 'Mouvements', Michaux's chaotic squiggles and blobs conjure up images akin to those of dancing or battling humans, and are reminiscent of black and white transcriptions of certain petroglyphs (see Fig. 9.5). But more often, Michaux's signs seem to celebrate polysemy, the pen alluding to, yet never spelling out, any single signified. As Dupin puts it, 'the sign captures energy by its very indeterminacy'.

Applied to the incisions of the Val Camonica, such parallels are enlightening. Granted, many Camunian signs do appear to refer to a single entity. Yet many are less definite, or are otherwise ambiguous. One set of marks on a rock near Montecchio di Darfo, known locally as 'I Corni Freschi', is conventionally held to represent a cluster of halberds or pikes. Yet, at another sighting, the pikes may easily look like a flock of herons. Again the recurrent motif often called a 'paddle' – it consists of a square from which extends a straight appendage or 'handle' – might prompt a variety of inter-pretations. It could just as well be a ladle, a mallet, an axe, an animal-trap, even a diagram of an enclosure. The fact that we lack all evidence of that oral culture, which at one time must have acted as the guiding context for the 'proper' appreciation of the meanings intended by these graphic propositions, should not perhaps inhibit our appreciation of the unfettered eloquence we are now encountering. Polyvalence and convertible signs are integral to our

9.5 Henri Michaux, ink drawing © ADAGP, Paris and DACS, London 1988.

current experience of visual meaning, and we ought not automatically to censor our responses as being anachronistic.

'It is signs that have no exact meaning that provoke the sense of magic', Miró once remarked. The very fact of indeterminacy may be an irreducible factor in our latterday reception of these ancient messages. But then who is to say that, even at the time of their making, they were necessarily perceived as being singular, univocal statements? A surrealist approach to the Val Camonica marks would happily allow for there having been experimental and exploratory impulses operative at the time of composition. Might not the prehistoric scratchmaker have occasionally begun a given design with no particular shape in view, simply letting his hands and the relative controllability of the tool against an uneven surface dictate the progress of the scratches? Why should we only ever impute earnestness and forethought to the primordial mark, denying its maker all capacity to doodle and to dream?

Whichever model of creativity we invoke, and whatever specialist research we consult, we are in the final analysis left with the task of drawing together a sense from these marks for ourselves. The Primitive Scratch has its intrinsic virtue, being at once precise and mysterious, apparently deliberate as an expression left on the rock surface, yet richly elusive in its import. To help pinpoint a meaning for a given sign, one may refer to technical studies or to the various analogies I have indicated. Equally one should not overlook the more immediate resources of one's own sensibility. Roaming about the great outcrops at Seradina a few summers ago, when I was able to pad barefoot across the hot smooth rocks and thereby to engage in the most immediate and satisfying way with the emblems of the Primitive beneath my very feet, I experienced a fundamental sensation of contact which held its own deep meaning. Prior to any intellectual knowledge, this experience of being at an elective site was a fulfilment in itself. It was hardly an aesthetic experience. I can only recall that it had about it something of fragrance and poignancy. If I were to bend to the task of drawing some further lesson out of that sensation, I would have to say that what the marks were asking me to adduce was my own vulnerability. I begin to divine that the way to grasp the Primitive Scratch must be to advance without inhibition, to participate in its presence as generously as possible. To establish a dialogue across thousands of years, I must open my own sensibility as fully as possible to the transaction. *Camunnus artifex hic fuit.* Now I am here. The authentic apprehension of Otherness is perhaps grounded in some form of self-knowledge; or rather, knowledge of the Other is indissociable from the knowledge we concurrently gain of ourselves. Upon the high granite of the Val Camonica, a minimal sign speaks to me across the dimness of time, and voices a primitive truth, what I and its maker most authentically share: it is only ever desire, imagination, and fear that hasten understanding.

Select bibliography

Anati, Emmanuel (1964) *Camonica Valley*, Cape, London.

Anati, Emmanuel (1976) *Evolution and Style in Camunian Rock Art*, Edizioni del Centro, Capo di Ponte.

Dupin, Jacques (1982) *L'Espace autrement dit*, Editions Galilée, Paris.

Lewis-Williams, J. David (1981) 'Rock art and semiotic', in *Believing and Seeing. Symbolic meanings in southern San rock paintings*, Academic Press, London/New York, pp. 3–14.

Michaux, Henri (1950) *Mouvements*, Gallimard, Paris.

Penrose, Roland (1970) *Miró*, Thames & Hudson, London.

Roy, Claude (1966) 'Naquane, ou la signification des signes', in *Naquane*, Editions Clairefontaine, Lausanne, pp. 9–21.

Tomkins, Calvin (1974) 'A reporter at large: thinking in time', *New Yorker*, 22 April, pp. 109–28.

Viatte, Germain and Wilson, Sarah (1982) *Aftermath: France 1945-54. New Images of Man*, Barbican Centre, London.

Worringer, Wilhelm (1963) *Abstraction and Empathy*, Routledge & Kegan Paul, London.

Chapter Ten

How young children give meaning to drawing

John Matthews

This chapter is about how meaning is given to drawing by children. If analyses and diagnoses are based on their drawings, then it makes considerable sense to attend to how meanings are first attributed to lines, shapes, marks, and colours by the children themselves in earliest infancy. This supplies the context and starting point of this chapter.

My work has been concerned with the genesis of representation in early childhood, when the meanings of images, events, and objects are constructed by the child. When we try to appraise the qualities and meanings of artworks, pictures, and other vehicles of representation, the forms out of which these are composed embody those spatial specifications and relations attached to them in early childhood.

Over a period of fifteen years I have studied the development of early representation and symbolic play. Detailed longitudinal studies of my own three children's drawing development have been made, in which virtually all of the drawings produced have been collected, up to the children's present ages of 5 years, 13 years, and 15 years at the time of writing. Forty nursery class children were also studied over a two-year period, as well as children between the ages 4 and 7 years over a six-year period in infants' schools. The data consist, however, not only of analysis of end-products – the finished drawings – but of the ongoing processes of painting and drawing as symbolic episodes through time. Testing procedures were not employed and the descriptions of drawings were usually derived from the children's spontaneous utterances made whilst drawing.

An account of how basic drawing structures are acquired has been the subject of other papers (Matthews 1983, 1984, 1986, 1988). Analysis of my own highly detailed recorded observations reveal that drawing processes form part of a holistic programme generated by the child to form descriptions of events and objects. These studies show that very young children are making graphic experiments of their own, in which actions, lines, marks, shapes, and colours are often part of exquisitely orchestrated spatiotemporal events. In these episodes children monitor a series of alternating representational possibilities, which are not usually elicited in the experimental setting.

It is in this four-dimensional language, of which so-called 'scribbling' sometimes leaves a recording, that the denotional values of lines are worked out. Basic spatial relations – inside/outside, higher than/lower than, in front of/behind – plus powerful vectors and co-ordinate axes are investigated at this level, in the first few years of life, and mapped into two dimensions.

These drawing structures are generated spontaneously in a process akin to language acquisition, in which imitation plays only a small part (Willats 1983). Rather, the child begins to perceive a relationship between the structures he/she is generating and structures in the perceived environment. Synthesis and differentiation of actions and the resultant forms allow children between 2 and 4 years to encode on to the drawing surface relations which they find extremely salient and to which they attach powerful symbolic values. These early structures not only form a substratum for later configuration, they also contribute to children's internal descriptions of reality. Important examples of these early structures must include the use of closed shapes to enclose nuclei. This structure encodes inside/outside relations. The attachment in various ways of lines to other shapes allows children to explore and represent connectivity.

However, children not only attend to the configural relationships between their drawings and objects; they also perceive dynamic relationships between the process of drawing through time, and events or motion sequences external to the act of drawing (see also Athey 1980; Wolf and Fucigna 1983). They employ the 'trace making effects' of drawing (Michotte 1963, p. 289) to specify temporal events in the world. I call these action representations (Matthews 1983, 1984) and have mapped out their interrelationship with other modes of representation. Here are some examples of that interaction.

Ben at 2 years and 1 month makes a configurative response to the contrasting edge of paintwork, which specifies to him a contour derivative of a 'car'. He says, 'There's a car there.' This is a configurative representation. It conveys the shape of an object. Yet an instant later he makes a distinctly different kind of representation. Making a rotational movement with the brush, he says 'It's going round the corner . . . it's going around the corner. It's gone now.' This is an action representation. Having considered the car's configuration, he now represents its movement passage or trajectory through time and space.

A drawing made a few days later is a clear example of a configurative representation. Using two of the earliest mark-making gestures which, when they flow into each other produce a cruciform structure, he says 'This is an aeroplane.' He has noticed that the salient structural features of the drawing correspond with those of the object, 'aeroplane'. But consider a painting made a few days later. Whilst the brush is in very intense, elliptical motion, he says 'This is an aeroplane!' Now it is the identical utterance, but the mode of representation is here discreetly different. He is monitoring or recording the trajectory of the aeroplane, its flightpath through time and space, in an action representation. It is doubtful whether these modes of representation could be distinguished by merely viewing the finished drawings and paintings.

Action representation can also encode events more complex than simple trajectories from A to B. In a painting by Ben at 3.1 there is an alternation between two modes of representation within the same painting, which Ben says is about 'someone washing'. In this painting configuration appears – two parallel vertical strokes represent the arms lowered into the wash basin – but Ben's swirling brush also represents the actions involved in washing one's hands. These alternations between action and configurative modes of response could not be discerned merely by looking at the finished drawing. These representational categories are not rigidly separate but flow into each other. In another drawing, dynamic tracing of the motion of the helicopter's rotor blades may lead Ben to perceive – within the completed drawing – the configuration of that helicopter. This is part of the process described by John Willats (1984) as the interaction between production and perception. Looking in more detail at this process tells us something about the route from dynamic event-tracing to configuration.

These behaviours are carried over from pretend or symbolic play, where movements through horizontal and vertical planes have been represented by using hand-held toy figures. These movements are synchronized with vocalizations, music, narrative, and duologue, and they are carried over into the arena of drawing and painting, where mark-making activities themselves become the pivotal phenomena (Vygotsky 1966) around which representations develop.

As Joel (2 years, 5 months, and 22 days) makes a rising arc with a red felt-tip pen he says 'It's a man flying ... a man running away.' It may be that he is encoding on to the drawing surface higher and lower relationships; the ascent and descent of the figure, like the graceful apogees described by hand-

Figure 10.1

Figure 10.2

held toys in his play scenarios at this time. These higher/lower relations demonstrated in play do become more explicit in drawing as the child grows older. Consider clear examples by Ben at 3.2 (Figs 10.1 and 10.2). About Fig. 10.1 he says 'The train is going over the railway bridge' and about Fig. 10.2 'The train has crashed under the railway bridge.'

Hannah at 3.8.20 also produces a drawing in which an inverted U shape represents a bridge. 'A train', she says, 'goes over a bridge, and water is under the bridge.' She, too, has followed a similar route in mapping these relationships on to the drawing surface. About six months earlier she creates a series of continuous ellipses which spiral away from her toward the farther edge of the paper. She says 'The bubbles are going up to the surface.' At 3.5.9 she makes a drawing in which the pen point travels away from her as she says 'A cat ... his head's growing', and then, as the pen line moves back towards her, 'It's going down again!' Immediately after this she makes another drawing in which, once more, a line is moved away from her toward the farther edge of the paper, as she remarks 'The baby grow'd.' Hannah is beginning to encode a vertical axis on the drawing surface.

At 2.8.15 Joel places a mark near the middle of the paper, saying 'This is a nose' and another mark at the edge of the paper nearest him saying 'This is a foot.' He may be saying that the nose is higher than the foot; that the higher part of the scene should be encoded on to the 'higher' part of the drawing surface and the lower part of the scene on the 'lower' part of the drawing surface. Given an entire series of drawings, the progress does become clear. As he traces lines from the bottom to the top of the paper he says 'It's mummy, daddy, Joel, and Ben.' He is representing the vertical axis of the figures in the family group (Joel 2.9.20).

The child actively seeks out invariant or deep structure across a range of different situations and media (see Gibson 1979). Ben at 3.3 builds constructions of wooden bricks. Some of these are towers, saliently extended along a vertical axis and actually representing tongues of flame in a fire. Ben, like other young children, builds up knowledge about co-ordinate axes which remain essentially unchanged despite transposition from one context to another – in this case from two dimensions to three dimensions and *vice versa*.

A longitudinal line and an approximate perpendicular attachment is a structure to which the child assimilates a wide range of different content. A month after Ben makes a drawing (at 3.1, Fig. 10.3) in which structure is investigated independent of meaning, he uses vertical parallels and right-angular attachments to represent his mother wearing dungarees (Ben 3.2, Fig. 10.4). Look carefully at how physically similar lines specify a range of quite different denotional values (Willats 1985). The outermost, roughly parallel, lines represent the occluding boundaries of her body. A line circumscribes the contour of breast, waist, and thigh, while another lines denotes her back, the small of her back, her behind, and the back of her thighs. Two other lines represent the straps of her dungarees. Like Joel, Ben created parallel/vertical lines at a dynamic level and now he actively seeks out, within the environment, any new manifestation of this structure. Whilst this is an unusual drawing, it does show the old dichotomy between intellectual *versus* visual realism to be an artifact of an inadequate model of drawing development.

Also contradicting popular opinion and the classic Luquet/Piaget theory of drawing development (Luquet 1927) is the evidence that children between 3 and 4 years convey projective understandings, when they specify two aspects or viewpoints of the same scene. This is achieved as a byproduct, as it were, of the child's dynamic enactment of events. In a drawing by Hannah (3.3.2), for example, there occurs the embryonic specification of two basic aspects of the

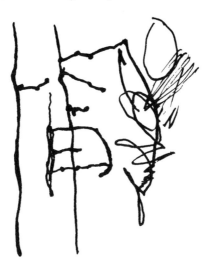

Figure 10.3

131

Figure 10.4

same phenomenon. She says 'The clouds are moving along ... the rain is coming down' and she employs two contrasting mark-making gestures with which to represent the falling rain. Firstly, an oscillating zig-zag represents the rain's movement along and down through a vertical plane, but to the right of this she impacts the pen against the surface, enacting the collision of the rain drops at right angles to the ground.

Although in its germinal phase, the child's use of two distinct mark-making actions to enact two axes within the same event – the flight path of rain drops – results in the encoding of two viewpoints of the same scene – lines of sight which are notionally perpendicular to each other. Lines of sight, or viewpoints, are performed in symbolic play. In games by Joel at around 3 years, two figures pursue each other around and around, up, over, and down, and also through a coffee-grinder. These axes are mapped on to the drawing surface at about the same age. In Fig. 10.5 the rotational line to the upper left represents figures going around and around a mountain, and at the bottom right going up, over, and down the mountain. The outcome of enacting this ascent/descent is a configurative profile of the mountain which is so powerful to Joel that he is prompted to draw the two climbers, linked together by a rope, which itself is trailed up and over the summit. Joel then encompasses this mountain profile with its rotational axis, showing in effect two aspects of the scene simultaneously. And back to the upper left of the drawing, in the centre of the original rotation, Joel pokes the pen right through the paper, attending carefully to how a form can go through a surface.

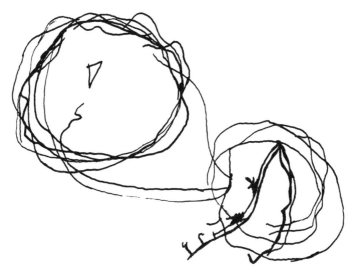

Figure 10.5

Contrasting lines of sight are also represented by Ben at 3.2 (Fig. 10.6). Here Ben spills a glass of milk from one hand, whilst holding a slice of beans on toast in his other. We have a notional line of sight to the plane of the human face at 90°. But we have a line of sight of 0° degrees to a flat plane here – the slice of beans on toast. This is an edge-on view – a totally foreshortened view of a flat (or flattish) plane. Planes can in effect be rotated through 90° – an ability not predicted by Piaget, who thought children below 4 years of age showed 'a complete lack of understanding of any sort of pictorial perspective' (Piaget and Inhelder 1956: 173).

Figure 10.6

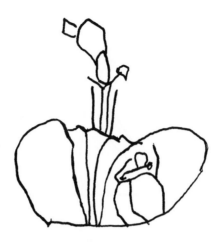

Figure 10.7

Frame-by-frame analysis of video recordings reveals however that children between 3 and 4 years practise the interrelationship between lines of sight in symbolic play. Joel, at 3.2, for example, manipulates two toy figures so that figure A hides from figure B before figure A descends through a tube, figure B's line of sight being adjusted at this instant to track the other's descent visually. The same dynamic structure – that of going through – is encoded into two dimensions. Santa Claus goes down and through a tube – a chimney; those vertical parallels now represent the section of a tube (Ben 3.3, Fig. 10.7).

The child actively seeks out within the environment any new manifestation of the same dynamic invariant. So, if Santa Claus can go through a tube, then music can go through a trumpet (Ben 3.3, Fig. 10.8).

Considering going through leads to consideration of section – a wholly imaginary line which marks the interface between one medium and another.

Figure 10.8

Figure 10.9

A line, in a drawing by Ben at 3.3, specifies a section through the ground; a man digs in the ground for the bones of animals (Fig. 10.9).

For Ben at 3.3 it is not always sufficient to place nuclei – figures, objects – simply inside a closed shape. Higher and lower relations are stipulated – or 'upstairs and downstairs', as Ben says as he draws a house (Fig. 10.10). A line divides the closed shape laterally, representing a section through the top floor. The two vertical parallels again represent the section of a tube. Smoke goes through this chimney. The chimney is in vertical linear relationship with the fireplace on the top floor and the fireplace on the ground floor. Ben is depicted in bed. We have a foreshortened, edge-on view of the table top, on which rest objects. His mother vacuum-cleans the floor. Santa's reindeer are parked on the roof. Santa Claus himself moves from position one to position two in space and time, where he is about to descent the chimney.

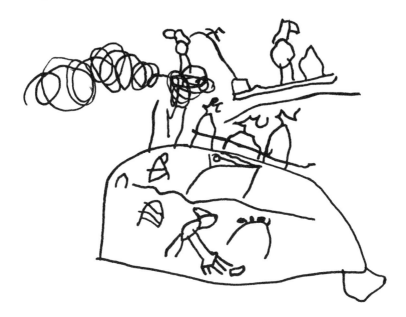

Figure 10.10

Figure 10.11

Periodic succession and temporal sequence are explored from the earliest drawings, where the beginnings and ends of sequences and lines are demarcated or when continuous linear journeys are broken down into their rhythmical constituents. Sometimes vocalizations are synchronized with marking actions in a one-to-one correspondence – early counting in fact. These concerns have been shifted to a new conceptual level in drawings by Ben at 3.3. One king jumps off a castle and his descent is shown in stages until his moment of impact with the ground is registered with a vigorous squiggle of the pen (Fig. 10.11). He loses his crown on the way. Ben is plotting and co-ordinating two trajectories through space and time. A series of drawings follow in which Ben investigates and represents, in serialized images, permutations of these vectors: the king ascends a hill to catch a flying kite; the king jumps off the castle and goes for a walk.

Figure 10.12

Figure 10.13

Fig. 10.12 shows one boat ascending from the surface of the water, shedding trails of water as it moves through positions one to four. 'It takes time' says Ben. The trails of water are represented by vertical grouped parallels. In drawings produced over the next few weeks a wide range of very different content is assimilated to virtually identical graphic structure – including those powerful parallels.

At 3.6 Ben draws one stagecoach receding away from us through the picture-plane in a controlled, three-stage decrease in apparent or optical size of shape to convey its recession (Fig. 10.13). The use of optical or apparent size change to specify recession into the third dimension means putting constraints on one's knowledge about invariant volumes (see also Pratt 1985). There is also an inferred oblique line here. The child will eventually realize further the significance and use of oblique lines, as we shall see.

Oblique parallels are used in Fig. 10.14 to show what in reality are horizontal edges of planes – the sides of the carriage – receding away from us in this drawing of a steam train coming straight toward us (Ben 4.3). Two sides of the carriage are shown, plus a front view of the engine, and a plan view of the railway tracks. This drawing then conveys both object-centred and

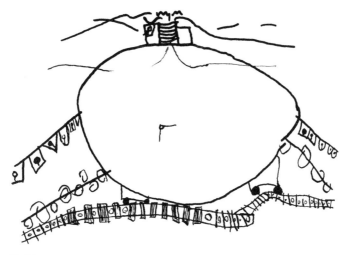

Figure 10.14

Figure 10.15

view-centred information (Marr 1982; Willats 1985). But he continues over the next few days and weeks to consider projective dimensions.

In Fig. 10.15 he excludes the carriage from the problem, concentrating on optical size grading, using a dot to stand for a disc-like plane at optical infinity. And gradually one side of the carriage dominates as object-centred descriptions give way to the need to convey view-specific information (Fig. 10.16). An oblique line can now specify a horizontal edge receding back through the picture plane. Willats (1985) has suggested that part of the child's problem in using a projective system perhaps is the symbolic difficulty of using a sloping line – an oblique line – to represent a horizontal edge; one month before, you see (at 4.2, Fig. 10.17), a sloping line usually meant a slope.

Once one viewpoint has been considered Ben goes on to construct others. Fig. 10.18 shows an extemely low-angle view – a 'worm's eye' view – of a giant

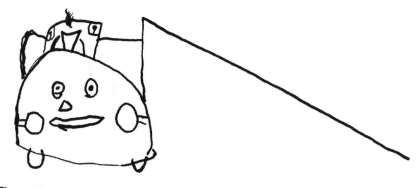

Figure 10.16

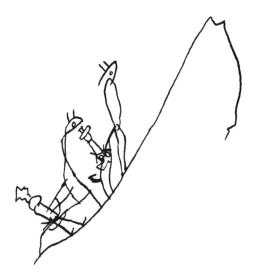

Figure 10.17

stepping over some people (Ben 4.3). The legs of the giant signal, perhaps, a move towards using convergent oblique lines to show depth.

In Fig. 10.19, a wonderful drawing of two pirates fighting (made by Ben at 4.6), forms are superimposed over one another, but the next day in-front-of/behind relations are conveyed by hidden line elimination (Fig. 10.20). A drawing may now specify the viewer's own position relative to the scene.

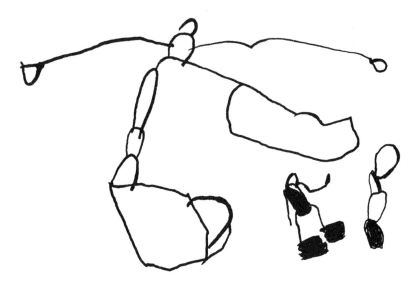

Figure 10.18

Figure 10.19

Distant forms are occluded from the viewer by nearer ones which interrupt his/her line of sight. Disc-like planes – the hilts of swords – can, in effect, be rotated through 90°.

These discoveries about representation of spatiotemporal events are investigated in a process which includes the first scribbles. Traditional accounts of drawing which consider its sole purpose to be the encoding of view-specific information cannot help us understand the uses to which very young children themselves put graphic media. Action representations in play and drawing are not simply abandoned in favour of projective geometry: on the contrary, they assist in the construction of basic vectors, co-ordinates, and axes, on which projective systems are mapped. More than this, they are part of a mutually reciprocal array of expressive and representational responses which humans develop to form descriptions of objects and events.

I have attempted to show some of the links between thinking which is embedded in actions and the use of symbolic systems, and how meaning is given to drawing by children. The analysis of drawing is inevitably complex and multi-layered. This chapter has shown some of the reasons why this is so. It is easy to make mistakes in analysis if one is ignorant of the deep structure which organizes the formation and development of drawing. Drawing is the only human behaviour in which a trace is made of actions performed. Children's drawings are literally recordings of their vitality and life. Denotional and aesthetic sensibility to lines, shapes, and colours probably comes about from an identification and a total participation with the

Figure 10.20

unfolding process of drawing, at a level when the multifarious expressive and representational potentialities are still in embryo. At this level the child is forming the 'double knowledge' (Furth 1969) that drawings are structures in themselves, yet simultaneously they refer to events and objects outside themselves. It is perhaps to this dimension of 'meaning' that therapists – and educators – should attend.

References

Athey, C. (1980) 'From marks to meanings: the language of lines'. A chapter from a book to be published. Froebel Institute, Roehampton, UK.

Furth, H. G. (1969) *Piaget and Knowledge*, Prentice-Hall, New Jersey.

Gibson, J. (1979) *The Ecological Approach to Visual Perception*, Houghton Mifflin, Boston.

Luquet, G. H. (1927) *Le dessin enfantin*, Alcan, Paris.

Marr, D. (1982) *Vision: A Computational Investigation into Human Representation and Processing of Visual Information*, W. H. Freeman, San Francisco.

Matthews, J. (1983) 'Children drawing: are young children really scribbling?', original version of a paper presented at the British Psychological Society International Conference on Psychology and the Arts, University of Cardiff, Wales.

Matthews, J. (1984) 'Children drawing: are young children really scribbling?', *Early Child Development and Care*, 18, pp. 1–39.

Matthews, J. (1986) 'Children's early representation: the construction of meaning', *Inscape*, 2, pp. 12–17.

Matthews, J. (1988) 'The young child's early representation and drawing', in Blenkin, G. M. and Kelly, A. V. (eds) *Early Childhood Education: A Developmental Curriculum*, Paul Chapman, London, pp. 162–83.

Michotte, A. (1963) *The Perception of Causality, Methuen Manual of Modern Psychology*, Methuen, London.

Piaget, J. and Inhelder, B. (1956) *The Child's Conception of Space*, Routledge & Kegan Paul, London.

Pratt, F. R. (1985) 'A perspective on traditional artistic practices', in Freeman, N. H. and Cox, M. V. (eds) *Visual Order: The Nature and Development of Pictorial Representation*, Cambridge University Press, pp. 32–57.

Vygotsky, L. S. (1966) 'Play and its role in the mental development of the child', *Soviet Psychology*, 12.6, pp. 62–76.

Willats, J. (1983) 'The role of conscious knowledge in the development of drawing ability', *Art Education*, March, pp. 78–83.

Willats, J. (1984) 'Getting the drawing to look right as well as be right: the interaction between production and perception as a mechanism of development', in Crozier, W. R. and Chapman, A. J. (eds) *Cognitive Processes in the Perception of Art*, North Holland, Amsterdam, pp. 111–25.

Willats, J. (1985) 'Drawing systems revisited: the role of denotation systems in children's figure drawings', in Freeman, N. H. and Cox, M. V. (eds) *Visual Order: The Nature and Development of Pictorial Representation*, Cambridge University Press, pp. 78–100.

Wolf, D. and Fucigna, C. (1983) 'Representation before picturing', transcript of symposium presentation, Symposium on Drawing Development, British Psychological Society International Conference on Psychology and the Arts, University of Cardiff, Wales.

Chapter Eleven

Working with defence mechanisms in art therapy

Mary Levens

In this chapter I intend to discuss briefly the psychoanalytic concept of defence mechanisms, and restrict myself to an examination of only two of these, with particular reference to art therapy. Psychoanalytic theory holds that the unconscious mind exerts a dynamic effect on behaviour, known as psychic determinism, and that all behaviour is motivated and goal directed.

Dynamically-oriented art therapy recognizes that man's fundamental thoughts and feelings, deriving from the unconscious, may reach expression in images rather than words. Freud (Brown 1961) appeared to put the creative impulse on a par with instinct, and developed theories in which imaginative modes of mental functioning were characteristic of primary processes. Art is seen as a compromise between the pleasure principle and the superego. The ego, working under the direction of the reality principle, balances these two tendencies, and therefore a reconciling of the reality and pleasure principles is required in the process. In analytically oriented art therapy the therapist is dealing with resistance, in the guise of various defence mechanisms.

Ultimately, all defence mechanisms are designed to secure the ego and to save it from experiencing unpleasure, from within and from the outside world. When all is well, the ego notes the onset of an instinctual impulse, the heightened tension, and feelings of unpleasure which accompany this and relief when gratification is experienced. The id, using primary processes, prevails. There is no synthesis of ideas, affects can be displaced, opposites are not mutually exclusive. The ego, using primarily secondary processes, demands that the impulses can no longer seek the required gratification and have to respect the demands of reality, of moral, ethical laws by which the superego controls the behaviour of the ego. The defensive measures of the ego, against the id, are carried out invisibly. We can only reconstruct them in retrospect. For example, in the case of successful repression, the ego knows nothing of it.

From the study of memory, it is known that recognition is an easier task than pure recall. Painting, which may contain unconscious elements not yet remembered, may act as an aid to the development from a purely visual memory to a more communicable one. The use of art, for most of us, is less amenable to control and unconscious material may bypass verbal defences which we are more adept at manipulating than imagery.

Guntrip (1982) explains that in the case of projection, a distortion of perception of the outer world occurs by unconscious projection on to it of the inner world, to such an extent that it reaches a degree of psychical reality. One may externalize that which is personally intolerable and consciously disowned, and therefore have to defend oneself against these dangerous, externalized objects. This primitive attempt to externalize internal pain leaves the self much impoverished.

Projection also refers to the constant means by which we structure our view of the world and bring to it aspects of our internal world. This process operates constantly in art; projection in art produces an investment of external objects with libidinal or aggressive energy and the psychological attachment of unconscious phantasies to that which excites interest. Even collage may unconsciously be designed to become a better recipient of the projected phantasy. The client may use art to test out his dangerous thoughts and ungratified wishes in a safer way than directly in relation to the therapist. In this way his art can act as a mirror in which to see himself more clearly, or as an intermediary between self and non-self, inner and outer worlds.

Turning to regression, as a second example of a defence mechanism, this can be understood as a retreat to a more dependent position. Winnicott (1980) suggests that therapeutic regression may allow the client to get in touch with his 'true self'. From this position one aims to aid the regrowth of the regressed ego. One often sees in art therapy images associated with earlier levels of functioning; Fairbairn (1952) suggests that bodily gratifications easily become the area which the client is forced back to for solving problems of unsatisfied needs, and this may be an important component of some portrayals of body image which so frequently occur.

For the regressed client, the edge of the paper provides an important boundary, the working out of inner and outer spaces, in the 'enclosure' stage of children's drawing development. Regression as a defence against anxiety can be seen to be determined by fixation points. Even sublimations can undergo regression, so that painting becomes smearing. Regressed art may take the form of scribbles or other pre-representational styles. Milner (1971) suggests that in these instances, ideas and feelings have not yet been sufficiently worked over internally to become communicable, i.e. have not yet taken on a symbolic form by having been sufficiently sublimated. So one may consider that the more regressed client is using the impulses and spontaneity of the id without making it communicative via the ego.

Regression in painting may serve immediate needs, in which case creative work is out of the question at that stage. It may be necessary to allow some release before the client is able to tolerate the frustration involved in the sublimation of their drives. The regressed painting may be more impulsive, perhaps with more emphasis on colour than form or organization. The therapist's task must be to recognize when interpretations are therapeutic or unconstructive. A client's need may be more for containment, a metaphorical 'holding', before symbolic use of their work can be undertaken. In this case, even transference interpretations require symbolic functioning, and should perhaps be delayed.

Winnicott (1980) suggests splashes and scribbles may represent a lack of separation, and he further develops the links between paintings and transitional objects, suggesting that as the client gradually adds form to their work, they are also involved in separating from a more fused position with the object. Rollo May (1975) discusses regressive elements in painting, symbols, and myth. He suggests they all bring into awareness not only infantile, archaic, unconscious longings, dreads, and other psychic contents, but also new meanings, new forms, and disclose a reality which was literally not present beforehand. They therefore serve a progressive function as well, which he is concerned is omitted in a traditional psychoanalytic approach.

It is extremely hard to limit myself to a selection of salient points for discussion, but I would like to highlight a few points in relation to other defence mechanisms. Repressed material includes data which have never really entered consciousness, as well as that which has. In recovering this material through art, the client may be faced (literally) with images or ideas which he had no awareness of having owned. Repression is of course essential for healthy functioning, as well as being used as a specific defence, and in art it may lead to images being disguised to avoid recognition, by both the client and therapist. Interpretations made too early may easily be wasted, or actually promote greater use of defences. One value in keeping artwork is that it allows images to be re-used at a later stage.

The process of sublimation, considered by some to be a defence, covers all transformations by the artwork, making it possible for phantasies to be partially expressed and fulfilled. Part of the constructive energy that goes into making art may derive from neutralized aggression. One may deliberately use clay to provide a greater physical resistance, allowing a symbolic acting out of aggression, but with the potential for sublimation.

If one considers restitution as a defence, one can see how the creating of art is considered by Kleinians to recreate the early wish to repair and restore an object derived from the guilt and fear the infant experiences due to his aggressive impulses towards his mother. His fear of actually destroying her leads to a desire to recreate her, or find her again, in what he makes – to make good again.

In art therapy the symbolic transformation that occurs, when it does, allows the phantasy content to undergo a series of changes to become more consciously acceptable, whilst the artist remains unconscious of much of the reason for each minute change to his work. Any mental mechanism may be demonstrated in art, for instance, splitting ego functions into separate and unrelated parts, but I want to end by stressing that defences are not purely contained in the image. The client's resistance to creating his images, or using them, may only be part of the resistance to engage in a therapeutic relationship. I believe the relationship issues are as important in art therapy as in other forms of therapy, and the work should be understood to relate to that relationship.

Freud held that the interpretation of resistance, along with that of transference, was crucial to his technique. He concluded that defence mechanisms directed against former danger recur, in treatment, as resistances against recovery. Recovery is treated by the ego as a new danger. The art therapist should therefore understand the nature of resistance, in all its guises, and be able to credit it with the respect it demands.

References

Brown, J. A. C. (1961) *Freud and the Post-Freudians*, Penguin, Harmondsworth.

Fairbairn, W. R. D. (1952) *Psychoanalytical Studies of the Personality*, Routledge & Kegan Paul, London.

Guntrip, H. (1982) *Personality Structure and Human Interaction*, Hogarth Press, London.

May, R. (1975) 'Values, myths and symbols', *American Journal of Psychiatry* vol. 132, no. 7, pp. 703–6.

Milner, M. (1971) *On Not Being Able to Paint*, Heinemann, London.

Winnicott, D. W. (1980) *Playing and Reality*, Penguin, Harmondsworth.

Chapter Twelve

The picture within the frame

Joy Schaverien

In this chapter I will attempt to clarify some of the issues which distinguish art therapy from therapy where art is 'employed', such as when it is used as an 'aid' to psychotherapy. In art therapy the relationship between client and therapist may at times form a background, while the foreground of the therapeutic work is the picture. Pictures may reveal more than is clearly apparent in the dialogue; they may exhibit the transference, contain it, and powerfully influence the counter-transference. This is in distinct contrast to the pictures which are sometimes 'employed' in psychotherapy. Here they are a background, an aid to understanding, or an illustration of feeling, but are not considered to be central. Such pictures are peripheral to the main task, which may be considered to be the analysis of the transference. (In art therapy it is always important to be aware of the transference and counter-transference, but analysis of the transference may not always be the main aim, as the picture may carry some of that function.)

A central feature of any context of therapy is the person of the therapist. It is the therapist who establishes what is on offer, the 'shape' of therapy, or what is to be considered within the boundaries. Therefore the background of the therapist, her formative learning experiences, her beliefs, fears, and personal philosophy, as well as the way she presents herself, all communicate and influence the setting. If the therapist is primarily an artist she will have encountered certain formative learning experiences, which are based on trust of the intuitive. At the best colleges of art in the UK, the student learns to court discomfort, to abandon obvious or well-tried solutions, and to test that which is new and different in her experience. Such an approach fosters emergence of inner reality, however chaotic, this being shaped into outer, more objective, imagery and objects once the raw material is manifest. Art, if not a direct instrument for social and individual change, is certainly a reflection of such change and an indicator of direction for those who are open to read the signs. In contrast to the artist, the formative experience of the medically trained is initially in gaining from received knowledge, through books, lectures, and observation of other people's behaviour. To become a psychotherapist such a person will need to relinquish the primacy of the outer world to allow space for acceptance of inner experience.

It would seem that these two opposite formative trainings equip the pro-spective therapist with very different skills; each may benefit from learning a little of what the other has to offer in order to work effectively. The danger is that the artist/therapist may feel a need to relinquish the artist part of her experience in the face of an institution or a system dominated by the scientific approach. In medically oriented environments such as hospitals, the scientific approach is dominant, and the various therapies are frequently required to justify themselves in terms of objectively identified criteria. This is a rather alien task, and in order to survive in this situation it is imperative that, as artists, we establish what it is that we bring to therapy which is special or unique. Art not only enriches the inner world of our clients and ourselves; it also enriches the approach of any therapeutic team. In this chapter I shall attempt to redress the balance by relating art therapy to its own antecedents, the private art process, the framed picture within the gallery, and the public framed space of the art gallery.

In addition to its prior base in art, art therapy is also closely linked to psychotherapy and psychoanalysis. The title of this chapter, 'The picture within the frame', refers to the therapeutic frame, that is the setting for therapy. The therapeutic frame includes the time, space, place, and the limits of therapy. Part of this frame, responsible for it but also a part of the picture within, is the therapist. In any psychotherapeutic encounter the setting and the person of the therapist are the main constants. In art therapy, in addition to these, and central within the frame, are the pictures made by the client. At times when the boundaries of the outer frame are unclear, such as very often in a psychiatric hospital, the picture, the inner frame of therapy, remains the stable factor.

Framed experience is not a strange or unusual concept; there are many analogies to draw on. For various reasons we go to special places, spaces 'set apart' for a particular purpose. One space 'set apart' in this manner is the theatre. We go there for the specific purpose of being entertained. By choosing to go to this place we are entering a particular relationship to the situation which requires a certain set of mind. We relinquish our usual self-concept and suspend disbelief in order to allow the action that is played in front of us to affect us. We are enabled in doing this by the fact that the action takes place in a space 'set apart' from everyday life.

In that they are experiences 'set apart', separated from everyday reality, psychotherapy and some forms of art therapy are comparable to the theatre. For the therapy hour the client steps out of material life, the demands of job, family, of unemployment, or loneliness, and into a room, a space and person 'set apart', a theatre with an empty stage. On this stage she can enact her own drama, she can direct it, and she introduces all the characters. Whatever takes place in the privacy of this room, time is suspended and the two people are both involved in observing the drama. Similarly to the spectator in the theatre, these two people may experience powerful emotions. What is important here, what makes this distinct from any other relationship, is that the two people involved have an agreement to keep the relationship within this particular frame, within the established boundaries of time 'set apart'. These boundaries include the agreed task of the search, within the person who has identified herself as the client, to find some kind of meaning in the material she brings. Like the theatre, this also requires a suspension of disbelief and the agreement to give serious attention and imaginative space to aspects of life which might ordinarily be denied. Whatever happens here is split off from everyday existence and is observed, rather than acted upon. This is crucial because, without this space set apart, there is the inclination to behave and respond spontaneously, as we do in our social relationships. Here the frame provides the setting where the therapist can maintain a certain objectivity, a therapeutic distance. This allows the client to make a split which enables her both to regress and also to function as an observer of her own behaviours. Not all art therapists are able, in their workplace, to establish such clear boundaries; they thus encounter problems which are particular to offering treatment which is based on psychotherapeutic models in an unclear frame. Leaving the theatre and psychotherapy aside, I will now consider the art gallery. As the theatre is analogous to psychotherapy, so the art gallery is to art therapy..

The art gallery is also space 'set apart', a space set apart for viewing pictures. The viewing of pictures also requires a suspension of disbelief and of judgement. In order to permit the aesthetic qualities of a work of art to affect one, it is necessary to be open to the experience. In art therapy the pictures which are viewed within the therapeutic frame require similar regard. In the following part of this paper I will attempt to make some connections and also distinctions between 'gallery' art and art therapy, and between art therapy and psychotherapy.

The pictures we see in galleries are usually framed. They are framed in many stages and in many different ways. The most obvious is the frame made of wood or metal which is fixed around the outer edges of the paper or the canvas. This frame is a convention which states visually 'This picture is finished.' The frame sets the picture apart from its surroundings and again, like the theatre and the therapy hour, presents the picture to the world as a separate, framed experience. Such a frame is reminiscent of a window, which also has the function of separating us from the world. When we look out of a window we see the outside world in a frame; it is like a picture, in that we can see but cannot feel the conditions. If it rains we can see the rain but do not get wet. Alternatively, if we are outside, we can look into a room and again we see but cannot feel the inner scene. Its atmosphere or warmth can be imagined but not felt. It is usually more difficult to see in through a window than out of one: unless the room is artificially lit the pattern of the inside may be indiscernible. In art therapy it is as if the therapist, looking at the client's picture, is the person attempting to look into the room from the outside. She peers beyond her reflection on the glass (the counter-transference), and tries to discern the atmosphere of the room beyond the frame. It is only when the picture is illuminated by the transference feelings that we start to be able to discern the inner pattern of the image. It is when the picture is animated in this way that the therapist who attempts to empathize, to feel what it is like to be inside the client's room, the frame of the picture, risks being overwhelmed by the power of emotion invested in the image. In the art gallery the picture may at times have a similar effect. More often when viewing a picture in a gallery we are like the person looking out of a window; we see what is consciously presented to the outside world. This is a rather extreme polarization but the point is that the pictures in galleries are for public view, the ones in therapy for private. This is an important distinction which is determined by the outer frame of each situation. The art gallery is a space set apart for the public viewing of pictures, the art therapy room is space set apart for private viewing and making of pictures.

Before a picture is framed by its wooden or metal boundary or by its place in the gallery, it will have been through many diverse stages which will have included decisions regarding other frames, limits, and boundaries. The artist is in total control of decisions regarding the boundaries of her picture; she can choose to alter the frame according to her will or personal preference. The essence of a work of art is the intuitive and conceptual interplay, the interplay between sensation and idea, a constant toing and froing between action and thought. Decisions regarding marks and limits produce a tension which eventually achieves a successful work. This is a personal reflective process and is totally the responsibility of the artist; no one else is involved. Any decision to alter the frame or boundaries does not have to be negotiated with someone else; this is clearly the artist's personal responsibility.

For the client in art therapy the picture she makes is likewise totally her responsibility. The inner frame of therapy, the picture, is hers alone. In contrast, the outer frame, the setting in art therapy is, just as in psychotherapy, carefully negotiated with the therapist and any move to alter it is only agreed after consideration of motives, conscious and unconscious. Here we start to clarify some important distinctions between the boundaries in art therapy and in psychotherapy. In art therapy, as in psychotherapy, there are ideally boundaries around the session. The difference is that within the session a degree of behaviour is permitted for both client and therapist which could be seen by a psychotherapist as pathological or 'acting out' behaviour on the part of either or both. Pictures may be made in the session and this may entail people moving about and discussing materials. There is too, even when pictures are brought to the session, a physical gesture, a moving towards them, in looking at the pictures. The point here is that 'acting out' is a term which implies a negative judgement and usually indicates behaviour which breaches agreed or accepted boundaries. As therapists we frame our client's experience. We do this whether we intend to or not, usually in terms which we understand ourselves and within our own limitations. Our stance is, in part, determined by who we are and from whence we come. It is therefore likely that the art therapist expects and accepts slightly different behaviour and tolerates different boundaries than her colleagues. The important point about boundaries is that they should be clear to the people involved.

When an artist makes a mark on a piece of paper or canvas, that mark is framed immediately, in that the piece of paper, the canvas, has edges which are predetermined boundaries. The limits and dimensions of the piece of paper are thus the first boundaries encountered by the artist. The artist may choose to accept these limitations, making marks within the boundaries of the paper. Alternatively she may reject these limitations, extending the edges in one of several possible ways. Maybe the paper starts to feel too small, there is a need to extend it in one direction. The artist may cramp everything within this space or she may extend the paper, perhaps by carefully sticking an additional piece of paper to the original so that the join is invisible. Conversely she may tear the second piece of paper and stick it on top in a careless ragged way, so that the edge sticks over the original. This latter would make it obvious and part of the image that the boundary of the edge of the paper had been violated. There are other ways in which an artist may challenge the limits of the paper; she may splash paint around the room, paint on the walls or floor. There may be many reasons why the artist may do this, some rational and some irrational, some conscious and some unconscious, but as an artist whatever she chooses to present as finished is what people see and respond to. When an image is presented as 'art', we accept the image and respond to it as just that. We may then possibly consider the extended boundaries as an interesting concept, a thought-provoking gesture, or as a comment on space. Our response is, in part at least, conditioned by the place where we view and by our familiarity with the way we are expected to look at art in galleries. In therapy we are similarly influenced by the setting. In psychotherapy the motivations behind breaking the boundaries of the paper might be focused on in terms of emotional decisions. In some kinds of therapy the whole might be interpreted as 'acting out'. The art therapist, with her experience of the art process, will be less likely to interpret such behaviour reductively. She will be more likely to accept the 'artist' aspect of her client's decisions and regard it as a need for extra space. This may or may not be significant in the therapeutic context and can only be assessed in the full knowledge of the current affects of the therapeutic relationship. Here again the frame of reference of the therapist will clearly influence the therapeutic interaction and affect the 'quality' of therapy.

The therapeutic situation differs from that of 'pure' art in the process of its conception. For the client in therapy the process of image-making may have been similar to that described above, but it would have been influenced and affected by other considerations, most prominently the therapist. The picture may have been made with the therapist in mind. It may have been made to show her, for her, or just with the knowledge that she would see it. It may have been made to shock, frighten, or to please her. The client may have wanted to reveal how she felt, perhaps intense sadness or anger, the complexity of which words could not parallel. This picture, although the process of making marks may have been similar to that of the artist, is made in the context of a specific relationship. In this respect it differs profoundly from the picture produced for the gallery. The artist's intentions are different, and in addition the picture is viewed in a different institutional relationship. The picture in the gallery, and therefore its maker, is protected, defended by its frame and the thought that went into presenting it as framed or finished. The picture in therapy is far from finished; it is part of a continuing story. It is seen within the frame of therapeutic time, space, and place which establishes a boundary within which the picture can be ragged, undefended, or unfinished. The work shown to the art therapist is in a more raw state than the gallery picture.

The artist who has finished her picture has now to consider where to show it. She may choose not to show it, to hide it, keeping it private. It exists then as her private framed experience which perhaps feels too precious or powerful to risk showing. It may be a dialogue with herself, or something of which she is ashamed, or maybe she anticipates others' rejection of it. Quite possibly her motivations are unclear; it just feels wrong to show it. The client in therapy may well go through similar feelings in deciding whether to show her picture to the therapist. This transition from private to public is a common feature of all art. It is the step from the process of image-making to acceptance of the picture as a product.

The artist may at this stage decide that she will show her picture to the world, exhibit it, so she offers it to a gallery. At this point something changes. The artist is making a statement, she is entering into an institutional relation-ship to the world; her picture is public. Her work is to be considered a 'work of art', to be viewed, praised, and criticized in so-called 'objective' terms. She is taking on the identity and myth of the artist which renders her immune from certain comments, limits the frame and the questions asked about her relationship to her work. To present her work in this way the artist has to step outside it, objectify herself from it, and take a critical stance in relation to it. She will pre-empt her critics and see if she considers it will stand in this competitive and potentially demanding situation. It is really only when an artist shows her work publicly that she has social credibility as a professional artist. She may paint all day, every day, but unless the product of this activity is accessible to the world, her professionality may be in question.

Once the picture is accepted by the gallery it is seen in the context, the frame, of the gallery. This 'sets apart' the picture, takes it out of its usual context, the artist's studio, and presents it to the public. This is the first setting-apart, the first frame within which the picture is viewed. The second frame is the frame around the picture within which this picture is contained. This frame separates it within the gallery from works by other artists and other works by the same artist. It is separated within time and space of its own; it is a framed finished piece of work with the stamp of approval of the institution.

The picture in the gallery is now viewed by the public, for the sake of argument, spearheaded by the art critic, who may or may not know the artist personally. The critic will view the work, open herself to its effect, question herself in response to it. She may criticize the picture in terms of its success or failure as a work of art, probably regarding the whole work in its context, in the gallery with other works. There are other contexts which inform her judgement. The current fashions of the art world, her political stance, her knowledge of the history of art, and her assumption of the artist's awareness of art history. There are also various aesthetic criteria which will inform her, personal preferences about certain marks and theories of art. The critic may speculate as to the motives of the artist, her intentions and moods, trying to understand how she may have felt in making the picture. On the other hand it is quite possible that she may not be interested in motives. She may respond in terms of surface pattern and relationships, merely responding to what she sees in front of her. This may be the case whether the picture is figurative or abstract. If the picture is figurative it is more likely to evoke a literal interpretation. Even in such a case, what the person who knows about art is unlikely to do is merely to focus on the apparent in the subject matter, or on one aspect of the picture to the exclusion of the others. The trained eye moves around and through a picture, from one relationship to another and back, always perceiving the connections – the whole to the particular, the detail in context of the whole, this red in relation to that blue in relation to the other red, this figure in relation to that patch of orange, and so on. Pictures, even when apparently finished, evoke movement and relationship but cannot be read. Maps can be read; on maps the figures act as signs which refer to a specific place or meaning. Pictures are not like that; meanings are not clearly fixed in pictures; the figures and marks do not necessarily signify something outside themselves. Even a two-dimensional image is three-dimensional in the sense that it is full of multiple potential meanings which reverberate and echo against one another. No picture can be fully explained in words; if it could there would be no need to make it.

The art therapist working seriously with the client and the pictures, although the situation may be analogous to the art critic in the gallery, is in a very different relation to the pictures. Like the critic, the art therapist is informed by the context of art and art history; very often their initial training will have been similar. Looking at images in therapy, we draw on our familiarity with images and styles and with our knowledge of how it feels to make this type of gesture as opposed to that one. Like the critic, we take an overview at first, only later focusing down to details which are seen in the context of the whole picture in its physical and historical context. There is a very definite contextual distinction between pictures in galleries and pictures in therapy, in that in therapy the artist is present, and usually we look together at the picture. This, and the agreed task of looking deeply into and behind the apparent in the images, distinguishes the role of the art therapist from that of the art critic, and from the person viewing pictures in galleries. In therapy the picture reverberates outwards again, from the inner frame of the psycho-therapy setting, to encompass the person of the client. The therapist then, unlike the art critic, sees the visual relationships in the context of the personal relationships. In addition to moving through and round the relationships within the picture, the therapist is also aware of the artist's connection to the marks and the feelings to which they may refer. The visual relationships reverberate in this context with the personal ones – this patch of red next to this figure in relation to how it may have felt to do that and what that might mean in the context of the therapeutic relationship.

Most, if not all, psychotherapists work with images. Usually these images are verbally expressed by the client or they are mental images which the therapist may form of the client as a result of the material she brings. Since Freud's *Interpretation of Dreams*, the stuff of psychoanalysis or analytic psychotherapy has been imagery, and, most often, mental imagery described. To report a dream is a different experience from dreaming it. Similarly, to describe an image is different in many subtle respects from actually making it. Thus, just as a dream analysis might depend on a knowledge of what it is like to dream, so, too, to work with pictures in psychotherapy or art therapy, it is reasonable to expect the therapist to know how it feels to make her own images – to know from personal experience how exposing it can feel to picture her world in paints or clay and how powerful, even at times devastating, the revelations of one's images can feel.

Within a psychotherapy session the picture is sometimes used as an 'aid' to the psychotherapy; it is employed to extend what is being said, to describe a feeling. It can be seen or 'read' by the therapist, treated rather like a map with signs which point to a certain meaning. The loss in such a case is that by fixing one meaning of an image, in talking about it prematurely, or in too fixed a way, other multiple potential meanings may be ignored. Unlike the ideal art critic described above, who responds to the relationships within an image, the person who has not personally experienced art or art therapy will be inclined to see the figures but not the figure–ground relationship in a picture. Pictures are frequently seen in this way by the untrained eye; the figures are picked out, the ground unseen. Thus, in a figurative picture, the people may be seen but their relationship to the space and colours within the frame of the picture will be missed. Meanwhile an abstract picture may present a set of problems which may well be ignored. When art is an aid to psychotherapy it is usually seen as merely descriptive.

Alternatively a picture may offer the possibility of expanding a set of potentialities and relationships of meaning. Empathy is an attempt to identify, to feel, with the other person, to find a place in ourselves which can recognize what it is the client is experiencing. So it is with pictures; we empathize, entering into the picture, taking the risk of exposing ourselves to the content – the risk of being overwhelmed by the power of the emotion invested in the image, by its subleties and ambiguities. Familiarity with art and image-making provides the solid ground from which we can risk this imaginative identification. The therapist's ability to make this leap has a teaching function; if the therapist is able to demonstrate an attitude of acceptance, without fear or repulsion, to the depth of the meanings in an image, the client will be more likely to take this mode of expression seriously.

It is not my intention to undermine other professionals. Most psychotherapists are aware and sensitive to their clients' needs and to their own limitations. I draw on this polarization of the situation rather to expand the ground under the feet of the art therapist, so that a firmer foothold may be established. In our professional contacts we meet psychotherapists and psychiatrists who are a part of the dominant culture in our places of work – hospitals and clinics. Art therapists are usually the only one in a team whose background is that of an art training. Often the art therapist is only too aware of how little she knows about medicine, or psychiatry, and is usually for this reason only too ready to defer to those who, because of their formative experiences, take an authoritative stance. Art therapy is in the position of being between two fields; rooted in art, it is a hybrid of cross-fertilization with psychoanalysis. Thus, it has roots in art history, aesthetics, in psychoanalysis and psychotherapy. Different art therapists choose paths at varying distances from each of these positions, some nearer to one aspect, some nearer another, but what distinguishes the art therapist from her psychotherapist colleague is her knowledge and formative experiences in art.

Bibliography

Greenson, R. (1974) *The Technique and Practice of Psychoanalysis*, Hogarth Press, London.
Kant, I. (1980) *The Critique of Judgement*, Oxford University Press.
Neumann, E. (1959) *Art and the Creative Unconscious*, Routledge & Kegan Paul, New York.
Szasz, T. (1965) *The Ethics of Psychoanalysis*, Routledge & Kegan Paul, London.
Wittgenstein, L. (1985) *Philosophical Investigations*, Blackwell, Oxford.
Wollheim, R. (1975) *Art and its Objects*, Peregrine, London.

Chapter Thirteen

Group analytic art groups

Gerry McNeilly

It is my intention to explore specific dynamic processes within group analytic art groups. The main theoretical formulations are presented in earlier papers (McNeilly 1983, 1984), and are based upon the writings of S. H. Foulkes. I will also explore the image and groups of images as multiple layers which one sees as the final picture. Although Foulkes (1983) and Bion (1961a, 1961b) are central to my thesis, I suggest that the framework of this particular type of art therapy is a development of my own, although other colleagues work in this way today.

Basic hypothesis

With my earlier papers I found myself striking at some well-held views of the art therapist as a gentle, nurturing, and caring therapist. Their approach was to facilitate the patient with their creative productions within the therapeutic setting. Sometimes the images would be created outside the session, and a view exists that this has a validity in art therapy. Such therapists following this line of belief often get caught up in the following session discussing the completed picture. This may have the effect of sidestepping any transference/counter-transference exploration between the therapist and the patient. In reality terms there is no proof that the patient did the picture, as the therapist didn't see it created.

My earlier formulations addressed the interactive processes in art groups, particularly those that were set in motion by the therapist via the use of instilled themes. This particular discussion I entitled 'Directive and non-directive approaches in art therapy' (McNeilly 1983). This paper brought strong negative and positive reactions. Part of the aim was to look critically at long-held and cherished beliefs in art therapy.

However, there is still a basic philosophical struggle. There is the art therapist who leads his group with high levels of order through his implanting a theme of his choice, without prior consultation with his group or patient. On the other hand, there is the group analytic art therapist who nurtures the dynamics of his clientele and takes his lead from this process; in return he conducts the group.

I have now abandoned the term 'non-directive', replacing it with 'group analytic'. It was with the combination of my art group techniques, and my later training as a group analyst, that I finally settled upon the term 'group analytic art therapy'. With this more solid avenue, I began to formulate the many processes that occur in art groups alongside parallels in group analytic theory. These findings covered the main Foulkesian cornerstones and went further into such dynamic concepts as 'resonance' and the 'group matrix' as portrayed in group analytic art groups (McNeilly 1987).

Some of the basic tenets which structure group analytic groups are:

1 No set direction or topic.
2 The aim is self (group) exploration, group treating itself.
3 Figure/ground and here and now understandings.
4 The major part played in understanding the group inclusive of the conductor. 'Group analysis is analysis of the group, by the group, including the conductor' (Foulkes 1983: 33).

In applying some of these thoughts to group analytic art therapy, the merits lie with the high level of involvement in the whole learning process with the interchanging of positions. The approach is psychodynamic, allowing for the totality of the group experience. The image-making is but a part of the process. As with Gestalt principles, the art production shifts from fore to background. There is less pressure in this type of art therapy to justify the triangular arrangement of patient, therapist, and artifact, and to explain the imagery and find meanings.

Five types of image presented in group analytic art groups

I will now focus upon a particular typology of images which emerge time and again in the groups that I have conducted. Some individuals use these types, while certain groups use 'types' as a form of identification. I can only highlight some of my ways of viewing them.

The blank page

Strictly speaking this does not constitute an image, but in this context it is a very potent image against the background of the total group activity. This is initially seen when a person comes into a group for the first time and they can, or will, not commit themselves to paper. Similar dynamics occur in individual art therapy, and the blank sheet is equivalent to initial silences in verbal therapy. Blank sheets and initial silences carry very powerful messages, and signify a threshold between the world and the therapeutic setting. Anxiety and trepidation are two dynamics that are manifested in the blank sheet and silences. There may be an opposing battle between the wish to let go in order to fill the space, but at the same time a fear of 'doing so'. The individual's inner fears are therefore met with either fantasized, or real, expectations that they should fill the space with shapes and colours on paper, and put words into the silence. Another facet that exacerbates this is the individual's expectations of the conductor, who initially will be held in great awe. If we consider Bion's (1961a) 'basic assumption dependency' the element of passivity may also be a factor, where the person is waiting to be fed and given a cure. This wish for gratification is not therefore met and the blank sheet may be seen as a paralysis in the face of anger and frustration.

Of course it is not just at the beginning of a group that the blank sheet is most prominent; it will recur throughout the client's therapy. Each new blank sheet, although visibly the same, will carry a different meaning. Another variation on the blank sheet is when the paper is painted over with another colour, but is primarily still kept blank. Here no form is portrayed and one sees a colourful layer over the original feeling of blankness. Other messages that often lie under blank sheets are those that are generated by ambivalence, and under this there is an unexpressed rage. The blank sheet then comes to represent a striking presentation of the conflict between withholding the fullness of feelings that constitute the rage, while there is a great feeling of emptiness which is waiting to be filled. The blank sheet, therefore, is so full that to incur a mark on it would herald release of rage. It is also empty and stands as a seduction for others to come inside and fill the space. In my work with the anorexic/bulimic conditions this paradox of empty and fullness is central. The inner void is a bottomless pit or blank sheet.

Foulkes (1983) has spoken of silences in groups as a 'double-edged weapon' which should not be used aggressively. One should try and understand them for what they mean. The same applies for the blank sheet, which should be seen as just as valuable a piece of communication in the group as members' work which is laden with paint. The blank sheet is therefore accepted as valid communication but the aim is to make the 'uncommunicable' 'communicable'. Persistent blankness, either by the individual or the group, is therefore not used by the client as their double-edged sword against the conductor.

The written word

This is very common, and I seldom recall any group where at least one person did not use single words or sentences. On a simple level, a person may write as a way of expressing what they feel, but on an intellectual level, if he is new to art therapy, he may do this because he feels he is expected to draw or paint and this he can't do. However, I think that the use of words diminishes in time when he sees that artistic proficiency is not necessary.

In my experience, a dynamic of a person using words is a complex one, which has its roots set in the use and maintenance of control. To set aside words and use abstract symbol formulation or other marks is to give oneself over to a primitive part of one's self, as well as making it more possible for group members to have a say in how they see each other. The written word in the art group leaves little apparent room for other meanings – if accepted at face value. The writer is trying to express certain feelings with written words but in my experience this recipe rarely is successful on a deeper level. One reason why this is so is that other feelings emerge when the client uses pictorial symbols and colour, which are then restricted by the language form. However, not all is lost with people who use the written word. Like the use of the blank sheet in the group, it should be explored as meaningful. There are, after all, many dimensions: for example, the size, shape, colour, spelling, slips, capitals or not; the emotive quality of the message; precision, poetic form; to name a few. An example of this follows.

Two members of two separate groups used words continuously. One would produce reams of words which would take hours to sort through. The other would produce one picture but the writing was either too small or written in flowing artistic fashion. The messages from the first (male) were mainly shocking to others. He seldom showed an appropriate feeling in connection to his words and never worked through to any conclusion what he presented (over two and a half years). Clinically he presented as a schizoid character with strong potential for psychotic episodes. He took delight in his professional patient role. Like the second person (woman), he was highly controlled and controlling – she much less.

With the second example, her primary messages in the words were portrayed in an aesthetic, poetic manner. She conveyed herself through language in an evasive and ambiguous way. She did not always guard her controlled areas, and did remarkably well considering this. Her history was one of severe anorexia which had become almost a forgotten memory in the ending months of therapy.

In her very last session I was led to a new formulation upon her writing. She became in touch with her feelings and was partially crying, which she found difficult to tolerate. She was speaking in a much fuller (fatter) way, before becoming sad about leaving, while talking about the words in her picture. From here her voice changed into a much thinner, or quieter, tone which we could hardly hear – the way she had begun therapy. She then moved the focus to others in an attempt to show a certain concern for them. She felt she was getting too much attention.

Although I can't recall exactly what I said, I suggested that she was moving to others as a way of not staying with her feelings, and she was pushing the attention and her last meal away. I said that she was using an anorexic (thin) voice which we could not hear rather than her previous full (fat) voice. She appeared to be trying to leave in the same way as she had come.

Generally speaking, to have picked up in each session in any depth the individual words, sentences, numbers of pages, would have meant being seduced into high levels of control. Most of the work in these groups was to explore what these seductions meant. On many occasions I didn't even read the writing and treated these as abstract forms of communication, rather than specific meanings connected to language. In such groups a lot of energy is invested by the other members, particularly at the beginning of the verbal section, in discussion of the written pictures, so much so that there is a strong diversion from other images and abstractions. There was often a group feeling that because these were clearer statements, then the process of the group getting solutions would be easier.

The shocking image

With the former illustrative example in the previous type, I had referred to shocking messages which were portrayed through written words. Here I want to look a little more in depth at what it means to shock in the therapeutic setting. The strength of the feeling behind the word or image is now in question. With the first 'type', the blank sheet, there is very little shock attached. This shocking image may be connected to the narcissistic struggle, where the shock would be more in the sphere of 'object relations' conflict. It is with this in mind that I am addressing how one sees this in group analytic art groups.

There are two points to look at here.

1   Is it shocking to the creator, and, if so, is there any unconscious drive to consciousness?

2   Is it intended consciously to shock the group, along with an unconscious attack on external objects?

One dimension that is often present is that 'he whoever shocks the therapist most will be treated better'. The person who produces shocking images may well be acting out many things for himself, but likewise it may also be statements for the group as a whole. An equivalent position in a verbal analytic group would be the monopolizer or hysterically oriented individual, who uses words and actions to shock and impress.

Shocking images are numerous in many art therapy settings, and we have all come in contact with them. For example, they range from the written statement 'I'll kill myself' to pictures of broken windows, burning houses, cut wrists, car accidents, people falling off cliffs, abortions, deformities, stabbing, sexual abuse, and wild angry abstractions that are more evident by the way they've been created. There are no hard and fast rules about how one responds technically to these messages, but it is important to try to understand and locate the individual meaning within the group context. To achieve this with some success will help the therapist use his art and technique more appropriately. According to Foulkesian group analysis, the individual is central in the group matrix, the group being more than a composite of its parts. Therefore a sound understanding of the individual and the group is necessary. When one comes up against such shocking images they must be taken seriously so as one can eventually reach the underlying meanings. Tolerance and understanding may therefore be equated with containment.

It may be easier to ask oneself in the session 'Why at this time is this image being produced?' I have often tested out in my own thinking a number of questions before speaking: 'Is this person really afraid of what they've produced?' 'Is he trying to worry me that he will hurt himself or others unless I act?' 'Should I do or say something?' 'Am I afraid of this?' 'Is this conscious or unconscious?' 'Is he angry or depressed?' 'Does this show disguised messages for, and towards me?' 'What does he want from the group and how will they deal with the power of this image?' 'Is there a pattern to this?' 'If it is a pattern, will the group eventually become immune to it, and will we have a 'cry wolf' situation?'

As I am having all of these personal questions, likewise others in the group may be having the selfsame, and other, questions. A couple of group questions are also present. 'Is he expressing something for the whole group, which others can't put across?' 'Is there more than one shocking image and, if not, then what level of resonance is occurring and to what is the resonance?' When there is an expression of the group as a whole upon a particular dynamic, then the task of the conductor is much easier, as it dilutes a potential, singularly explosive situation. One could simply see this as safety in numbers. With these deeper resonances to focal dynamics (birth, death, marriage, therapist's illness, new and lost members, etc.) it gives rise to many more group associations. To accommodate the group working, the conductor has to change by widening his field of vision, and therefore act as a greater container.

The shocking image should therefore be freely expressed without censorship, which I believe leads to greater exploration. There should also be freedom for the person who has produced such an image to do with it what they want, i.e. tear it up, or wipe it out, or disown it. However, the one limit I put categorically on the group, is that people should not burn their pictures in the session, as I feel this is too dangerous a situation. The power of fire is much greater than any individual, and full of many meanings. It should not be called into the session in real terms as it can easily get out of hand, and, besides, I think it is possibly the greatest attack on the boundaries of any group. The ban on burning of one's picture I would place alongside the rule that people are not permitted to attack another member physically in the verbal group analytic session (likewise in group analytic art therapy groups).

Apart from these two rules, then, we should aim to put the making of, and reactions to, shocking images into context. They should be contained and not over-reacted to, which would lead to states of anxiety, panic, or early dampening interpretations by the conductor.

One example was a man who each week produced many shocking images which revolved around violence, sexuality, and an absence of and yearning for love and attention. Here he struggled with his unconscious breaking through via his images, dreams, and day-to-day behaviour. His inner world was in disarray and the art groups acted as the receptacle for the projection of these impulses. During this time, he gained an inner strength which eventually enabled him to reclaim what he had left, but in a modified form. In many ways he could not see me as separate from him (this was not conscious) until the day that I was leaving the therapeutic community. He then began to recognize me more as a person in my own right. While I was there, my main (unconscious) job for him was as a symbolic extension of his unconscious processes. With this process I believe that by my acting in a fairly passive non-anxious way (which does not mean I didn't challenge or confront) this provided a mirroring process. As well as a deposit for the unconscious and infantile parts of himself, he was able to take from me a structural way of dealing with himself. His old adult framework did not make allowances for this emerging material and repressed it, which was showing up through his shocking images. With this whole process of change then fear became less dominant, whereas in his initial stages of therapy any emotion that was evident, either pictorially or in words, was splintered into anxiety and panic.

As he was not the only member of this specific group to produce such shocking images, then the process of how I worked with him was in effect similar with the others in relation to myself. However, as one of the major differences between Foulkesian group analysis and other schools (i.e. Bion groups), the 'transference' to other members and the 'group as a whole' contributed greatly to this man's therapeutic success.

The recurring picture

Within the 'types' I have spoken of so far there may be either individual or group repetition of that particular type. This may be either compulsive (every session) or sporadic. Primarily there is a normal component here, where the individual is trying to gain some balance and structure. One only has to look at repetitive squiggles and patterns of children's pictures to see the normality in such recurrences. However, many recurring pictures in art therapy have a negative component, where the recurrence is repetition of a more neurotic functioning. In this setting such repetitive patterns can partly be understood theoretically under Freud's 'compulsion to repeat'. In Laplanche and Pontalis's dictionary, they define the repetition compulsion:

> I. At the level of concrete psychopathology, the compulsion to repeat is an ungovernable process originating in the unconscious. As a result of its action, the subject deliberately places himself in distressing situations, thereby repeating an old experience, but he does not recall this prototype; on the contrary, he has the strong impression that the situation is fully determined by the circumstances of the moment. (p. 78)

With recurring shocking images, it is easy to see the repetition of the distressing situations, but not so easy to comprehend the recurring image that has little 'affect' pattern. With this latter expression, it often feels as if the repetition is a form of guarding against the distressing content that is being withheld.

Here the idea of the expression being a form of repeating the 'prototype experience' in order to work through to a resolution does not apply. These same viewpoints are as applicable to the group repeating the expression of particular types of image and may either be with the aim of resolution or repression.

Winnicott's concept of the transitional object may also be equated with a recurring image. The image, like the 'teddy bear or blanket', serves the purpose of transition from the inner autistic position of the child to that of object relations, when the transitional object melts into the inner self. These recurring images, if they become fixed, I see as similar to the transitional object that maintains its real molecular structure – it is then no more than an image of paint on a piece of paper. The recurring pattern continues its familiarity and is hardly susceptible to change. If the art therapist does not assist his group to explore these images and their defensiveness, the individual and the group will move into obsessional systems that become increasingly intransigent.

On the face of things, recurring images may be viewed as a two-horned dilemma: resolution or defence. I think it is triangular in structure. The hidden feeling behind the repeated image is a fear of change from the rigid and inferior presentation of the self. In the group this would lead to competition, feelings of superiority, conflict, and the fear of destruction of self and others via the consciously denied omnipotence. This hidden area is a container for rage and anger, whereas the defensive patterns present flatness and passivity. Often this acts as a guard against the anxiety of the mess that can be generated in art groups which, if experienced, would lead to a breaking in the pattern and the emergence of the hidden feelings. Art therapists who work group analytically and with individuals in a psychotherapeutic method should not be wary of anxiety if generated in such groups and individuals. In fact with the obsessional repetition of particular images, they should promote an 'optimum' level of frustration and anxiety. Generally speaking, an individual in a group who is a passively obsessional image maker may function with such statements to others as 'That's a nice picture (wild and free) I wish I could do that!' In turn this passive admirer may be harbouring much envy and rage, packaging it in admiration. The group as a whole may likewise be continually churning out 'pretty pictures' week after week, while their lives are unhappy and in pieces. Here they deny themselves the opportunity of doing awful pictures which would show their awful lives, and this would go a way towards resolution. As with verbal analytic groups, in group analytic art groups the whole group may become entrenched in trying to persuade the recalcitrant pattern-maker to change his ways and be like everyone else, particularly if he is the only one. Here is a very difficult situation which will have many meanings according to that particular group. Here, like the verbal group, there is a battle ensuing between the group as a whole, which is naively perceived as getting everyone to be the same, where they all have to march to the same tune. This is not group analysis. On the other hand there has to be an acceptance that if John wants to keep painting this pattern, then that should be accepted. However, the group should be disavowed of the idea that they will cure or change John. Once John sees this, and these points have been clarified, the group as a whole stops acting out John's and the group's conflict. He expresses passivity and stubbornness and the group as a whole project high levels of hope into the most intransigent member. They try to change that part of themselves that they have projected on to John, which they can't do if they acknowledge it in themselves. On many occasions when I have pointed this conflict out, along with its paradoxes, it has the effect of modifying the struggles to make the group more analytic and changing, inclusive of the 'Johns' (as I'm sure you've guessed, John is a composite person of those who have carried this dynamic).

I believe that if the therapist has an understanding of the various dynamic points for the individual in relation to 'triangles of conflict', he will see the dynamic structure of the three poles (Malin 1979). Therefore it is illustrative of the part anxiety plays in the mediation between defence and hidden feelings, and likewise how the defence guards against the anxiety.

Copied pictures

With the previous 'types' of images, I am primarily concerned with what, in the first instance, comes directly from the individual. Their productions may be formed not solely from that which emerges from within, but are influenced by the groups to which they belong. We now move to a position where someone deliberately takes from another person's picture, and expresses this as part of themselves. In some instances members of a group do not apparently copy, and very similar images emerge from two or more people. On the one hand this may have resonant qualities, but on the other there may be pre-conscious links. Rather than forming value judgements about whether it is good or bad to copy, we should explore why there is the wish to – if it is conscious. Basically, I see that when someone copies they are taking, borrowing, from another member – with or without their permission. There is nothing wrong with that really, dependent upon the person being copied from. If we consider 'object relations theory', then one idea of taking parts of others is a positive process. In verbal groups, we do this all the time and here there is little comeback, i.e. 'I can feel for you', or 'What you said reminds me'.

Looking at copying from a different perspective, a driving force may be that the copier may feel devoid or empty inside, and they copy because they feel they have little to give to the world. There is a great ego deficiency here. There may be a fear of showing infantile feelings, as the only pictures they may be able to portray without copying would be matchstick people, houses, and scribbles. Here the process of copying is a pairing one in that there is a striving through another person for some form of sophistication. In line with Bion's basic assumption – pairing (which may be partially one sided) – there is a search for hope in the other object. This then forms a bond against the basic assumption fight/flight, but also forms a link with the basic assumption dependency. As with Bion's view that the hope must never be fulfilled in order for hope to remain, then also the copying should continue until it has served its purpose.

Therefore there should not be a rule that people can't copy in the group, but it should be worked with accordingly. The person that is being copied from also has a say, and possibly an investment, in such a process. They may find on the positive pole that this a boost to feeling more valuable. On the negative pole, there may be an obsessional transference which is not worked through if the copying persists. Finally, in process terms, consideration should be made to understanding what this pairing dynamic is saying for the group as a whole. Another simple message in copying is that the copier is re-enacting a schoolday experience and is trying to place the therapist in the teacher position, who will in turn tell him off for copying. The aim then is to explore the complexities that lie behind what would appear to be a simple action, and this may lead to greater individuality of the copier. Hopefully there will then be a taking back of their projections from the object of their choice.

Pairing in groups is often a defence against the group as a whole, and if we consider further Bion's 'basic assumption pairing' there is the underlying wish to create a saviour. This ideally is a creation of the pair who will save the group. Considering this we can also accommodate the investment by other members of the group, and the 'group as a whole'; for example, the new person may copy the oldest member, the weakest copies the strongest, the one who feels unnoticed by the therapist copies the one he feels that is most in the therapist's thoughts. Another variation is that a number of pairs of copiers emerge and this may be understood in subgrouping terminology. It is necessary here to explore just what each pair is searching for and the meanings that underlie such a splintering process. This has a parallel in verbal analytic groups, when conversations occur between different pairs of people simultaneously. I have been in groups where up to six different conversations have been going on concurrently.

On an unconscious level I view the process of copying in the art therapy group as a guard against one's self, and that part of the self which is chaotic and spontaneous. The guard I feel is placed in order to ward against such fears as being out of control and even of disintegration. If art groups become fixated with such a controlled process of excessive copying, one may look at this as the members guarding against the fear of potential 'psychotic like' states. This would be along the lines of such a group attaining the opposite of its conscious presentation, where there would be no boundaries between people, with everything flowing together nebulously.

As I pointed out briefly, copying has nothing to do with synchronistic images of similar form, i.e. everyone painting houses without apparent awareness of what the person beside them is painting. When such a phenomenon occurs, I see it as one of a healthy group. Here the members are in tune, both consciously and unconsciously. Resonances on particular focal dynamics are therefore much clearer. There is often, at such times, a great deal of surprise at the similarities when recognized. Over my years of working in groups, I recall actual copying occuring minimally.

Conclusion

The 'types' I have spoken of here are but a small number of many that are evidenced in such groups. Here I have offered them as a beginning to looking at these presentations in group analytic art groups. I'm sure the reader will have experienced these images emerging in other types of groups and individual art therapy and psychotherapy. Maybe the reader will find connecting clarifications to their own therapeutic approaches.

References

Bion, W. R. (1961a) *Experiences in Groups and Other Papers*, Tavistock, London.

Bion, W. R. (1961b) 'The psychoanalytic study of thinking. A theory of thinking', read at the 22nd International Psycho-Analytic Congress.

Foulkes, S. H. (1983) *Introduction to Group Analytic Psychotherapy*, Maresfield, Reprints, London (originally published in 1948 by W. Heinemann, London).

Laplanche, J. and Pontalis, J. B. (1973) *The Language of Psycho-Analysis*, the International Psycho-Analytic Library no. 94, Hogarth Press and Institute of Psycho-Analysis, London.

Malin, D. H. (1979) *Individual Psychotherapy and the Science of Psychodynamics*, Butterworths, London.

McNeilly, G. (1983) 'Directive and non-directive approaches in art therapy', *The Arts In Psychotherapy*, vol. 10, no. 4, pp. 211–19.

McNeilly, G. (1984) 'Group analytic art therapy', *Journal of Institute of Group Analysis*, vol. XVII, no. 3, pp. 204–10.

McNeilly, G. (1987) 'Further contributions to group analytic art therapy', *Inscape*, summer, pp. 8–11.

Chapter Fourteen

Five years on: further thoughts on the issue of surviving as an art therapist

David Edwards

Introduction

In a paper originally presented at the Eleventh Triennial Congress of the International Society for the study of Art and Psychopathology[1] in 1985, I outlined some of the problems I faced when, as a recently qualified art therapist, I began working in a large psychiatric hospital in the north of England. In this revised version of my paper I intend to return to the issue of 'surviving' as an art therapist in a large institution or organization. However, while many of the problems art therapists face remain the same as those originally described, five years on it is I hope possible to offer some further insights into the nature of these difficulties and a more personal appreciation of the kind of strategies and resources available for beginning to resolve them.

During the time I have been working as an art therapist it has often become apparent to me – sometimes quite forcefully – that there is a marked discrepancy between the way I would like things to be with regard to my work and how it very often is. Our awareness of this state of affairs is, unfortunately, all too often experienced as disillusioning or distressing. Putting our principles into practice can be, and very often is, fraught with difficulties far from easy to resolve. The issue seems to me to be an important one, primarily because it often appears to be the case that art therapists generally, and recently qualified art therapists in particular, greatly underestimate the complex nature of the difficulties to be faced in the workplace and the impact these will have upon their work.

This is not to imply that the postgraduate art therapy diploma courses currently running in this country are producing inadequately trained therapists. Rather it is to suggest that away from the nurturing environment provided by these courses, art therapists may face possibly new or unfamiliar problems which may in turn lead them to conclude that, for example, working single-handed as the only art therapist in the district or institution is not simply a difficult undertaking but may very well come to feel like an impossible one. Art therapists are, of course, far from being alone in arriving at such a conclusion; many staff employed in the field of mental health find they must struggle to overcome indifference or resistance to their work.

Despite the fact that as a profession art therapy has undoubtedly made important advances in recent years, many of the difficulties art therapists face today are not unlike those experienced by the 'pioneers' of the profession in its early days. Indeed the struggle to integrate our work into those institutions which increasingly employ us may be felt all the more intensely, not simply because art therapists usually continue to find themselves working in relative isolation (institutions rarely employ more than one fulltime art therapist), but also as a consequence of the internal and external expectations now placed upon our status as professionals. As a result, the fate which may await the pioneering art therapist who enters the institution and attempts to change things, however modestly, may prove to be an unpleasant one. Such a fate has been described by Georgiades and Phillimore in terms of the tendency institutions have to devour hero innovators just as dragons devour brave knights.

> This then is the myth of the hero innovator: the idea that you can produce, by training, a knight in shining armour who, loins girded with ... beliefs, will assault his organisational fortress and institute changes both in himself and others at a stroke. Such a view is ingenuous. The fact of the matter is that organisations such as schools and hospitals will, like dragons, eat hero innovators for breakfast. (Georgiades and Phillimore 1975: 315)

Despite such cautionary tales, the professional self-image of the beginning art therapist is often such that the warnings go unheeded in the enthusiasm to embrace the challenge presented by the seemingly docile dragon. Contrary to the hopes many of us may have regarding the acceptance of art therapy as a valid way of working with people in need, all too frequently art therapists discover that their way of working is not readily accepted and that they are in conflict with the institution. As this conflict may be internalized it may be experienced all the more painfully. Because the experience of conflict is so common to many art therapists it is vital the origin and nature of these conflicts are addressed, not simply because of the resulting distress – though that would be justification enough – but because without any serious and sustained attempt to resolve them they may have a serious and detrimental effect upon the work we trained for and are employed to do.

In order to begin to understand and come to terms with the difficulties art therapists experience in the workplace, and to appreciate more fully the reasons why these may lead art therapists to becoming engaged in a struggle for survival as opposed to growth and development, it is necessary to recognize that our practice takes place in a context; that the nature of the institutions – with or without walls – in which we work will inevitably influence to a greater or lesser degree our ability to establish and maintain a credible therapeutic practice, no matter how committed or well trained we may be. The point may well be an obvious one, though it is one easily overlooked in our day-to-day work. At the risk of over simplification, the problems art therapists face appear to fall into three main areas; the problem of recognition, integration, and validation.[2]

The problem of recognition

Although painting, drawing, and sculpting, and the role these artforms may play in the 'treatment' or 'rehabilitation' of those in emotional need or distress, has long been acknowledged as a professional discipline in its own right, art therapy has only very recently received any formal recognition.[3] While the term art therapy predates this recognition by a considerable time, it is nevertheless true that many myths and fantasies continue to circulate regarding the nature of our work. Perhaps the two most commonly encountered of these are that it is essentially recreational in orientation, or concerned with diagnosis. The mythology surrounding art therapy is further complicated by both the tradition many institutions have of inviting artists and art teachers in to organize art-based activities, and the fact members of many other professional groups claim a degree of expertise in the use of images in the context of therapy. As the members of all these diverse groups bring with them a particular approach to the image, it need hardly be surprising that the work of art therapists may be obscured in the resulting confusion regarding who does what. It is also sadly the case that suspicion or antipathy may result when the interests or expertise of any of these groups is felt to be challenged.

Where art therapists are in danger of making a crucial error of judgement in their attempts to gain recognition for their particular way of working with images and people is through assuming whatever misunderstandings or suspicions may exist about it will be allayed simply through arguing its merits. Attending multidisciplinary meetings, giving talks, and producing handouts may, amongst other things, prove useful and even necessary on occasions. As a strategy for gaining recognition in the long term, however, it is one I believe to be unlikely to succeed. Almost certainly it will do little to help art therapy reach a position of influence within the institution, a position from which it would be able to exercise its own voice in the decision-making process.

Although a degree of recognition has now been afforded to art therapy within the National Health Service, at a local level many art therapists are not recognized as belonging to a separate profession, and continue to remain linked to, or be managed by, other professional groups. More often than not this link will be with occupational therapy, and in many situations this arrangement is clearly detrimental to the development of art therapy. The issue of professional autonomy and recognition so often discussed by art therapists was one it was necessary to grapple with shortly after taking up my post. At that time the art therapy service was managed by the head occupational therapist and there appeared to be little immediate prospect of any change in this arrangement. Still more disheartening was the realization that art therapy was widely regarded as an essentially diversional activity, with the art therapy hut being seen as a place to send patients *en masse* in order to keep them occupied. As a newly qualified art therapist keen to apply his recently acquired therapeutic 'skills', this situation was one I considered both demoralizing and untenable, and so set about changing.

Fortunately in my own case it was possible to negotiate successfully a move out of the occupational therapy department, although the process took many months of frustrating and patient work to conclude. This successful outcome was, it needs to be emphasized, more significant than simply helping to boost my morale, important though that was. Crucially, the recognition of art therapy as a separate profession has since provided the means by which it has proved possible to develop the service offered by the department. While the advantages of professional autonomy seem to me clear enough – not least through whatever benefits having an independent voice within the institution may offer in terms of negotiating for additional resources – the means of achieving autonomy for art therapy on a wider scale are unfortunately far from clear. Some art therapists have achieved professional autonomy with relative ease, others only after arguing for it for many years against all manner of objections; objections which usually find their origin in the institution's need to preserve the *status quo*. While art therapists have become increasingly skilled in recent years in overcoming such objections, and as a result an increasing number of precedents for establishing autonomous art therapy departments now exist, the problem of gaining the formal recognition so necessary for the development of the profession inside and outside the NHS will undoubtedly remain for some time.

The problem of integration

Even in those situations where the work of art therapists is formally recognized as functionally different from that of other professional groups, the day-to-day task of successfully integrating this work into the institution is always likely to prove problematic. In those institutions where art therapy is not so recognized, or in those functioning with a very different philosophical orientation to that of the art therapist, the issue of integration is likely to prove problematic in the extreme. One consequence of this is that the art therapist may risk becoming isolated. Certainly courage, patience, sensitivity, and the ability to compromise are qualities all art therapist need as they struggle to fit in and avoid the fate of the hero innovator. However, my own experience has led me to conclude that the difficulties art therapists face in this area cannot be overcome simply by gaining professional recognition, or explained away in terms of personal issues, philosophical conflicts, or confusion over roles. Rather I believe we need to examine the nature of the institutions in which we work in order to understand their dynamics as social systems. This is necessary because, as Bannister has argued, therapy takes place within an institutional and social surround and whether this dominates the process or not, depends, to a large extent, on the degree of awareness of that institutional and social surround which the therapist and client can develop. What we are not aware of we cannot effectively contend with. (Bannister 1983: 147)

The institutions in which many art therapists work are, more often than not, large, bureaucratically enmeshed organizations with their own, long-established, routines and procedures. Much of the isolation and frustration experienced by art therapists working in such institutions would appear to find its origin in the way they resist our attempts to innovate change. As Parry and Gowler (1983) have observed, this may involve the therapist in a struggle to weld together contradictory ideologies. They note, for example, that

a common task for the therapist is to help the client experience and honestly face painful, primitive or destructive emotions. In opposition to this the organisational structure of the hospital can be seen as adapted to defend against the anxiety of facing the realities of mental pain and suffering. (156).

Perhaps the most visible way such defences manifest themselves is, as Aitken has remarked, through the 'military ethos' which continues to pervade institutions like the large psychiatric hospital, where the wearing of epaulettes and uniforms denoting rank, and terms such as duty rosters, going on leave, and nursing or medical officers are so frequently encountered (Aitken 1984).

Amongst the many existing studies of the ways in which organizations function, the work of Isabel Menzies is particularly helpful through offering a psychodynamically based model to explain why the structure, culture, and mode of functioning of organizations like hospitals develop as they do into what she terms 'social defence systems' (Menzies 1977). Menzies argues that social defence systems develop because of the needs of the members of the organization to create structured defence mechanisms against anxiety – anxiety aroused in the individual as a result of the difficult or frightening tasks they are required to do.

A social defence mechanism develops over time as a result of the collusive interaction and agreement, often unconscious, between members of the organisation as to what form it will take. The socially structured defence mechanisms then tend to become an aspect of external reality with which old *and new* members of the institution must come to terms. (10)

Menzies' work has important implications for art therapists wishing to integrate their practice successfully into the institution in which they work, not least through helping us to understand the difficulties experienced by other groups of staff. This understanding may provide a workable basis for the development of tolerance and trust, as it is important to remember that social defence systems evolve in response to a need to reduce anxiety – anxiety which, to cite but one example, may be aroused in the form of hostility or suspicion when established norms are threatened or challenged through the art therapist's insistence upon confidentiality in respect to certain aspects of their work. To protect a confidence may all too readily be perceived as with-holding a secret and call into question one's loyalty to the team.

Like all defence mechanisms, however, social defence systems are only partially successful in their attempts to do this, and may in addition produce anxiety in those for whom such defence mechanisms are inappropriate. As de Board has observed,

> opposition and resistance to change can be understood by seeing it as the fear people have of relinquishing established social systems that have helped to defend them against anxiety in the past. The old system will reflect the power and influence the previous generation had to shape the system to fit their own psychological needs. ... Unless people have the opportunity to participate in the changes they will not be able to influence the formation of new social systems and the result will be an increase in suspicion, hostility and aggression. (de Board 1978: 143)

Clearly such issues need to be approached sensitively if art therapists are to have their work understood and accepted by others, and are to avoid having it sabotaged or marginalized. It is equally clear, however, that the problems which may arise when new or unfamiliar ways of working with patients are introduced into the institution are far from easy to resolve. The successful integration of art therapy into any institution cannot be expected to be achieved quickly. Trust takes time to establish itself.

The problem of validation

Given the value systems which currently dominate our society and its institutions, at the end of the day no matter how clearly art therapists argue the case for their work, or how sensitively they approach the problem of integration, for many final acceptance of art therapy's worth will not be forthcoming until such time as it is able to provide 'objective' evidence of its utility; until, that is, the claims made for it as a valid form of therapeutic intervention have been subject to 'scientific' appraisal. Such attitudes tend to be most commonly encountered amongst those in the mental health profes-sions who themselves come from largely scientific backgrounds. As Males, a clinical psychologist by profession, has for example commented, 'in terms of objective research based on scientific measurement that can be put to general use, there sometimes appears to be an element of resistance amongst art therapists' (Males 1979: 5).

In addition to this perennial problem, the recent introduction of general management into the NHS will without doubt result in an intensification of the pressures placed upon art therapists to demonstrate that their work is both valid and cost effective. Indeed one of the central recommendations made in the Griffiths Report on the management of the NHS[4] is that service managers should set objectives, measure output, and evaluate clinical practices on a cost effective basis; all of which is aimed at securing the best deal for patients within the available resources.

It is clear, therefore, that questions such as 'Does art therapy work?' or 'How does it work?' resonate with increasingly important implications, for art therapists, their colleagues, their employers, and ultimately for those patients or clients art therapists seek to help. Such questions also pose important questions concerning the means art therapists choose to validate their work. My personal concern regarding this issue is not one of principle. I fully accept that art therapists have a responsibility to evaluate their practice and that patients are entitled to expect the best possible service. Rather my concern stems from two major but interrelated problems art therapists face with regard to validating their work. First, that of devising appropriate ways of evaluating art therapy. And second, that of the purpose such evaluations might serve. Far from providing the means by which practitioners might be helped to work more effectively, the kind of cost-based evaluations currently being developed to measure performance and output within the NHS cannot, in my view, be separated from the government's commitment to and faith in the values of the free market economy; although the reassuring rhetoric of contemporary managerial and political Newspeak would often have us believe otherwise.

When considering the problem of developing an appropriate methodology for evaluating art therapy it is necessary to acknowledge that while art therapists in general feel more comfortable with ideas and influences drawn from the humanities, it is within a world very largely dominated by science that we must live and work. It is from science that traditional forms of psychiatric treatment draw their authority and power, and it is with these forms of treatment and the ideology that accompanies them that art therapists must find ways of coexisting. As empirical science is primarily concerned with the accumulation of facts, facts moreover drawn from dispassionate observation and experimentation, it is facts – preferably in a statistical form – which art therapists are expected to come up with in order to validate their work. Before embarking upon such a fact-finding mission it would be wise to question the assumption that scientific knowledge is necessarily objective. Commenting on this issue in relation to research in psychotherapy, David Smail has observed that,

> The very word 'scientific' is still frequently used to convey a total freedom from values, a noble state of pure objectivity from which our wants, wishes, beliefs and prejudices have been purged.... The whitecoated scientist is seen as a kind of high priest of truth, toughened by his exposure to the cold

blast of actuality, immune to the subjective errors of bias and sentimentality to which the rest of us are prone.... Once the realisation has been made, however, that the way things are cannot sensibly be detached from the way we see them, we can begin to see that the scientist's knowledge is not an especially privileged insight into reality, but a certain kind of knowledge, a particular way (and a particularly human way) of looking at the world. (Smail 1978: 66–7)

Smail's argument, in line with that put forward earlier by Polanyi (Polanyi 1973), is that scientific truth, far from being dispassionate, is both partial and selective. To work as an art therapist in a field of knowledge such as psychiatry where orthodox methods of scientific enquiry have long been applied in an effort to understand human conduct (and to a lesser extent the psychopathology of art; see Cunningham-Dax 1953) is quickly to become aware that certain kinds of knowledge are invested with enormous influence. It is also to become aware of how often our own insights into reality and the perceptions of those with whom we work may be set aside in favour of the relevant expert. There is, I believe, a danger that in our attempts to validate art therapy we may seek to do so by employing methods which effectively devalue it through reducing a sophisticated body of knowledge and experience to a rough and ready set of demonstrable facts.

This is not to state that empirical evalations in art therapy are necessarily misguided or wrong. Indeed, as I have argued elsewhere, thoughtfully conducted research may reveal,

a considerable amount of clinically useful information concerning the most potent processes involved in promoting change through art therapy, and provide a much clearer picture regarding who gets selected, who drops out, and who benefits. (Edwards 1987: 67)

It is, however, important to recognize that through emphasizing the 'technical' aspects of art therapy we run the risk of overlooking much that is fundamentally important, and in many ways radically different, about it. To attempt to validate art therapy by seeking to demonstrate the superiority of one approach in comparison with another, or to discount the possibility that the personalities of those engaged in it play a significant role in what goes on, seems to me not only to lack sense but to miss the point. As it is the personal relationship established between the therapist and the patient – a relationship mediated through images – that is central to art therapy, it is essential that the subjective experience of this relationship from the perspective of both the therapist and the patient be taken account of in any process of evaluation.

Those critical of approaches emphasizing subjective as opposed to objective evaluations of art therapy such as are frequently found in case studies tend to regard them as idiosyncratic or untrustworthy, not because they lack the rigour of serious enquiry, but because they fail to provide data of the kind believed to be necessary to attain the status of verifiable fact. While I would not wish to deny the limitations of the case study approach to evaluating art therapy with respect to providing information that is of 'general use', it is, nevertheless, one which does at least pay serious attention to the unique and interactive nature of the relationship between therapist and patient. As such, it is an approach which has validity in so far as it challenges the popular view of therapy as a process through which the expert therapist changes the passive patient in a way the former believes desirable. To adopt more seriously such a view of art therapy seriously would be to abandon the evidence of its validity presented through our own subjective experience, and to assume that the language and concepts available to help us understand the nature of our work – particularly when drawn from literature, philosophy, aesthetics, and psychotherapy – are somehow inadequate or inferior to those drawn from the realm of science.

Supervision

In each of the preceding sections of this paper I have argued that art therapists are likely to experience a number of conflicts arising directly from the nature of their work and the context in which it takes place. If prolonged these conflicts may result in the art therapist experiencing stress and strain affecting both their feelings of well being and their therapeutic work. In conclusion, I intend to focus upon the role personal supervision may play in helping art therapists survive these conflicts and continue to develop as practitioners.

Whether we are just beginning or art therapists with many years experience, our first concern should be that we do not harm those with whom we work. In part, this involves the art therapist establishing secure boundaries within which it is safe enough for those in need or distress to explore their inner world. Successfully doing so will inevitably involve working through some of the problems previously outlined. In addition, however, it is essential that if art therapists are to develop following their training they will continually need to find ways to clarify and refine their practice. Above all, as the psychotherapist Robert Hobson has so succinctly put it, 'We need to go on learning how to learn – about others, about relationships, about ourselves' (Hobson 1985: 206).

There are many ways we might choose to do this. We might, for example, attend conferences, read accounts of the work and ideas of other therapists, engage in research of one form or another, seek advice from colleagues, or continue developing our own artwork. We may even choose to risk going public with our own ideas by publishing papers or giving talks. None of these are mutually exclusive, and all may prove helpful. In my own experience, however, it has been the availability on a regular basis of personal supervision which has proved to be the most helpful and enriching way of continuing to learn.

As many different models of supervision exist (Hess 1980), and the term itself is open to widely differing interpretations, it is first of all necessary to clarify what I mean by the term before proceeding to discuss its relevance to art therapy. In many situations the term supervison refers to the process whereby one person directs or oversees another's work from a position of authority. As applied in many organizations and institutions – including those in the health or social services – what this means in practice is that supervision is regarded as the main means by which control is exercised in order to ensure subordinates within the hierarchy remain accountable and conform to accepted norms. In the sense that I am using the term, the process of supervision is not synonymous with the management of personnel; neither is it to be confused with personal therapy. Supervison, unlike therapy, is primarily oriented towards helping the therapist help the patients or clients they work with.

If supervision is to prove helpful it should enable the therapist to increase their awareness of what is going on in therapy. While the relationship between supervisor and therapist may, therefore, at times concern itself with the provision of guidance through stimulating new ideas or fresh approaches, it should also reflect aspects of the patient–therapist relationship. The relationship between supervisor and therapist may be conceptualized as one providing emotional support for the therapist through helping them feel safe enough to explore and work through feelings emerging out of their work with patients. As the process of supervision with which I am familiar inevitably involves the re-experiencing of those interpersonal and intrapersonal issues and conflicts which have the potential to inhibit personal growth or therapeutic change – involves, in other words, the capacity for self-reflection and willingness to be open to experience – it is essential the relationship between supervisor and therapist be based securely upon mutual trust, and be one in which confidentiality is preserved.

In order to practise and survive in the kinds of difficult situation many art therapists find themselves working in it is important that ways of coping are found which are not defensive or destructive. Common anxieties and difficulties often experienced by therapists – particularly, though not exclusively, by those as yet unfamiliar with the role – frequently focus around feelings of not being good enough for the task of helping. Therapists can, and do, defend themselves from such uncomfortable feelings by distancing themselves emotionally from contact with patients, or by investing enormous effort in attempting to become the all-knowing, all-seeing, ever-effective professional they imagine they could or should be. Although we may try our best to meet the needs of the patients we work with, few therapists are entirely able to transcend the ordinary human failings to which most of us are prone. It can, therefore, be immensely helpful, though possibly also distressing, to share the fantasies we may have about our ability to help others without fear of being judged a failure or incompetent. That these fantasies may be extremely powerful and potentially destructive invests the issue of the availability of supervision for art therapists with considerable ethical importance.

Empathy and caring require great emotional effort, especially when the patient or client has many difficulties, resists the help available, or despite our best efforts may not only fail to 'get better' but may visibly deteriorate. Coping with the work-related stresses encountered in many institutions may only further deplete the energy available for this task.[5] Unless art therapists are able to find emotional nourishment outside the context of their work, and discover constructive and creative ways of coping with the demands their work involves, they are likely to feel progressively drained and helpless. I do not believe such a fate is inevitable. I do, however, believe the key to our own survival, and the survival of art therapy itself, is through a recognition of our own needs. It is perhaps only through recognizing these needs – be they practical or emotional – and through having these needs met that art therapists may truly be in a position to meet the needs of others without the risk of exploiting them.

Notes

1 An expanded version of this paper, 'Three years on: surviving the institution' was published in the Summer, 1986, issue of *Inscape*, the Journal of the British Association of Art Therapists.
2 For an alternative view of this issue, see Dr A. R. K. Mitchell's paper 'Art and drama therapy as part of a multi-disciplinary team'. This paper was originally presented at a two-day conference on Art Therapy and Drama Therapy at Hertfordshire College of Art and Design, St Albans, in 1982.
3 For art therapists working in the National Health Service, formal recognition of their status, training, and pay and conditions of service followed the publication by the Department of Health and Social Security of Personnel Memorandum PM(82)6 in 1982.
4 A summary of the main points and findings made in the Griffiths' Report was published in the 3 November 1983 issue of the *Nursing Standard*, p. 3.
5 Recent concern regarding work-related stress experienced by members of the caring professions has spawned a plethora of literature on emotional burnout. For a more thoroughgoing discussion of this issue see Cherniss, C. (1981) *Staff Burnout: Job Stress in the Human Services*, Sage, New York; and B. A. Farber (ed.) (1983) *Stress and Burnout in the Human Service Professions*, Pergamon, Oxford.

References

Aitken, S. (1984) 'The patient as enemy – notes from a fifth columnist', *Changes* 2, no. 2, pp. 54–5.
Bannister, D. (1983) 'The internal politics of psychotherapy', in Pilgrim, D. (ed.) *Psychology and Psychotherapy*, Routledge & Kegan Paul, London.
Cunningham-Dax, E. (1953) *Experimental Studies in Psychiatric Art*, Faber & Faber, London.
de Board, R. (1978) *The Psychoanalysis of Organisations*, Tavistock, London.

Edwards, D. (1987) 'Evaluation in art therapy', in Milne, D. (ed.), *Evaluating Mental Health Practice*, Croom Helm, London.

Georgiades, J. M. and Phillimore, L. (1975) 'The myth of the hero innovator and alternative strategies for organisational change', in Kiernan, C. C. and Woodford, F. P. (eds), *Behaviour Modification with the Severely Retarded*, Associated Scientific Publishers, London.

Hess, A. K. (ed.) (1980) *Psychotherapy Supervision*, Wiley, New York.

Hobson, R. F. (1985) *Forms of Feeling*, Tavistock, London.

Males, J. (1979) 'Is it right to carry out scientific research into art therapy?', *Therapy*, 3 May, p. 5.

Menzies, I. (1977) *The Functioning of a Social System as a Defence against Anxiety*, Tavistock, London.

Parry, G. and Gowler, D. (1983) 'Career stresses of psychological therapists', in Pilgrim, D. (ed.), *Psychology and Psychotherapy*, Routledge & Kegan Paul, London.

Polanyi, M. (1973) *Personal Knowledge*, Routledge & Kegan Paul, London.

Smail, D. (1978) *Psychotherapy: A Personal Approach*, Dent, London.

Acknowledgements

There are many people I would like to thank for helping me to 'survive' the writing of this paper – in its original and revised forms – and those experiences which made this writing necessary for me. Special thanks, however, are due to Julie Leeson, Terry Molloy, Sally Skaife, and Polly Blacker.

Chapter Fifteen

Musing cross culturally

Diane Waller

Presumably the reason for holding international conferences is so that an exchange of ideas with people from varying social, cultural, and historical backgrounds can take place. We hope that this will enable us to distance ourselves from the assumptions underlying our own practice, or to challenge them.

Working abroad in a country with a language, social structure, and educational system very unlike one's own gives an excellent opportunity to rethink one's approach to work – and to life in general. It is easier to spot where the differences in values lie. However, we are apt to assume that if the language, and, superficially, the culture, are the same, then there should be few problems in communicating. That this assumption is often not true was confirmed for me following the many stimulating hours of discussion I spent with Harriet Wadeson, Director of the Master's Art Therapy programme in Chicago, and also from experiencing the difficulties which American art therapy students encounter when they come to study at the Art Therapy Unit at Goldsmiths'. I am indebted to Harriet for sparking off many of the thoughts in this chapter and for her contribution to our joint presentation on the similarities and differences between British and American art therapy education at the 1985 Société Internationale de la Psychopathologie de l'Expression (SIPE) conference. I am also deeply grateful to my Bulgarian friends and colleagues for their participation in an on-going debate about art therapy and psychoanalysis.

I once heard a psychoanalyst at a British Association of Art Therapists' conference declare that he could work in Hampstead or in Japan and still use the same approach to his patients. That remark stuck in my mind. I remember being uneasy about it, and assumed that he meant he could work with a middle-class (professional) English speaking Japanese in Tokyo; that the patient would have a familiarity with the theories of the unconscious and the concepts that have permeated our culture since Freud. 'Freudian slip' is a term that most people understand, likewise 'phallic symbol', 'a strong ego', 'my subconscious tells me', and so on. I supposed that he was not referring to a villager from a remote province who spoke no English. I did not check as to whether or not this psychoanalyst spoke Japanese; perhaps he did, but I rather think not.

Some years later I got to know a Greek child psychiatrist. He worked half the year in London and half in Athens and specialized in family therapy. He told me it took him weeks each time to readjust his approach, for the family structure was so different that he had to change his method of conducting sessions in order to feel comfortable in his work and to be acceptable to both groups. He could not exactly explain what the difference was, but thought it was to do with gender roles in the Balkans seeming to be more clearly defined; for example, the father would definitely be expected to be the head of the family and the therapist would need to support the family in their expectations. In London he found roles to be more blurred. I said, but surely all families are different and the Greek family may have the same problems as the London family, regardless of the fact that they are in Hampstead or Athens. He confessed to feeling 'not at home' in either place, as a result of living constantly between two cultures.

When I started to work at the Medical Academy in Sofia, Bulgaria, several years ago, I had at the back of my mind these discussions. I was working with a group of medical personnel, introducing art therapy and group analysis at the early stages of a project to incorporate art therapy into the Bulgarian NHS. Just about everything was different from what I was used to in Britain, yet I had spent many months in Bulgaria over the years, and lived in Yugoslavia, so the culture was familiar and I had a lot of friends and colleagues.

The students were mainly psychiatrists and women, with little or no art experience whatsoever. There is no tradition of 'lay' psychotherapy in Bulgaria, and indeed the students had no experience of psychotherapy, either from personal involvement or training. There has been a deep mistrust of psychoanalysis within Bulgarian psychiatry, due to the fact that, apart from Eric Fromm, few authors have argued for the 'strong convergence between Marxism and Freudian theory' (Corrigan and Leonard 1979: 117). There is, however, a strong and developing interest in group psychotherapy, and the students' reading in this area was in some cases impressive, especially considering that they had to read the books in a foreign language and obtain them from colleagues or on visits abroad.

A useful challenge to my assumptions occurred in the first art therapy course I conducted, when I advocated the provision of a wide range of materials in art therapy sessions. The students had thought that paper and pencil or felt tips were enough. They had not seemed to grasp the importance of having a variety of types and qualities of material available, so the patient could have choice for their image-making. They told me art materials were nearly impossible to find in some towns, and that they were very expensive, often only obtainable from the art academy shop, by art students. I realized that the assumption I had made about the value of different materials stemmed from certain models of British or American art education, namely that the type of material used affects the type of expression produced. Alschuler and Hattwick, for example, psychologists working in 1940s America, wished to determine that there was a relationship between the child's personality as evidenced from their social behaviour, and the form and content of their paintings, including material used. They suggested that as children matured their preoccupation shifted from 'self-expression' to 'literal representation' (1947). In the course of their research they made clear distinctions between the functions of materials, suggesting that 'crayons tend to be associated with awareness of outside standards and with the desire to communicate with others. ... With painting, on the other hand, children tend to express how they feel, regardless of what others think' (1943: 616–25).

Whether or not we agree with their conclusions, it is certainly the case that provision of a choice of materials is regarded as essential by most British art therapists. This assumption does, however, need to be explained in a country where models of art education have different roots and tend not to be about 'self-expression', which is not particularly valued either in art or in society generally. 'Self-expression' is considered in relation to the concept of 'the individual' which, in the west, has become increasingly important under capitalism. It is not only alien to Marxist-Leninist philosophy, but also to Bulgarian traditions in art. These have arisen from the folk-arts, where whole families and villages could be identified by their identical costumes; from religious art, including icon painting and frescoes; from Bulgaria's historical heritage and the celebration of her total liberation from Ottoman rule in 1908. It is only in the past few years that some influences of 'child art' can be discerned, as Sofia has played host to UNESCO-sponsored exhibitions of children's paintings.

Having pondered about these issues with the students, we set about defining 'art materials', and I suggested raiding hospital stores for 'junk' of various kinds, buying raw pigment and brushes from the hardware store, and getting rolls of newsprint free from the printing presses, collecting old magazines and posters, and so on. The notion of using 'junk' as art material was very new and strange to the Bulgarian students. They were reassured when they learned that 'scavenging' is a regular preoccupation of British art therapists.

Another tricky issue arose during an art therapy workshop designed to explore students' problems in working with their own groups, when members refused to discuss their families. This incident is fully described in *Inscape* (Waller 1983), so I will merely summarize here that I became fully aware of how loyalty to one's family – in Bulgaria usually an extended one – is so strong that any request to discuss the family in other than positive terms among strangers arouses the suspicion that the knowledge will be used or abused. The network of extended family – including first, second, and third cousins – is crucial in Bulgarian society. It provides a system of mutual aid and support in all kinds of situations, from weddings to building a house, sharing anxiety over children, mourning the loss of a parent, helping less affluent members, and so on, and anything which threatens this is rejected. It was very important for these student therapists to understand why their patients were unwilling to disclose family matters. They had not realized the strength of resistance until they themselves were faced with the task during the art therapy session.

Helen Landgarten, in her *Family Art Psychotherapy*, warns us to 'pay heed to the techniques that evoke strong emotions, bring about confrontations, and/or expose family or individual secrets' (Landgarten 1987: 8). Art therapy is useful in that the products can be viewed on many different levels. The clients can choose to talk or not to talk about them, to talk about them as form and structure, or to try and get in touch with feelings elicited during the making. They therefore have control over the session and the speed and depth at which they want to proceed. In the Bulgarian group there were many networks of relationships spreading throughout the small medical/psychiatric profession and through the country itself. It was not a question of being in a group which did not associate outside the group (a standard 'rule' in group analytic psychotherapy); it was inevitable that the students and their own patients would have plenty of contact across the networks.

During the break in that very long and tense 'family' workshop, I remembered how reluctant I had felt to talk about my own family during my group training, from a sense of 'disloyalty'. In my family, matters pertaining to the family were rarely discussed outside. It was, in fact, a large extended family so there was plenty of chance to share, to quarrel, to make up, to support each other. But neighbours were neighbours, friends were friends, and family was family. Relationships were somewhat formalized and boundaries rarely crossed. In our street this was the culture, and hinting at things being less than 'going along fine' would be to betray the family unit. After many years in the culture of psychotherapy, I still had a clear memory of my amazement and discomfort in the first groups I attended, as other members laid into their relatives with gusto and betrayed family secrets by the dozen.

I understood what my Greek friend had been trying to tell me after that experience. When a community is tight knit and dependent on formal sets of relationships, any attempt to disrupt the set is considered not only as potentially damaging to the individual, but also to put the whole family at risk. For me, the workshop highlighted the difficulties which exist in many groups about the critical presentation of one's own family, for fear of retribution of some sort. In some cases, this may be a fantasy; in others it could be a reality.

I have often been asked, when mentioning that I work in Bulgaria, 'But don't you find the language a problem?' As a matter of fact, this is not particularly so. How many people would ask that question if one was off to work in the USA, I wonder? In the introduction to this chapter I mentioned that we often assume that because Britain and the USA have the English language in common, then our cultural assumptions are likely to be shared.

(That there are even significant differences in the meaning of certain words or phrases became hilariously clear to Harriet when the hotel reception asked if she wanted to be 'knocked up' in the morning!) In the course of our discussion, we discovered that the language of academia often differs, even in the meaning of 'course', 'class', 'programme', so that, for instance, the 'art therapy course' could be a small part of a degree programme in psychology in the USA. Or *vice versa*. There are more fundamental differences in 'course' philosophy, symbolized by the USA favouring 'grading' as a means of assessment, whereas in Britain assessment is continuous and carried out on an individual basis with the student concerned. As Harriet pointed out, the giving of an A or B, or, horrors, a C, becomes imbued with all kinds of transference, such as 'Am I special', 'Am I wonderful', 'Am I useless'. Somehow, grading seems linked up to the 'time' difference in the USA and Britain. Harriet experienced things moving generally faster in the USA. She felt that this was to do with not having long traditions of history – no 500-year celebrations, etc. 'There are few significant precursors of the fact that things take time to evolve and develop, we want to do it yesterday ... we are a relatively young organization, yet we developed thirty training programmes since 1969.'

This statement has certainly been born out by our experience of students from the USA coming to the Art Therapy Unit at Goldsmiths'. They get impatient with what they perceive as our 'let it happen' approach, and the 'non-directive' approach which we tend to favour is somewhat alien. I, on the other hand, have to adapt to a society which dislikes planning far ahead (on everyday matters at least) and where things tend always to get done at the very last minute when you have practically given up hope. Then the pace of life in Britain seems fast in comparison.

We sometimes say that art therapy is a useful medium for people who have little language or have difficulty in expressing themselves, as the images help to put across a message. The statement 'art therapy is non-verbal' (which I have used on many occasions) quickly becomes meaningless, however, unless we are talking about silent communication, when in fact neither party is sure that they have picked up the right message. This issue was raised recently by current art therapy students at Goldsmiths', who were struggling to find a means to communicate with patients who were both deaf and unable to speak. They role-played an art therapy group with deaf people, and in playing back the video we turned the sound right down to cut out extraneous noises. We were struck by how exhausting and difficult it was to watch the ten-minute tape, and how isolated we felt without the background of language and sound. It gave us a little insight into how it must feel to be a deaf person in a hearing culture, and also into how much, as art therapists, we rely on words for communication, the finer nuances of which are lost unless both parties have a sophisticated grasp of gesture and body language, not to say symbol interpretation. Another assumption, about the non-verbality of art therapy, was tested and found wanting.

Being aware of one's own assumptions is obviously something that all therapists see as desirable. Or is it? According to Maurice Lipsedge and Roland Littlewood in their book *Aliens and Alienists*, there are serious problems to be faced in the way that immigrants to Britain and their descendants are treated within our psychiatric services.

> The experience of migration and of discrimination in housing, employment and everyday life were frequently expressed by patients not as conscious complaints, but symbolically in the actual structure of their illness. We continually found ourselves looking upon a particular type of behaviour first as abnormal, but later as 'only a cultural phenomenon' – or the reverse. ... Other doctors regarded our concern with cultural background as a self-indulgent pursuit of the exotic, if not an expression of our own identity problems. (Littlewood and Lipsedge 1982: 7–8).

One assumption that these two doctors confidently make is that the expression of mental illness is a meaningful reaction of the individual to his or her situation. The difficulty arises when that individual cannot communicate their feelings because of a set of assumptions which are held by the possible recipient (e.g. the therapist) about the client and the client about the therapist. They explain that:

> While we have tried to situate our own theories within the relativistic framework we have applied to others, we are still white, male, middle-class doctors discussing the private experiences of patients who are frequently black, female and working-class – part of what Michel Foucault calls the monologue of reason about madness. (8)

It was precisely these considerations which led Jafar Kareem, a psychotherapist of both Indian and Chinese origin, to found NAFSIYAT (meaning 'Mind-Body-Soul') Intercultural Therapy Centre in London. NAFSIYAT staff share the conviction that clients should have some choice as to who their therapist is to be – female or male, white or black, of the same or different nationality. (How rare it is for any client to have access to a psychotherapist in the NHS, let alone a choice; for when emotional crises and traumas of life are construed as 'illnesses', then psychotherapy is seen as irrelevant.)

At the time of NAFSIYAT's foundation in October 1983 there were only three African/Caribbean consultant psychiatrists working in the NHS in Britain. During a NAFSIYAT conference last January, we noted that 'schizophrenia' is more likely to be diagnosed when the client is from a different ethnic background (usually a black person) from the psychiatrist. There are problems of language, cultural and social mores. Littlewood and Lipsedge comment 'A not uncommon situation is the Indian junior psychiatrist attempting to interpret the experience of an East European patient to a white British consultant on the basis of reports made by Malaysian or West Indian nurses' (1982: 24). It is not surprising that the patient, who brings to the situation his or her own set of expectations, ends up thoroughly confused and frightened. Unconscious racism exacerbates the already unsatisfactory situation.

In his book *The Mismeasure of Man*, a critical account of intelligence testing, Stephen Jay Gould gives us an important and terrifying insight into how easily suspect data can be accepted if they conform to current political ideology. He describes a particularly pervasive example, that of biological determinism – the view that shared behavioural norms and social and economic differences between human groups arise from inherited, inborn distinctions, and that society is a reflection of biology. Gould points out that:

> Since biological determinism possesses such evident utility for groups in power, one might be excused for suspecting that it also arises in a political context. ... After all, if the status quo is an extension of nature, then any major change, if possible, must inflict an enormous cost – psychological for individuals or economic for society – in forcing people into unnatural arrangements. (Gould 1981: 21)

Gould draws our attention to the phenomenon of 'recapitulation', a nineteenth-century general theory of biological determinism in which all 'inferior' groups – races, sexes, and classes – were compared with the children of white males. It was one of the most influential ideas of late nineteenth-century science and spilled into other disciplines, notably psychiatry. Unfortunately, we discover that both Freud and Jung were 'convinced recapitulationists' (Gould 1981: 114).

Four groups of 'lower human forms' were identified by the palaeontologist E. D. Cope in 1887: non-white races; all women; southern as opposed to northern European whites; and lower classes within the superior races. For example, he believed that southern Europeans are caught in a more childlike, hence primitive, state as adults because of the warmer climate which imposes an earlier maturation! Cope had quite an influence on G. Stanley Hall, in 1904 the leading educational psychologist in the USA, who in turn had influence on art education in the USA and in Britain. Hall declared 'Most savages in most respects are children, or because of sexual maturity, more properly, adolescents of adult size' (Hall 1904: 649). He was moved to compare prehistoric art with the sketches of children and living 'primitives' and impressed the English psychologist James Sully, who compared children with savages:

> In much of the first crude utterance of the aesthetic sense of the child we have points of contact with the first manifestations of taste in the race. Delight in bright, glistening things, in gay things, in strong contrasts of colour, as well as in certain forms of movement, as that of feathers – the favourite personal adornment – this is known to be characteristic of the savage and gives to his taste in the eyes of civilised man the look of childishness. On the other hand, it is doubtful whether the savage attains to the sentiment of the child for the beauty of flowers. (Sully 1895: 386)

As art therapists working today, we may look at the date and content of these comments, feel horrified, and reassure ourselves that 'it was a long time ago'. Yet much more recently, in Marie Petrie's *Art and Regeneration* published in 1946 we find a section entitled 'The Slum Child' in a chapter on 'Art and Therapy'. Marie Petrie tells us that:

> The emotional life of London slum children is vivid and has been revealed by pictures painted in schools, clubs, shelters and play-centres. The street urchin is proverbially a happy, irrepressible creature, but it is from his ranks that the young delinquent is recruited. The earlier, therefore, he can be 'conditioned' by better and healthier social settings, by the good habits inculcated in nurseries and schools, the better for the rest of the community. ... The need for education through art is still greater for the slum child than for the average child, but the means by which it can be achieved do not differ from those advocated earlier for ordinary education. (Petrie 1946: 107)

Later, she suggests a similarity between the art of children and that of 'deficients' and the 'insane' (adding in 'and the art of primitive peoples') in that they make repetitive patterns:

> which, is so integral a feature of most applied art and tends to turn these into more automatic occupations, favouring a rather lazy state of mind, as opposed to drawing, painting or modelling, for which awareness and a certain emotional and mental excitement are required. (90–1)

Petrie suggests it is up to the psychiatrist and occupational therapist to decide whether a patient needs the 'calming' effect of crafts or the more 'rousing, stimulating nature of the arts'. There seems little doubt which is the more highly ranked in her mind.

Some prickles of discomfort were felt as I recognized the origins of some of the rationalizations justifying the 'superiority' of 'fine art' over 'applied art' in many of our leading art schools – a sense of this has been about at least since Plato's time, and tends to permeate all levels of art education. Marie Petrie advises us that 'If the artistic and the nervous temperament are as closely connected as it would seem, a dose of art might be a kind of homoeopathic treatment for neurotics' (92). Such views of the artist's temperament are liable to affect art therapists working today, about whom there are many myths and misconceptions.

We find a clash of cultures – that of art and science. Many members of the clinical team, coming as they do from a medical/scientific background, are unable to grasp why there is an artist in their midst and wonder what on earth art therapy is all about. (Andrea Gilroy and I have elaborated on this point in 'Art therapy in practice' (Waller and Gilroy 1986).) Both groups find it hard to communicate to the other, and on occasions hide behind their own jargon. Freud thought of the artist as:

one who is urged on by needs which are too clamorous ... so like any other with an unsatisfied longing, he turns away from reality and transfers all his interest and all his libido too onto the creation of his wishes in the life of phantasy. (Freud 1922)

Ursula Le Guin among others takes issue with Freud's assumptions, citing Emily Brontë as but one of Freud's overlooked female artists:

Freud seems to assume that the artist is male: not only is the pronoun 'he' used throughout his descriptions of the role, but the artist was supposed to be motivated by the 'desire to achieve honour, power, riches, fame and the love of women'. (Le Guin 1977)

In *Civilisation and its Discontents* he declares 'Yet art affects us but as a mild narcotic and can provide no more than a temporary refuge for us from the hardships of life; its influence is not strong enough to make us forget real misery' (Freud 1930: 30).

Freud appears to be cautioning both the artist and those who would advocate art as a panacea for the ills of individuals. As present-day art therapists, we are, one hopes, most unlikely to do this. We must be equally careful, it seems to me, not to confine the ill of the individual to him or herself alone, and thus avoid the realities of social, cultural, and ethnic differences, however painful and difficult these are to confront.

In this paper I have tried to share some of my preoccupations with the term 'cross-cultural', to consider briefly some of the differences between working as an art therapist in Britain, and in the USA and Bulgaria. Working in a country with a history and culture very unlike that of Britain has caused me to reflect much more rigorously on the way that I practise and teach in Britain and, in particular, on the foundations of some of our most cherished assumptions as art therapists.

I'll end with a quote from Lenin: 'It is impossible to live in a society and to be free of that society.'

References

Alschuler, R. and Hattwick, L. (1943) 'Easel painting as an index of personality in preschool children', *Amer. Jnl. of Orthopsychiatry*, vol. 13, pp. 616–25.

Alschuler, R. and Hattwick, L. (1947) *Painting and Personality: A Study of Young Children*, vols 1 and 2, University of Chicago Press.

Corrigan, P. and Leonard, P. (1979) *Social Work Practice under Capitalism. A Marxist Approach. Critical Texts in Social Work and the Welfare State*, Macmillan, London.

Freud, S. (1922) *Introductory Lectures on Psychoanalysis. Collected Papers*, vol. I, Hogarth, London.

Freud, S. (1930) *Civilisation and its Discontents*, Hogarth, London.

Gould, S. J. (1981) *The Mismeasure of Man*, Penguin, Harmondsworth.

Hall, G. Stanley (1904) *Adolescence. Its Psychology and its Relation to Physiology,*

Anthropology, Sociology, Sex, Crime, Religion and Education, Appleton, New York.

Landgarten, H. (1987) *Family Art Psychotherapy*, Bruner Mazel, New York.

Le Guin, U. (1977) *The Word for World is Forest*, Gollancz, London.

Littlewood, R. and Lipsedge, M. (1982) *Aliens and Alienists: Ethnic Minorities and Psychiatry*, Penguin, Harmondsworth.

NAFSIYAT Intercultural Therapy Centre (1985) *A Report 1983–1985*, London.

Petrie, M. (1946) *Art and Regeneration*, Paul Elek, London.

Sully, J. (1895) 'Studies of childhood XIV. The child as artist', *Popular Science* 48, pp. 385–95.

Waller, D. E. (1983) 'Art therapy in Bulgaria. Part II', *Inscape*, October, pp. 15–17.

Waller, D. E. and Gilroy, A. J. (1986) 'Art therapy in practice', in Steinberg, D. (ed.), *The Adolescent Unit*, Wiley, London.

Chapter Sixteen

The psychic roots of drama

Rosemary Gordon

Much of this chapter will represent my attempt to explore the question of man and drama. I will do this in terms of what I, as an analytical psychologist, can contribute to elucidate it further by drawing on my clinical experience and on my store of those theories that have proved to be useful models. Such elucidation may then also help towards a firmer assessment of the healing potential of drama, drama when enacted on the stage, in the therapist's consulting room, or in real life.

The discussion of drama in any of these situations leads one inevitably to examine the experience of 'being oneself' – true and real or false and alien. Looking carefully and deeply at the experience of 'one's self' seems to lead quite naturally to an awareness that we carry inside us a number of different selves, different 'internal personages'. These internal personages furnish our inner world and derive from a least three different sources.

1 The images of our own body and its parts, and the many sensations we receive from them.

2 The objects and persons we encounter and relate to outside us, though modified and often even distorted as they may be by the particular psychological processes through which they have arrived in our inner world – processes such as idealization, denigration, projective identification, rationalization, etc.

3 The archetypal images, that is the themes and goals of our basic drives.

As regards the definition of drama, I have been guided by Martin Esslin (1978), who ascribes to drama four major features.

1 Emphasis on action, or at least the preparation and planning of action.

2 The experience of emotions that belong to several characters.

3 A happening in the here and now, that is in the 'eternal present'.

4 The simulation of reality, in other words 'play' in Winnicott's sense (1971).

Unlike my usual procedure I want to begin with a description of my analytic work with a young man, Bob, who was 37 when he started analysis. It was not until quite late on, as the analytic work with him progressed, that I suddenly realized that so many features of his case are features that also characterize drama.

Bob had been in analysis for several years. He was a designer and desperately anxious to become a good and inventive designer. He longed to find, to reach, and to use his own creative resources. Longing to achieve this goal had been one of the main reasons for coming into analysis.

He was the older of two boys. His father, a doctor, a quiet and somewhat withdrawn man, had been away fighting in a war when Bob was between 8 and 12 years old, the very years when he most needed the presence, encouragement, and inspired companionship of a man. His mother had been a professional singer, who, after the birth of her two sons and then the absence of her husand, became a teacher of singing. She was – as she came to appear from Bob's description of her – a very lively person, somewhat self-centred, devoted to her work and profession, with easy access to her feelings and her creativity, but not really interested in, or talented for, making a home, enriching such a home, or giving much time and attention to her children. She had a close woman friend with whom she collaborated in her professional work.

Bob was a tall, thin, quiet, shy, timid, diffident, insecure, and passive person, who looked ten to fifteen years younger than his age. He had great difficulty in asserting himself, either in his work, in relation to colleagues and bosses, or in his personal relationships with friends, partners, or acquaintances. He seemed very cut off from his affects and impulses, and his feelings in the transference were subdued. Only when he could tell me of some new failure, or of some new loss of prestige, achievement, or argument did a flash of triumph, of masochistic triumph, enliven his facial and verbal expression.

But the analysis jogged along – quietly. Yet he had many interesting dreams and some of them were filled with quite strong emotions. There were several about a birth-giving; either he himself or some domestic animal was bearing a baby. But even this potentially forward-looking theme tended to be vitiated in some way or other: either there was not enough food for the new baby; or instead of milk the baby was offered shit; or he, the mother, the birth-giver, was neglected and socially excluded and shunned; or else the baby was damaged or disposed of as rubbish. There was in these dreams so much hurt and pain, but he would tell them in his quiet, gentle, and bland manner, as if they had been dreamed by someone else.

Strangely enough, my own feelings for him in my counter-transference remained consistently patient, affectionate, and maternally caring. Why, I often wondered, did I not – at least sometimes – react with impatience, anger and/or irritation – as indeed his father had shown and expressed to him when he did return from his war service and did not, as Bob remembered, seem to be particularly pleased at the way his eldest son had developed. (It may well be that his father experienced Bob as a part of his own shadow, as a caricature of himself, representing his own lack of a positive masculinity.) I began to suspect that perhaps there was no lively and potentially creative centre to be found in Bob. When both of us came close to a loss of hope (and yet there were the dreams!) he decided that he would like to try his hand at some art therapy. The results were truly surprising. Bob brought his paintings to his analytic sessions. They were a revelation. The paintings were quite remarkably lively, colourful, and full of imaginative forms – of persons, of creatures, of objects – expressing joy and fun as well as fear, anger, violence, and even horror. They showed a capacity to be playful – playful in Winnicott's sense of 'play' – that he had, until now, been unable to draw on and use and enjoy consciously. But at first, as with his dreams, Bob displayed and discussed them without much affect, enthusiasm, or even involvement.

But now my own reactions to him changed. I became more fierce and challenging. I felt anger, as if on behalf of those pictures, his pictures, at what seemed to me to be his dismissal of them, and his churlish and almost sadistic refusal to acknowledge as his own the paintings before us. And, as I began to express some of these reactions, it seemed as if a father – a more potentially enabling father than he had actually experienced in his own personal history – had become activated inside each one of us and between us. At first Bob reacted with sullen, sulky, and hurt withdrawal into more silence. But then, slowly, he rose to my challenge. He became overtly more resentful, a bit abusive, and finally openly and honestly hostile and aggressive. This then seemed slowly to enable him to protect and to defend what he had made and created and to relate to it as coming from him. It seemed also to enable him to stand by and to protect that part of himself from where his pictures had drawn their existence and their aliveness. It seemed to me that he was now beginning to extricate himself from the envy and from the sense of total and hopeless impotence in relation to his lively and artistic mother; emerge also from the delusion that all creativity is feminine and belongs to the woman, the mother who castrates males and leaves them with only one way of associating with the forces of creation – that of being her vassal, her slave, or, at best, of being her flirty and admiring eunuch.

However, before Bob had achieved this extrication, and while he was in the midst of this battle in and through the transference to both the mother-analyst-me as well as the father-analyst-me, he had a pretty bad accident in his home. It had not been altogether his fault, but had he been more alert and attentive he could have avoided it – as he himself explained to me. Indeed it took many months to discover and to understand the many meanings of this accident, and to work through, in the relative safety of the consulting room, the emotional upheaval and the catastrophic emotional experience of this accident.

What emerged is that the accident was indeed a murderous attack on the much admired and much envied mother. It was also a murderous attack on the father, whom he thought of either as absent and unavailable, or, if present, as inadequate and impotent because he had not succeeded in taming and containing the mother; he had also been unable to guide Bob into true and enjoyable manhood. But, inasmuch as Bob – when in somewhat less hopeless and less depressed state – was identified with the enviable mother, or, when in a more depressed state with the inadequate and impotent father, the accident was also a suicide, a killing of himself who had been swamped and taken over by one or both parents. This suicide was then provoked by the despair that he would never be able to shed the incorporated and introjected 'others'; that he would never manage to overthrow their domination inside him; despair that he could ever become his own self. As we worked and worked through the emotional experience and the symbolic meaning of the accident, it took on the quality, not only of murder and suicide, but also of birth, of parturition, of sacrifice – sacrifice, that essential and always present constituent of all rites of passage.

What then are the features thrown up in Bob's analysis that seem to me to be so particularly relevant to drama? First and foremost, there are the conflicts engendered by the presence of alien, of 'not-me', personages inside one. Then there is the uncertainty, the problematic, of what one may, at any one time, regard or experience as being one's own real and true self. There are the actions that are – or are not – (in terms of one's own conscious plans and intentions) appropriate as regards space, time, conditions, and circumstances. There is the experience, inside one, of struggle – struggle between life and death, hope and disillusion, and battles won and battles lost. And finally there is the search – conscious and deliberate, or unconscious – to discover one's own destiny.

Before I discuss some of these in relation to Bob I will define and view some of the key terms. What are the qualities that mark a psychic content or process as archetypal? I think of four main qualities that distinguish it.

1 Universality – across epochs and cultures.
2 Bipolarity – good and bad, creative and destructive, powerful and impotent.
3 The presence of very powerful affects.
4 An 'all-or-nothing' quality, evoking a more or less ruthless attitude.

The need to create was regarded by Jung as one of the five main instincts in the human being. It is the expression of our two basic but contradictory needs: the need for order, for continuity and for meaning on the one hand; and, on the other, the need for excitement, and for the discovery and the making of something new.

Closely interdependent and interacting with creativity is the process of imagination, that cluster of images which have been brought together and, as it were, 'produced' in association with other more cognitive mental processes such as past experiences, memories, thoughts, as well as wishes, hopes, fears, and so on. Imagination must be distinguished from phantasy. Phantasies embody instinctual and archetypal experiences, and belong predominantly to our unconscious world, our dream world; but imagination depends on the interaction of both conscious and unconscious processes.

As for symbolization, its essential character is the 'as if' attitude. It is really the most powerful and decisive function in the processes of creation and imagination. Through the process of symbolization man is helped and enabled to perceive the links between disparate, separate, and individual objects and events on the one hand, and, on the other, the universals. He can thus attend to and concern himself with both facts and meaning.

I regard the concept of 'the self' as an abstraction, as a model which, like a geographical map, refers to and represents a whole system composed of various phenomena, but all of them tending to move in the direction of cohesion, integration, and synthesis. Joseph Redfearn (1986) suggests that there are many selves in all of us (have poets and artists not always known this?). Redfearn illustrates the migratory nature of the feeling of 'I' by saying that this 'I'.

migrates hither and thither to various locations in the total personality, like the spotlight at a theatre picking out first one actor and then another ... each of them may take the stage and relate to other units in sometimes familiar, sometimes novel dramas and stories. . . . I call these various actors in ourselves 'sub-personalities'.

Redfearn calls our attention to the fact that there can be shifts and changes in our relationship to, and in our identification and de-identification with, the various sub-personalities in our inner world. Surely we saw this happening to Bob, particularly when, after the accident, the spell that had held his inner world static, as if frozen, began to break and lose its power. This then brought, at last, movement and change to the scene and to the personages – the characters – inside him.

It seems to me to be very illuminating that Redfearn should have used theatre and actors as his metaphors to describe the intrapsychic world, peopled by our many selves, and marked by so much ebb and flow of our inner states. All art involves the translation of something immaterial – vision, affect, experience – into the making of something material. However, while some art forms need only the collaboration of the body and its skills, in others – in particular in music, dance, mime, and drama – the body itself is the actual instrument for artistic expression. This means of course that we need to explore the relationship a person has to his body, and here three processes are particularly relevant.

1 Identity – we need to know with which of the many internal personages

the artist identifies, at least in the present context and at the present time.

2 The artist's body image – does it fit his/her actual body? Or does it distort it? And in what way? In what direction?

3 The quality of a person's narcissism – is it healthy? Is it love for one's true self, warts and all?

Of course the actor's very task is to step into the 'other', the 'outsider', the 'not I'. But in the case of the actor we are not dealing with phantasy, that is with a uni-dimensional reality which dominates dreams and hallucinations, but with imagination, where conscious and unconscious processes interact.

The importance for the art-creating person of a valid and growth-promoting relationship with his body and with the various internal personages – in other words the presence of a healthy narcissism – was clearly shown by Bob. His identification with a mother whom he really wanted to humiliate and defeat, if not murder, was certainly responsible for the absence, the lack of healthy-enough narcissism. It had lured him into an artistic-creative profession, only to trick him into failing and ridiculing the professional mother-self. Hence the expression of triumph whenever he could report to me a new failure, a new humiliation. Yes, he could draw. He did, as far as he consciously knew, want to be a good designer. He did want to be able to translate his images into perceptual forms. But, somehow, his imagination kept faltering and his hand kept blundering. However when, at last, after the accident, he got on better terms with himself, his work seems to have improved perceptibly, to judge by the approval of his boss and his progress and promotion at work.

Bob's case throws up another factor that one needs to consider when one examines the arts, creativity, mental health, and therapy. I am referring to a person's thoughts, beliefs, and phantasies about masculinity and femininity, and about his own relationship to either and/or both. Bob seemed to assume – unconsciously – that all creativity is the monopoly of the woman, the mother. It seemed to him clear that not only could she make babies, but she alone, he believed, had access to feelings, to imagination, and to the capacity and the technique to express them. Masculinity seemed to him to be sterile, and men seemed to be destined, seemed to be condemned, to be dull, subdued, and more or less impotent. Their role was to stand by, to admire the woman, to be her public, the consumer of her artistry.

The recognition that there are in each of us a number of sub-personalities makes it evident that our inner world also is really a stage on which one enacts and experiences many types of drama; for where two or more personalities coexist, be they outside us or inside us, there is, almost inevitably, conflict, confrontation, argument, dialogue, and debate. Thus we have inside us some of the very constituents that mark and belong to drama in the theatre as described and defined by Martin Esslin. It is thus not surprising that man should have tried to enact, have wanted to enact, from very early on through the art of drama the contentious, competing, and contradictory experiences of the many characters he meets both outside and inside himself. By externalizing the inner drama and rendering it into a form that is visible both to oneself and to others, one may discover parts of oneself, new sub-personalities, of which one had remained relatively unconscious and unaware. One might then even discover that there could be new ways in which the sub-personalities inside one might coexist and interact. Drama, whether extra-psychic or intrapsychic can therefore be the most direct means of self-communication as well as other-communication.

But between the happening of the inner dramas and the enactment of the drama outside one lies the field of the operation of creation. In order to transpose drama from inside to the outside, phantasies must be transformed into imagination. This is as valid for drama as it is for all the arts. Thinking of drama as the enactment – through words, mime, gestures, and actions – of conflicts engendered by the various incompatible human needs, the various sub-personalities, and the many different actual persons, we can think of drama as happening in four different settings and contexts.

1 Drama is enacted inside a person in a setting of solitude, a one-person situation. All the actors are the personifications of exclusively intrapersonal forms and functions. This happens in and through a process that Jung has called active imagination.

2 In an analysis, drama is enacted in a two-body relationship. It is thus an interpersonal event, although the 'actors' are predominantly intrapersonal figures that issue, primarily, from one person only – the patient.

3 Drama therapy happens in the context of a multi-body situation. The main purpose is still the translation of essentially personal intrapsychic characters, but here they are drawn not from only one, but from several persons present in the drama therapy group. Here then appear through drama both intra- and interpersonal forces and conflicts.

In the three settings described so far, drama is used primarily as a healing technique. One relies therefore mainly on relatively free improvizations.

4 But in drama in the theatre, which involves the active participation of a certain given number of actors and the passive-receptive presence of an unspecified number of individuals that constitute the audience, improvization is displaced by a disciplined, ritualized, planned, scripted, and structured text, the play. Here the embodiment of personal intra- and interpersonal protagonists may be complemented by characters that are transpersonal; that is to say they are drawn from a people's historic, cultural, and collective roots, and from personages that represent suprahuman or transhuman figures. Here then we are confronted not only with our personal internal dramas, or with the dramas that belong to our relationships with one another, but we are also

put in touch with the whole tragicomedy of the human situation and with our eternal quest for meaning.

When we speak of drama we refer really to two activities:

1 The construction or the composition of a story;
2 The acting, that is the portrayal, of the protagonists.

This then leads me on to compare and to discuss 'acting', in the sense of 'enacting' a part, a role on the one hand, and, on the other hand, what psychoanalysts call 'acting out'. By the latter is meant actions that occur outside the analytic room, outside the analytic sessions, and outside the analytic relationship; such acting out has tended to be thought of as counterproductive to the therapeutic work. However, nowadays we are no longer quite so certain that acting out is always and necessarily unhealthy and antitherapeutic. Admittedly, while psychoanalysis was thought of as only a 'talking cure', and while the expression in and through words was believed to be the only way through which unconscious contents could reach consciousness it was inevitable that all acting and all enacting should be considered to be an 'acting out'.

But with the more recent developments in psychoanalysis and analytical psychology, with the treatment of young children and of sicker and more regressed patients – here Jung and Klein are particularly notable as pioneers – and with the use of the arts as ways of helping the mentally ill, the exclusive reliance on words has diminished. Instead, making psychic experience visible and tangible is now recognized as another efficient and valuable way through which consciousness can be helped to expand. Consequently 'acting out' and 'enactment' need no longer be thought of as totally antagonistic and opposed to one another, but rather as being two points on a spectrum along which lie a number of 'actions' that represent a whole register of gradations of conscious–unconscious interactions.

Drama, whether enacted within the individual or outside the individual, is likely to play a major part in what Jung has called the process of individuation, a process that aims at the achievement of optimum synthesis of the conscious and unconscious functions. Jung had recognized early on that there is in man an unquenchable thirst for the development of his 'self'. Since drama and the techniques of drama therapy – such as role-reversal, playing the part of many and diverse characters, etc. – inevitably increase one's range of possible identifications, they have every chance to enlarge our knowledge and our experience of many of our sub-personalities. This must further the process of individuation, which includes the capacity to sympathize and to empathize with an ever-enlarging number of individuals outside us. Thus will a person be enriched in both the width and the depth of his knowledge, understanding, experience, and compassion.

To summarize, my discussions in this chapter have taken me to a place from where I can see that drama is ubiquitous and universal, happening as it does in the world inside all persons, between all persons, and in the world where man relates to universals, to the cosmic. The presence of multiple and often contradictory forces both inside us and outside us creates fields of tension and conflict. Our endowment with language and imagination, and our disposition to symbolize, to make and to create, all this make the emergence of drama and of dramatic forms natural and inevitable.

References

Esslin, M. (1978) *An Anatomy of Drama*, Abacus, London.
Redfearn, J. W. (1986) *My Self, My Many Selves*, Library of Analytical Psychology, Academic Press, London.
Winnicott, D. W. (1971) *Playing and Reality*, Tavistock, London.

Chapter Seventeen

Some aspects of art therapy and family therapy

Michael Donnelly

As a form of psychotherapeutic intervention, family therapy is a relative newcomer. Haley (1971) describes how the idea of trying to bring about change in the family, rather than in groups or individuals, appeared in America in the 1950s. This movement towards working with whole families came about at a time when the established psychiatric response to troubled individuals was to remove the individual from their social situation and to treat the intrapsychic problems causing their difficulties. The real world of the patient was considered secondary since what was important was his perception of it, his affect, his attitudes, the objects he had introjected, and the conflicts within him programmed by his past. The focus when treating the whole family was no longer on changing the individual's perceptions, his affect, or his behaviour (although this may happen, it is not the goal of a family therapy approach), but on changing the structure of a family and the sequences of behaviour and communication between intimates.

With this shift it became clearer that neither traditional individual therapy nor group therapy with artificial groups was relevant to the goals and techniques of family therapists. The problem was to change the living situation of a person, not to pluck him out of it and to try to change him.

Family and marital therapy are often used as terms to describe the interviewing and psychotherapy of natural groups. More strictly, however, the terms refer to a focus on the dysfunctions and treatment of the systems formed by individuals involved in such intimate relationships rather than a focus on the psychology of the individuals alone. It is assumed that in such systems the whole is more than the sum of its parts and cannot be satisfactorily explained or most effectively treated by means of theories that describe the parts taken separately (Skynner 1976). The practice of family therapy covers a wide range of approaches and models. At one extreme the therapist may see the family together for assessment but subsequently tends to concentrate the therapeutic efforts on the most responsive individual (who may not always be the referred patient), or the marital dyad, even when more generalized family problems exist. At the other extreme the therapist gathers together relatives, neighbours, friends, and others involved with the family in regular meetings of up to fifty individuals. In between these contrasting approaches, the majority of family therapists work with the nuclear family, supplemented by grandparents and other members of the extended family or social network who seem particularly relevant to the presenting problem. This wide range of approaches can nevertheless be described as family therapy because they are based on an attempt to understand, and seek to change, the total family system rather than its individual members.

Various models of family therapy have evolved and become differentiated since the 1960s, the classification of which still continues to undergo change and re-evaluation. Models that guide the therapeutic endeavour with families contain implicit or explicit concepts about what makes a family functional or dysfunctional, and are consequently of great interest when considering how art therapy and family therapy can work together. Out of the underlying concepts emerge the means to enable the therapist to observe the family and to create a language that reflects his experience of the family. In turn this enables the goals of therapy to be determined, which leads to the sorts of interventions that the therapist uses to achieve the therapeutic goals. Some models place much emphasis on the development of insight and the use of psychoanalytical concepts, while others are explicitly behavioural. Some concentrate on the context the problem occurs in, whether it is the social context or the cognitive context the family uses to interpret itself in relation to reality and its social ecosystem. Other models make extensive use of both cybernetic and general systems theories that emphasize the organizational aspects of family functioning.

All of these models pose particular problems for the art therapist seeking to practise in a family therapy setting. The model that underlies the thinking in this paper is one derived from the cybernetic and systems theories, that of structural family therapy. The structurally oriented family therapist sees the first task as 'joining' the family; that is, the therapist attunes himself to the manner in which the family thinks, speaks, and feels. Often the therapist will imitate the family's style and takes up their images, expectations, and metaphors. He assesses the dysfunctional structure of the family, such as blurring of boundaries, confusions in family hierarchy, and the existence of rigid coalitions (triangulation). The therapist may be seen to be following the family's interactions by allowing or even encouraging family patterns to unfold naturally before interviewing overtly. In general, when he does interview, it will be in one of two ways: first as a means of clarifying boundaries; or second to enable the family to practise new ways of relating to each other by enactment within the session.

Within a structural framework to family functioning, art therapy (and related visualizing techniques of sculpting – *tableau vivant*, role play, and doubling) can play a useful role, with its emphasis on its 'here and now' concrete qualities (enactment), as well as a sensitive means of the therapist and family becoming aware of their own style of communication and the particular images that they use (joining). The use of art expression in this context also presents opportunities for the promotion of changes in the family structure (boundary formation) and the establishment of a consensus about the way the family wishes to change (goal setting).

In general, the use of art expression or picturing (I very rarely use the words 'art therapy' with a family, as the term seems to cause some alarm) with families divides into three main approaches – individual, shared, and simultaneous. These are not mutually exclusive, and often blend and merge during the course of therapy. In the individual approach, a subgroup of the family such as the children or a particular individual, perhaps with a communication problem, will be the focus of the therapist's interest (Guttman 1975; Muller 1966; Kwiatkowska 1971). Other therapists seek the participation of all family members in a collaborative effort to create one product. This is typical of those who used the shared approach to family art therapy (Kwiatkowska 1967; Wadeson 1980). In the simultaneous approach all family members are encouraged to create their own individual images without any attempt at collaboration (Sherr and Hicks 1973; Jenkins and Donnelly 1983).

The use of simultaneous approach can lend itself to particular problems and stages in therapy, and while it has a generalized application as a diagnostic aid, a joining technique, or as a means of challenging ritualized and habitual family responses (Wadeson 1980; Kwiatowska 1971), it is proposed that the use of simultaneous expression can be of particular value in families who find themselves in conflict, either overt or covert, or in those families who exclude particular members or subgroups or invalidate their contribution to the therapy session. When using such an approach all the family members are asked to respond individually to a request from the therapist, using the art materials provided instead of responding verbally. One result of this is the placing of family members in a less hierarchically determined position, offering greater opportunities for clearer communication, unstructuring the family in order to establish how it sees itself.

This is facilitated by one of the intrinsic features of art therapy, the phenomenon of freedom from linear and temporal constraints that are so much a feature of verbal expression; in artwork a number of ideas can be expressed at the same time, all having different chronologies. While family members are engaged in making their own responses, there is a greater likelihood that material that may be of use to the family can emerge without the usual controlling mechanisms intervening to prevent disclosure. For example, the father, when his 15-year-old daughter begins to describe her version of the family problem, interrupts to say that he was sure that the therapist did not really want to hear her strange ideas, so that he attempts to censor her contribution and also makes clear that all communications should occur with his permission and consent. Simultaneous expression can give all family members a voice where previously they may have been denied or voluntarily excluded themselves from making a contribution.

Where conflict is present, the use of simultaneous expression can contribute to the reduction of the 'tit for tat' style of communication that can be a feature of such conflicts. It requires them to state their own point of view rather than chronically or habitually rebutting or confronting the other's position. Equally, in conflicted couples the verbal necessity for 'taking turns' in communicating with the therapist can create the situation where both partners can seem to be competing to form an alliance with the therapist against the other, perhaps perpetuating the avoidance of looking realistically at their difficulties by seeking to reinforce their particular point of view by bringing in a third person, be they neighbour, friend, relative, or therapist.

The giving of a 'voice' to all members of a family does not represent a view of family that feels that all family members have a right to have their point of view heard, or that the creating of equality in communication is in itself a solution to family problems. The underlying thinking is that in the types of couples and families already mentioned, the way that they solve their difficulties is either by denying the real issue or by creating a new problem. So that any attempts either to raise what is denied or to resolve the conflict will be perceived as a threat which has to be countered by the family. The intention in using simultaneous expression is to enable the family to learn about itself, in order that the whole family system is illuminated for both the family and the therapist.

Many of the themes used by art therapists in family settings are prompted by a view of family functioning that sees spontaneous and undirected art activities as liberating; particularly of repressed or denied emotions, or of transferences within the family. Hence the use of themes such as 'a free scribble drawing', a 'spontaneous drawing', or a 'collaboration by the whole family on spontaneous drawing' (Kwiatkowska 1971). Certainly the use of such themes combines the opportunities for the family process to be observed, as well as yielding items of interest in the manifest content. Other therapists focus on the feelings of individual family members, with themes such as 'a strong feeling', 'something you hate', or 'your feelings about the future' (Muller 1966). Such themes do not reflect the family process well, but may enable unresolved emotional conflicts and needs to become the focus of therapy. For some therapists the themes and content are subservient to the enactment of family patterns, such as dominance, collusion, openness, etc., through joint activity. This gives rise not so much to themes, but more to instructions to the family such as 'develop a well-integrated picture together, without verbal communication' (Wadeson 1980).

In using consecutive themes, themes that are conceived of in pairs, one following the other, the principle aim is to focus not on the individual images but on the relationships between them – such pairs of themes as 'family life with husband/father' and 'family life without husband/father', 'family life before things began to go wrong' and 'family life now', and 'family life as it is now' and 'family life as you would like it to be'. Particular themes which require the family to look forward, such as 'family life with our problem' and 'family life in the future' can often provide much useful information with regard to the motivation to change, what the family sees as a solution to its difficulties, and the outcomes that the various family members are prepared to accept.

While consecutive themes do not yield much information on the family process, as enacted in the creation of the images, experience to date suggests that they do demonstrate clearly, for both family and therapists, evidence of how the interpersonal relationships of the family and the family structure are perceived by its members (Jenkins and Donnelly 1983).

In the following case study the use of both a simultaneous approach to eliciting art expression, combined with themes that have a consecutive structure, is described. These approaches were chosen so that events and attitudes could be experienced and shared simultaneously, and so that family members have an opportunity to experience other members' views – in essence, the family encountering itself while at the same time providing a forum in which the family could look at their goals for the future. The important feature here is the role of the therapist as a catalyst, emphasizing family members' inherent ability to initiate therapeutic material, drawing on their own creativity and resources, and producing their own ideas from which to work.

Mr and Mrs H were married in 1950, and had two children, Valerie aged 27 and Kevin aged 17. At the time the family came into treatment, Valerie had married and moved a considerable distance from her family of origin, and was not included in the family sessions. The principal reason the family were in therapy was that Kevin had been placed on probation on the condition that he received some sort of psychiatric care.

There were a number of events that precipitated this family into crisis. The family home was burgled and £1,200 worth of goods were taken. This event prompted a 'nervous breakdown' in Mrs H and a few days later Kevin committed his first offence. In a single day he took and drove away three motorcycles which he claimed to be test driving. He was disqualified for three months and fined. He immediately paid the fine out of his own savings. When he regained his licence three months later, he took and drove away three cars on two separate days. He was unable to explain any of these events.

During the first session it transpired that Mrs H was very angry at her husband for being passive, both at home and in their marital relationship. No mention was made of Kevin's offences which brought the family into therapy. Each complained of living separate lives, while at the same time uniting to label Kevin as a 'slow starter' who had difficulty in communicating. Whenever he tried they would interrupt him.

The drawing task was introduced during the second session, with the therapist asserting that this was a usual thing to do at this point in therapy. Each member was given a drawing board with two pieces of paper, and a range of coloured wax crayons. They were encouraged to view this activity as one in which they could begin to help themselves with their problem. They were then asked to 'represent with the materials' (not to draw, nor to imply that this was art) the consecutive themes of 'their family as it is now', and when this had been done they were asked to use the second piece of paper to represent their 'family as they would like it to be'. They were neither encouraged to look, nor not to look, at each other's pictures while they were being drawn. When they were completed, they were invited to look at and comment on each other's drawings. As space prohibits reproduction of all the material produced, only Kevin's pictures have been reproduced, Fig. 17.1 and 17.2. A brief description of his parents' pictures follows.

Mr H's response to the first part of the consecutive theme of representing the family 'as it is now' was to draw three disconnected unidentifiable figures, far apart in a room, watching television. Mrs H drew herself at a cooker,

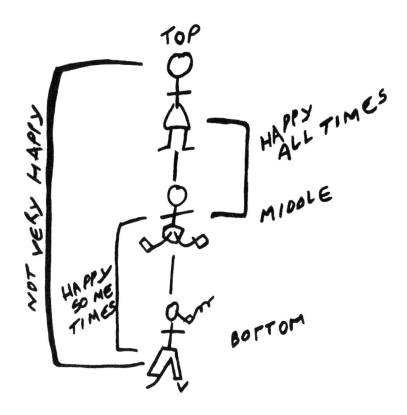

17.1 Kevin's response to 'your family as it is now'.

ALL HAPPY

NO ONE ON TOP

17.2 Kevin's response to 'as you would like your family to be'.

boxed off from the rest of the picture in the bottom corner. She placed Mr H in his garden shed and in the opposite corner to herself, with Kevin and his car in the upper centre of the page between them. In response to the second part of the consecutive theme, Mr H used the same scene in a room with a television but this time all three figures were playing cards, with the television off. Mrs H said she had felt unable to contemplate the future and had not drawn anything.

After listening to the comments that the encounter with the pictures produced, the therapist drew the family's attention to their first set of pictures and encouraged them to describe why they had represented the family the way they had. Both parents agreed that theirs was not really a family, they all lived separate lives, this for Mr H being typified by the way television discouraged conversation and for Mrs H by the way she was taken for granted and was expected to do everything including repairs around the house and managing all the financial affairs.

Kevin's drawings (Fig. 17.1 and 17.2) are of a different order, and are a good example of the advantages of simultaneous expression. When he spoke about his picture he communicated an understanding of the separateness of all their lives, but he also described the nature of the relationships in the family, with him in the role of intermediary between his parents. He described it like this: 'Mother tells me to go and ask my father when will he repair the cupboard, and my father tells me to say that he will do it when he is ready.' The first picture (Fig. 17.1) had the therapist and the family looking and talking about how the family was currently organized. Kevin's picture raised the issue of family hierarchy (Minuchin 1974; Haley 1976; Haley 1980), with mother placed on top, father underneath, and Kevin describing his discomfort in the middle. The use of simultaneous drawing confirmed the therapist's view of the family as being disconnected and with there being blurred boundaries between the parental dyad and the sibling subsystem (Kevin). In his second picture (Fig. 17.2) Kevin proposes a solution (restructuring), with himself removed from between his parents and on the outside in a much better position to 'graduate' from the family at the appropriate time. He also suggests that the hierarchical nature of the family structure needs to be modified and places all members as equals, with the consequent greater risk of open conflict.

Here picturing has enabled a previously silent or censored member of the family to have a voice and the consecutive themes have highlighted areas which, although known to the family, were not available for consideration as part of the problem. Both the content of Kevin's second picture and that of his other paved the way for a restructuring intervention by the therapists during the sessions. Mrs H had left her paper blank and this had been reframed as a positive statement which reflected how she was feeling about the future. She stated that the blankness was how she felt about the future with her husband. At this point it was suggested by the therapists, after discussion with the family, that although Kevin's behaviour had been the reason the family had come into therapy, the 'blankness' of the parental relationship and their anxieties about life without Kevin were the real issue.

The restructuring intervention was to invite Kevin to leave the sessions, and for only his parents to attend, freeing him from his enmeshed position, and providing a setting where the parental dyad could begin to tackle their difficulties in a more open way.

As can be seen from this example, the family and the therapists have been able to make use of an art therapy intervention using the concepts of simultaneous expression and consecutive themes, which has helped to clarify aspects of the interpersonal structure of the family and has enabled the hidden agenda of life without Kevin to become the focus of immediate enactment and of future family work.

In singling out simultaneous expression and the use of consecutive themes and describing them as 'techniques' somehow to be 'applied' to particular families, it is important to stress that they can only be used within the constraints of what the family will accept. Like any other form of intervention they are not in themselves solutions, nor are they shortcuts to effective therapy, and when applied in a mechanical or parrot-fashion way they can only satisfy the needs of the therapist. Minuchin (1974) describes the art of the family therapist as being the ability to join with a family, experiencing reality as the family members experience it, becoming involved in the repeated interactions that form the family structure and shape the way people think and behave. It means to use oneself to become an agent of change who works within the constraints of the family system, intervening in ways that are possible only with that particular family to provide a different, more productive, way of living.

When undertaking such interventions as described in this paper, it is important that the therapists are capable of being responsive and divergent in their expectations. It is all too easy to overlook important communications if they do not fit in with the therapists' view of what 'success' of the task should be. In this case the success of the task, if applied in an impersonal way, would have been for everyone to complete a picture, and the importance of the blank paper lost as an opportunity for the communication of Mrs H's apprehension about the future. When setting out to encourage a family to speak to itself and of itself to the therapist in its own terms and language, there must be an accompanying willingness and ability in the therapist to receive and consider all that the family communicates.

References

Haley, J. (ed.) (1971) *Changing Families*, Grune & Stratton, New York.

Haley, J. (1976) *Problem-solving Therapy*, Jossey Bass, New York.

Haley, J. (1980) *Leaving Home. The Therapy of Disturbed Young People*, McGraw-Hill, New York.

Guttman, H. A. (1975) 'The child's participation in con-joint family therapy', *Journal of the American Academy of Child Psychiatry*, 14, pp. 490–9.

Jenkins, H. and Donnelly, M. (1983) 'The therapist's responsibility; a systemic approach to mobilising family creativity', *Journal of Family Therapy*, 5, pp. 199–218.

Kwiatkowska, H. Y. (1967) 'The use of families' art productions for psychiatric evaluation', *Bulletin of Art Therapy*, 6, pp. 52–75.

Kwiatkowska, H. Y. (1971) 'Family art therapy and family art evaluations, indications and contradiction', in M. J. Jakab (ed.), *Psychiatry and Art*, vol. 3, Basil Krager, Switzerland, pp. 138–51.

Minuchin, S. (1974) *Families and Family Therapy*, Tavistock, London.

Minuchin, S. and Fishman, H. (1981) *Family Therapy Techniques*, Harvard University Press.

Minuchin, S. and Montatvo, B. (1971) 'Techniques for working with disorganised, low-socio-economic families', in J. Haley (ed.) *Changing Families*, Grune & Stratton, New York, pp. 202–11.

Muller, E. F. (1966) 'Family group art therapy; treatment of choice for a specific case', *Psychiatry and Art*, proc. IVth International Coll. Psychopathology of Expression, Washington DC, pp. 132–43.

Sherr, C. and Hicks, H. (1973) 'Family drawings as a diagnostic and therapeutic technique', *Family Process*, 12, pp. 439–60.

Skynner, A. C. R. (1976) 'Family and marital psychotherapy', *Brit. J. Hospital Medicine*, March, pp. 224–34.

Wadeson, H. (1980) *Art Psychotherapy*, Wiley, New York.

Chapter Eighteen

Drinking problems and short-term art therapy: working with images of withdrawal and clinging

Paola Luzzatto

Introduction

In this paper I will illustrate two cases of brief individual psychodynamic art therapy with patients with drinking problems. More specifically, I will present two images, symbolic of withdrawal and clinging respectively, which appeared to be particularly meaningful during the therapeutic process, because of their being recurrent and related to intense present and past emotional experience. I will describe some art therapy techniques I have used to facilitate the work of the patients.

Withdrawal and clinging are interpreted, within the psychodynamic object-relations perspective, as early defences against an unsatisfactory relationship with an absent, or threatening, or impinging, primary figure in childhood. They are seen as attempts of the young child to re-establish a harmonious antenatal situation where there would be no conflict with a demanding or dangerous environment (Guntrip 1982). They have also been described as two basic emotional positions of patients with addiction generally, and with drinking problems in particular. These two early ways of coping with the frustrating two-person relationship become dysfunctional to the adult, who, in time of crisis, may resort to alcohol or drugs in order to reinforce the early defence (Balint 1979).

The two examples presented here are brief therapies, and as such they share several aspects of brief psychotherapies in general (Beck 1976; Malan 1979; Mann 1973). I am referring particularly to the length of treatment (between ten and twenty sessions); to the early establishment of a therapeutic alliance; to the choice and maintenence of a 'focus' throughout the treatment; to the rather active approach of the therapist (in the consideration that a passive approach would lead to long-term work). The treatment does not attempt a deep personality change but centres on two main points, which have been called the 'interpretation' linking behaviour and feelings, present and past) and the 'confrontation' allowing, or encouraging, the exploration of alternative ways) of the defence (Ursano and Hales 1986).

As an art therapist working with patients with drinking problems within a short-term plan, I have been concerned with the following questions. Are some images produced in the art therapy session more meaningful than others? If so, is there any way of working with these images that may be more effective than others? What would be the most appropriate timing of the specific interventions? And how does this 'work on the image' fit with the work on the patient–therapist relationship? And how does it fit into the general treatment plan of the patient?

In these two cases, the images which appeared to be particularly useful in the therapeutic process started as representations of either an intensely negative – or an intensely positive – two-person relationship in the current life of the patients. They were later understood as representing their basic defence, which originated in childhood. In both cases, working on the image meant to move from that 'basic image' in all possible directions – in space and in time. This was done mainly using two techniques: stimulating 'free associations' to the image; and suggesting the exploration of 'alternative images'. This last technique is in line with Winnicott's theory of 'play' (Winnicott 1971) and Bowlby's concept of 'exploration' (Bowlby 1979). I have been particularly inspired by Sartre's study on the nature of imagination (Sartre 1983). Sartre emphasizes the importance of the 'imaginative attitude' as the capability of positing an 'hypothesis of unreality'; if man cannot envisage a given situation as possibly being 'otherwise' than how it is, then he would have no power to change it.

This chapter is focused on the use of the active technique of suggesting the exploration of an alternative image. The suggestions were made according either to an affirmative or to a negative modality, because imagination may work in both ways: either imagining that something *is* there; or imagining that something *is not* there. The most appropriate timing for this intervention appeared to be after the link with the past had already been established.

In this chapter I am not discussing the interrelationship between the art therapy techniques and the use of transference (that is, between the projection of the internal world of the patient on to the person of the therapist, and the projection on to the 'empty page' in front of the patient). I am also not discussing the interrelationship between the individual art therapy sessions and the various group therapies the patients were attending at the same time. The patients were bringing their 'withdrawing' or 'clinging' attitude also in the transference; and the patients were making their own connections between the individual sessions and some of the groups they were attending. These areas would need further analysis.

The setting and the patients

The work was carried out at ACCEPT, a London-based day clinic for patients with drinking problems, which offers individual counselling and psychotherapy, as well as a wide variety of group work. The two patients, whom I will call A and B, attended the Centre full-time for a period of a few months. At the time of being discharged they were considered quite improved, by both self- and staff-evaluation. At a one-year follow-up they had maintained their improvement. Both have given their permission to be mentioned in this paper, but their data have been slightly changed.

At the time of admission, A was a man in his forties. He was single, and living with his elderly parents. He had a job in the Civil Service, but was on sick leave because of his drinking problems, which seemed to be damaging his health. A had an older brother and two younger sisters. A had a long history of drinking. He used alcohol at first as a way of gaining confidence, in order to meet friends in the pub, but recently he had started to drink by himself in his room, ending up not being able to go out at all. In the Centre, A appeared to be sleepy most of the time, and this prevented him from gaining much benefit from the groups he was attending. He seemed to have difficulties in expressing himself verbally. He was referred to art therapy for individual sessions, while he continued to attend some groups, among which he particularly appreciated relaxation and assertiveness training. We had fifteen weekly art therapy sessions. During this time, A made thirty drawings, with an average of one to three during each session.

B was a man in his late fifties, married, with three grown-up children and one grandchild. B was well educated, and his profession was in the field of journalism. He had one younger brother, and was living with his elderly mother – only temporarily, in order to be able to attend the Centre.

B also had a long history of drinking, but things had got worse in the past few years after B lost his job as a result of his drinking. Being unemployed increased his drinking, and his wife started to talk about divorce. B reacted by taking an overdose. Now his wife would accept him back home, but B was afraid of his own feelings of hopelessness and despair. B appeared a pleasant, intelligent, and verbally sophisticated person. Individual art therapy was suggested to him because the use of a non-verbal modality seemed to the staff to be more appropriate in his case. B attended at the same time a variety of other groups; among them, he said he had been particularly helped by the transactional analysis group.

We had eleven weekly art therapy sessions. B loved to go to the artroom by himself during the week (this was one of the facilities offered in the Centre), and used to bring his work to the sessions. In this way B produced a great amount of artwork (125 paintings).

Working with an image of withdrawal

The image: the yellow barrier

Although A mentioned loneliness as his main problem, fear emerged as a basic emotion behind loneliness as soon as he made his first image during the second session. This image was the result of a casual combination of colours on the white page, using pastels and water colours. It was associated by A with the flashes of light during a thunderstorm, and the thunderstorm was associated with the experience of being bullied in school and later at work. Then A talked about being tormented by his senior brother, who was asked by his mother to look after him when he was a small child. A said he had always repressed his resentment against his brother, but he was afraid that one day he would lose control. So his fear appeared in the session, not only as fear of being attacked, but also fear of attacking others.

In the third session A decided to use fingerpaints, which he had never used in his life, to represent the relationship between himself and his brother (Fig. 18.1). He put some red on the right side, to represent himself, some black on the left side, to represent his brother, and a yellow line in between, to represent the feeling:

> The yellow is a special feeling I have had in the past about him, and I still have at times, and it is always there as a possibility. The yellow means that I am scared, that I would like not to be there; it is a difficult feeling, that I don't know how to describe.

18.1 The image – the yellow barrier (the relationship between A and his brother). 'Yellow means I am scared ... I would like not to be there.'

This yellow line seemed to be like another version of the flashing light of the thunderstorm of the previous session, but this time it seemed to represent a 'point of urgency' (Strachey 1969), the actual re-experience of an important emotion. The question for me was 'How can we use this image?' I could relate it to the transference; or I could ask A to say more, or to make more images, on the same issues; or I could be silent, waiting for him to proceed. I decided on none of these. I thought it was important to test how pervading his experience of being 'a victim' had been for him as a child. I asked him whether he could follow a phantasy of 'being a child – free to do what he wanted'. A came up with a real memory, instead of a phantasy. He remembered one day as a child going with a schoolfriend to visit his friend's grandmother, playing with him in the garden, feeling happy and free, but he was late when he came back home and was beaten up by his father. It became clear that the yellow line was a barrier against bad relationships, and also expressing a fear of good relationships. The bad world is threatening, the good world is unaccessible. It was also important to realize that A had experienced, at some point in his life, some happiness and freedom.

The early relationship

After a few sessions, A began to analyse his panic attacks which he had not mentioned before. He described them as feeling paralysed, and seeing 'flashes of light' in front of his eyes. They started when he was quite young. He had read in a book that flashes of light were often associated with attacks of migraine, and he said that maybe he was just suffering from migraine.

During the seventh session, A associated the yellow flashes with a recent event, when his brother came home drunk and threatened his old mother. After some silence, he remembered a very early episode of his life, and made an image of it (Fig. 18.2):

> I was very young, maybe 4–5 years old. I was in my room, frightened. My father was drunk, and I was afraid that he could hurt, or kill, my mother.... I put yellow as a separation line between my parents and myself: maybe it was the door of my bedroom.... I made myself black, because I was alone, isolated, paralysed. I chose green for my father, and red for my mother because I was on her side.

A was aware that this was an important image for him. It was the image of his early withdrawal, as a way of reacting to a weak mother and a threatening father. He realized that his present way of withdrawing was very similar – to shut himself into his bedroom, drinking. A commented on his fears as a child that his mother would die; he admitted that his mother was not so vulnerable after all, and that his father was not so threatening after all. A started to accept that the 'threatening world' was an image that he had brought with him since childhood, and that it was not necessarily the image of the real world.

18.2 The early relationship. 'Maybe yellow is the door of my bedroom ... I was in my room, frightened.'

The symbolic change

During the ninth session, A started to talk about wanting to overcome his apprehension at meeting new people. At the same time A was working in the same direction with his weekly group of assertiveness training. On the tenth session he talked about wanting to attend an adult education class, but of being afraid of having to ask for information from the receptionist. He made an image about this, again using fingerpaint, and said 'Red is for me; green is for the person I want to meet; yellow is the barrier between us.' Red and green were the colours he had chosen previously for his mother and for his father respectively. Now he chose red for himself (didn't he say 'I was on the side of my mother'?), and green for the unknown-frightening person he may meet – anywhere. After we had analysed these associations, I suggested A might explore the possibility of the barrier not being there, allowing the red actually to meet the green. The compulsive image was confronted. What happens if the image is different, if red and green find that they can face each other, without the barrier in between?

A decided he could try. He took another sheet of paper, and put some red and some green fingerpaint on it. He started to move his finger on them, and soon the two colours became one large spot of a greenish colour. A looked upset and said, in a fatalistic way, 'The green has taken over.' He then admitted it was his own doing, and wanted to try again. In the second trial he succeeded in making red touch green without losing its identity. On a symbolic level, A had been able to 'interact with the stranger' in a non-destructive way, without withdrawing behind the yellow barrier and without being swallowed into the other person's world. We discussed at length his feelings during the different parts of the exercise.

On the following session, A produced a kind of self-portrait (Fig. 18.3). There was a central yellow figure standing in a green meadow, surrounded by a blue arch and by a second red arch. A said:

> I made myself yellow this time. I don't know why. Maybe *I was the barrier*. The barrier is blue now. It is made of sadness, not of fear. The green is Nature. The goodness is the red outside, but there is a bit of red on this side of the barrier, too.

This was the last time A used any yellow fingerpaint. We had another four sessions, and A started to use felt-pens, and made some cheerful free drawings. When he resumed his job, his first comment was that his colleagues did not look to him as frightening as before.

Working with an image of clinging

The image: the Chinese Tao

B did not like the idea of art therapy at first; in fact, he looked quite angry during the first session. He said he could write poems, he could compose

18.3 The symbolic change. 'Maybe I was the barrier.'

music, but he had never attempted drawing, nor painting. So, why was art therapy chosen for him? He felt it was a way of making him feel faulty. Nevertheless, he quickly understood that he could draw very simple shapes, and they could become symbols of his internal world. From the very first session, B said he wanted to understand his relationship with his wife, and why he could not live without her; in fact, why he could not live with the idea that she would not need him. It became clear very soon that it was easy for B to talk about his wife, but it was difficult to talk about himself. He described her as a very independent, cheerful, active, capable woman, full of joy of life and of spirituality at the same time. What about him? Who is he? Without a job, without his wife, he is 'nobody'.

B brought to the third session a group of fifteen drawings, each showing a comparison between himself and his wife. Basically he was saying that she was almost perfect, and very reliable, and he was very imperfect, but maybe more creative – in every aspect of their daily life, from cutting butter, to managing their finances, to dealing with their children. One of the drawings was a circle divided into two halves, and B asked himself: Is she half of the circle with me? or more? or less? In the following sessions B kept returning to the symbol of the divided circle, and he was finally satisfied when he could visualize the idealized relationship between himself and his wife as the Chinese Tao, the supremely harmonious union of the opposites; the two halves get their meaning only as parts of the harmonious 'whole' (Fig. 18.4). Nevertheless, the need for the 'other half' was soon connected with feelings of anger (that she would not need him in the same way), of despair (that she could leave him at any time), of greed (wishing to have more, in order to be needed), of guilt (the need to succeed had led him to want too much, sometimes to want what belonged to other people). This image – which at first appeared as an image of peaceful wholeness – was soon understood by B as an image quite charged with painful ambivalent feelings of love and hate. B said he had never before looked at his ambivalence in such a close way – but now he wanted to go ahead.

The early relationship

As B kept bringing to the sessions the images of himself and his wife together, I pointed out how very difficult it was for him to focus on his own feelings and memories. B said he did not have any memory of his life before he was 10 years old. He made a drawing of a tomb, and said 'This is my childhood.'

For a few sessions B produced abstract paintings, based on colourful inkblots, and he phantasized freely on them. His imagination was very active. Phantastic castles, with the most strange creatures living inside and outside the castles, came to life. Then he threw himself into the rediscovery of his 'lost childhood'. During this time he was working on the same line with the transactional analysis group. He remembered wanting to run away from the

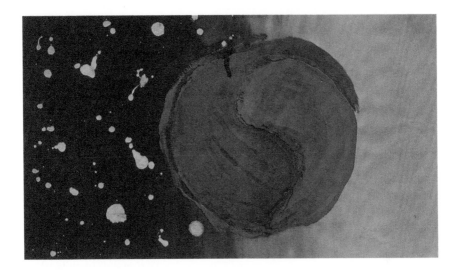

18.4 The image – the Chinese Tao (the relationship between B and his wife). 'Two parts of a completely harmonious whole.'

nursery school; he remembered being top of his class; and wanting to be good with his mother, who had so many worries, wanting to be 'special' for her. He remembered the death of a dear uncle; being left for some time with another family; his ambitions dropping dramatically after he was 16. These memories were made more relevant by the fact that, during this treatment, he was actually living with his mother, who was still seeing him in a very idealized light, and he found it difficult to cope with her.

B brought to the sixth session a drawing he made a few days previously, after waking up from a nightmare. In the dream he was clinging to the structure of a building, bleeding, and his mother was on his back, clinging to him, saying 'I love you, I need you' (Fig. 18.5). B interpreted the dream by saying that his mother's idealization of himself had been painful and destructive for him. He had always tried to be 'perfect' for her. B realized that his feeling 'special' was tied to his mother's need for him to be so. He had identified 'love' and 'need' for so many years. Was any other form of love possible? During this very intense session, B realized he had been trying to do with his wife what his mother had done to him. He was saying 'I love you, I need you', and could not allow her to be separate. Caught into the early symbiotic relationship, he could not see himself as separate.

18.5 The early relationship. 'My mother is clinging to me, saying "I love you, I need you."'

The symbolic change

One month before B was supposed to leave the clinic, although he was quite aware of his clinging attitude as a dysfunctional pattern, he was still playing with the image of himself and his wife as the Chinese Tao, the harmonious whole. I decided to confront this image, asking B to stop thinking of the relationship for a moment and to try to find 'his own shape'. The question was 'What happens if the other half of the circle *is not* there?'

During the following week, B went to the artroom almost every day, and he brought to the eighth session seventeen paintings. He said that for a few days he felt distressed. He could not find any image to represent himself. Suddenly he found it: the 'little blue shape' at the centre of a painting he had made to represent a vortex! Then he started to produce other images of his 'little self'. In the session we looked slowly at all these images. B had made them in different sizes, with different colours, in different positions. There was a 'little self' painfully bleeding, another one quite cheerful. Another 'little self' was growing into a flower (Fig. 18.6). Other pictures suggested 'growth' in a variety of ways, with strange plants, in surrealistic landscapes. B said he was experiencing something new, he felt 'real', he felt he 'existed'. He also mentioned that during the same week he had applied for a job (which he got, and started soon after he was discharged).

During his ninth session, B appeared quite sad. He said he had abandoned

18.6 The symbolic change. 'This is my little self ... I feel real ... I feel I exist.'

the idea of the symbiotic relationship, and of the 'fairy-tale marriage'. He said he accepted 'limitations', in himself, in his wife, in his marriage, but he found this a very painful process to go through. B also attempted a representation of himself as a father, and as a grandfather, which was quite new after having portrayed himself only as a 'partner'. We talked at length about his role as a grandfather. It seemed that for B now the main aim was to accept old age, imperfection, resentment, without despairing. He brought to the tenth session some images of 'Christ on the cross', which for him was the symbol of combined pain and hope. He started a re-evaluation of his religion, and the priest who performed the ceremony of his marriage appeared in one of his dreams. He planned to get in touch with him.

Before the last session, B attempted a representation of himself and his wife as two different shapes, not clinging to each other as in the previous Chinese Tao image, but separate, and talking to each other, even angry with each other. This was also a good image to express feelings related to the termination of our therapeutic relationship.

Conclusion

In this paper I have shown two images, produced in individual art therapy by two different patients presenting with a long history of drinking problems and referred to me for a short period of therapy.

These images, which I have called the yellow barrier and the Chinese Tao, have been recognized by the patients as symbolic of their own attitudes, of withdrawal and of clinging respectively, towards significant people in their life. These attitudes were dysfunctional, and it is reasonable to infer that they were conducive to drinking. This work supports Balint's interpretation (Balint 1979), and suggests that it may be important for the therapist to recognize images signifying a withdrawal or clinging attitude in order that they can be used in the therapeutic process. In this respect, I have shown a technique of active interplay through which the patients were encouraged to free-associate to the image (in order to understand the feelings and phantasies behind the defensive behaviour), and to explore alternative images (in order to gain some freedom from compulsive phantasies and behaviour). In this way A, who was locked into his loneliness and fear, 'played' with the idea of trust and interaction; B, who had projected his good side on to his idealized partner, 'played' with the idea of separation and individuation. Both of them first produced their 'basic image' (image representing a basic emotional position towards the world) within the first four sessions; they later connected it with an early primary relationship, around the sixth/seventh session; and they reached a most important moment in therapy soon after that (eighth/tenth session), when the possibility of change was considered, some freedom was experienced, and alternative attitudes were explored on a symbolic level. In both cases the process was reinforced by their attendance at group therapy, where the same issues were tackled from a different angle.

Acknowledgement

I thank ACCEPT (the institution where I conducted this work), Andrea Gilroy and Diana Burkitt who supervised it, and the two patients who trusted me enough to open themselves to me and from whom I have learned much.

References

Balint, M. (1979) *The Basic Fault, Therapeutic Aspects of Regression*, Tavistock, London, pp. 52–72.

Beck, A. T. (1976) *Cognitive Therapy and the Emotional Disorders*, International Universities Press, New York.

Bowlby, J. (1979) *The Making and Breaking of Affectional Bonds*, Tavistock, London, p. 156.

Gordon, R. (1985) 'Imagination as mediator between inner and outer reality', *The Arts in Psychotherapy*, vol. 12, pp. 11–15.

Guntrip, H. (1982) *Personality Structure and Human Interaction: the developing synthesis of psychodynamic theory*, The Hogarth Press, London.

Malan, D. H. (1979) *Individual Psychotherapy and the Science of Psychodynamics*, Butterworths, London, Chapter 10.

Mann, J. (1973) *Time-Limited Psychotherapy*, Harvard University Press.

Miller, Alice (1979) *The Drama of the Gifted Child and the Search for the True Self*, London, Faber.

Sartre, J. -P. (1983) *The Psychology of Imagination*, Methuen, London, p. 212.

Strachey, J. (1969) 'The nature of the therapeutic action of psychoanalysis', *Int. J. Psycho-Anal.*, vol. 50, no. 275, p. 286.

Ursano, R. J. and Hales, R. E. (1986) 'A review of brief individual psychotherapies', *The American Journal of Psychiatry*, 143, pp. 1507–17.

Winnicott, D. W. (1971) *Playing and Reality*, Tavistock, London.

Chapter Nineteen

Art therapy in search of a lost twin

Muriel Greenway

This case concerns unresolved grieving which affected a boy and his family. It presents an interesting example of the role art therapy can play in the multi-disciplinary treatment of disturbed children.

The unresolved grief at the death of the boy's twin shortly after birth was impeding normal family interaction. There is acknowledgement now of the need for careful support for such parents suffering stillbirth or neonatal death, if normal grieving is to proceed. At the time when his twin died the need for the parents to hold the baby and arrange a funeral was not recognized (Forrest, Standish, and Baum 1982). Art therapy was introduced, in this case with the surviving 9-year-old twin, and through his work and the concurrent family therapy their grieving was facilitated and their family interaction improved.

The boy, Peter, was admitted to a children's psychiatric hospital suffering from severe bouts of headaches and vomiting which had persisted for four years and occurred at home and at school. They were usually the result of minor confrontations with peers and teachers, or changes in routine such as trips and visits. Family life was dominated by fear of triggering the next bout. He had missed fifty days in school in the past year. The parents were anxious and angry, and the school concerned about the loss of time, though he had managed to maintain average levels of attainment.

Peter is the only surviving child of parents who themselves were only children, with a history of miscarriage on both sides of the family. The implication of this kind of experience for later generations is discussed by Pincus and Dare in their reference to family secrets which are unconsciously shared by parents and their children (Pincus and Dare 1978). The miscarriages, which were the basis of this secret, contributed to Peter's mother's anxiety and guilt relating to her mother's lost child, as she revealed later in family therapy. Her own subsequent pregnancy and the diagnosis of twins revived her childhood fantasy of having a twin which she had acted out with her dolls.

Peter was consequently born into a family eagerly awaiting the birth of much wanted twins. His brother died half an hour after birth and his own survival was in doubt during the first three days. The dead twin was buried by the hospital without parental involvement, a procedure common at the time. The boy went home after five weeks' separation from his parents and was given the name of this dead twin as his second name. The parents' recollection of the day of his birth was as the 'blackest day of our lives'.

He developed normally, apart from some temporary speech delay and a squint which was corrected at eight months. At school he seemed to be a loner and was picked on by his peers. He was inclined to exaggerate problems and involve his anxious parents in resolving them. At five he was admitted to hospital with gastroenteritis. During the history-taking at the time he first learned that he had had a twin. Soon after this hospital admission, and during his first school year, the symptoms of headaches and vomiting started. It is interesting to consider that these were some of the symptoms of the condition from which he was suffering when he first heard the news of the twin. He was seen by a paediatrician who, after trying various treatments for a year, recognized the emotional element and referred the family to a child psychiatrist. The psychiatrist saw them for a further eighteen months with no relief, though he noticed the parents' failed grief, their anxiety, overprotective-ness, and inability to set limits in their management of their son (Bryan 1983).

At this point it was decided to admit the boy for inpatient investigation as a last hope of relieving the symptoms and avoiding a permanent special school placement. It was arranged that a full battery of tests should be carried out first, to eliminate any organic problems. This also helped foster the parents' trust, as they still clung to anxieties in this area. When all such possibilities were removed it was necessary to obtain the parents' consent to a further period of admission for psychological treatment. They were worried by the suggestion of an emotional disorder, feeling that they must have failed. Their anxiety concerning their feeling of rejection towards the child was often expressed as anger. This was contained, and trust in the hospital encouraged during fortnightly meetings with a child psychiatrist and a psychologist.

Staff were asked to adopt a 'matter of fact' attitude to the boy's symptoms, while allowing him to express his fears where possible. He found it very difficult to verbalize his anxiety and in occupational therapy sessions, which he had twice weekly, he was limited and ritualistic in his play. In school he sat just inside the classroom door and did enough work and no more. It had been decided at the initial inpatient interview to use art therapy with Peter as it was hoped that the non-verbal approach would help him to communicate more easily. The start was deliberately delayed until the tests were completed. He was offered weekly non-directive sessions, which initially he declined unless they were arranged during school hours. It was decided to set clear limits for him by telling him that the sessions were part of his treatment and would take place after school. He acquiesced without enthusiasm.

Summary

1 A 9-year-old boy with a history of headaches and vomiting.

2 Parents who were anxious, overprotective, and unable to operate behavioural management techniques.

3 Art therapy was suggested by the child psychiatrist to take place after all tests had been completed.

4 Sessions were weekly, followed fortnightly by parents' sessions. The art therapist was not present at the family session but was kept informed.

The art therapy sessions

Twelve sessions of one hour took place in the course of one school term.

The first session was used to establish boundaries. Peter produced a very controlled and defended pattern and then went on to test me by wildly splashing paint into the sink, which was contained by showing him how to print the mess. In his school art sessions he continued to produce the same controlled patterns throughout the term. After the weekend at home his mother wrote to complain that he was now more sick at home, though he was not showing symptoms in the hospital at the time.

In the second session he engaged me in his work by questioning my understanding of each image. He painted a vivid picture of rockets and fireworks which suggested aggression and rivalry towards his father. His comments

19.1 The angry house.

about his family while he worked indicated that he was dealing with family issues. At the family session after this the parents expressed anxiety about focusing on relationships rather than Peter's symptoms. His father feared that confrontations could lead to his violent rage and the boy's vomiting.

Peter painted another rocket picture in the third session, continuing the theme of the previous week. When asked if the rocket was taking off he replied 'It's nowhere near ready for launching.' The next picture in this session was of a 125 train, which also seemed to relate to his feelings regarding his father. He removed this picture at the end of the session. It was the only picture not added to his folder. He said as he was leaving that day that he was glad that he had agreed to come to art therapy.

Peter arrived for the fourth session blotchy eyed and with a headache. The nurses at this time expressed worries that art therapy was making him ill. His first picture was of an 'angry house' with heavy roof and prominent drainpipes leading to sewers which he explained were to remove the water rushing off the roof (Fig. 19.1). This picture seemed to illustrate his own condition in which he spent a great deal of time with his head in the lavatory being sick. The second picture which followed quickly was of 'something really good and something really bad'. It showed the hospital and his home and his angry feelings about being kept in the hospital were expressed and worked with. He said that good is near home and bad is far away, using his clenched fists together and apart to express the distance. He left after this, saying that his headache was better.

The progress he had made in art therapy encouraged the doctors to suggest an extension of his stay in the hospital, realizing that this would cause concern to Peter and his parents. At the family session Peter and his mother were upset and his father angry, but permission was given.

The decision to extend the admission was a significant factor in the therapy. Peter arrived very late for the fifth session, anxious to know how much longer he would be coming. He said he thought three more weeks would be enough and then noticeably relaxed. In the short time left he painted a seemingly calm, peaceful picture of a seascape with two boats (Fig. 19.2). He appeared to be keeping his feelings firmly under control. I assumed a family connection in this picture, though he did not talk about it. Dr E. Bryan has written of children who have lost a twin whose drawings show a need to express their twinship (Bryan 1984). This was the first of Peter's twin images. Parts of the first green boat appear on the second blue boat and are an example of the incomplete bodies and objects with missing parts which Dr Bryan has found to be typical of these children's work. Peter left after this short session with no discussion.

His punctual arrival for the sixth session, after his lateness the previous week, was emphasized by his enquiring if I had expected him to come. He started work immediately, saying he would 'do a steam engine'. After he had outlined the shape in brown (Fig. 19.3) the fire alarm sounded. His level of

19.2 Seascape with two boats.

19.3 A steam engine.

anxiety rose sharply and he held my hand while we left the room to invest-igate. It was a false alarm, so we were able to return quickly. When we were settled in the room again he was still worried and he asked me what his parents would have thought if they had arrived to take him home and found the hospital gutted. I took this opportunity to say that as he is their only child, of course they would be very worried. He then informed me that he had had a twin brother who had died after half an hour. He went on to say that he was very worried because he did not know where the baby was buried. When walking one day with his parents in a nearby cemetery he had asked for details and his father had collapsed in tears. For this reason he said he could not ask again. He wanted his brother to be buried in the cemetery near his home and indicated this with his fists together in the way he had described 'good' in the fourth session. While he was talking he had completed the picture, putting a fierce fire in the boiler while he was describing his worries. The firm ground was added at the end when he was discussing the location. I suggested that the doctors could help by talking to his parents. He agreed but was still very anxious.

In the parents' session that evening the work from the art therapy session could not be discussed as Peter had not yet seen his doctor and given permis-sion to use the material. The parents were still persisting in their search for physical explanations for Peter's symptoms, but were beginning to respond to the support they were receiving.

There followed an unfortunate delay of three weeks in therapy sessions, due partly to half-term. When Peter returned the nursing staff considered he was too ill to attend the seventh art therapy session. He knew that I had spoken to the consultant, but because of half-term he did not know the outcome. He was seen by his doctor before that evening's family session and he gave permission for discussion of the material from art therapy.

The parents were relieved when they were told that he had raised the issue of his twin through his work and felt better able to cope with it presented in this way. His mother then revealed that his headaches had started after he had heard the twin mentioned in the history taking. Father was able to vent his anger about the way they were treated at the time of the birth. They had never seen the dead baby and recalled the day of Peter's birth with distress. They agreed to talk to the boy about his twin and bring him to the next parents' session.

In the eighth session Peter said that he still did not know what would happen as a result of his talk with his doctor. This anxiety was expressed in a picture based on a book which he had taken home from school to read with his mother. Although she was communicating with him, he felt that he was not hearing important facts. The picture represented a dark, threatening castle with turrets, repeating the rocket symbol from sessions two and three.

Peter came to session nine very sick and still very anxious about what would happen. He produced a letter which he had brought from his father to deliver to the consultant. He had retained this for five days until he felt able to hand it over in the safety of the session. The letter worried him because he thought his father was expressing anger in it concerning Peter's admission. We delivered it together later. During the session he regressed to paint mixing and splashing, as in the first week, and referred to 'naughty paint', to Dad putting paint on the fire, and then asked 'Can the vapour kill you?' Next he painted another rocket picture, this time saying 'It's taking off now', indicating that things had moved on from session three.

At the parents' session they admitted 'forgetting' to talk to Peter about his twin as they had agreed to do. This was discussed as a feature of their anxiety, and they were able to identify with the boy's difficulties. Father acknowledged the helpful route provided by the art, which made it possible for them to talk about sensitive issues. When Peter came into the meeting his father said that they wanted him to feel that he could talk to them about his brother, even if they were sometimes upset.

Peter was very restless and mixed paint until the last few minutes of the tenth session. He was feeling ill and asked if he could go out to be sick if necessary. At the end of the time he reproduced the picture of the 125 train which he had removed from the third session (Fig. 19.4). He added white smoke, asked if I knew what it was, then painted the first bird, asking again if I understood it. He quickly drew the arrow and the second bird, painting over them in black. He dashed out to be sick, saying something as he left. When he

19.4 The second 125 train, with twin birds.

returned he said that he had said 'Kersplat' illustrating the fate of the bird. The death of the twin bird was due to vapour which, in the last session, had been caused by 'naughty daddy'. The repeat of the train image representing male power and its involvement with the actions of his father allowed him to express his feelings of anger concerning the death of his twin.

In the eleventh session Peter made a blot picture, another twin image, which he called 'Sunsets' but which looked like two babies. He said that he preferred the more indistinct image which was incomplete. The rest of the time was spent mixing, pouring, and controlling paint. He was pleased to be in charge and able to change the colours. They were clear colours, not muddy as in session one, and I did not need to contain his feelings in any way. It was nearly the end of therapy and I was pleased that he was more in control.

In the family session he only attended the first half and left when he had resolved the issue of his twin's name. He was told that his twin was buried in an unmarked plot and seemed able to accept it.

He did not return after his usual weekend at home because his mother considered he was too ill. During his absence he missed an art therapy session. The family's anxiety was recognized and needed firm, sympathetic handling to ensure that Peter returned to complete his therapy. During this time he was taken to see his new school, the family having moved early in the admission.

He returned during the week before the end of the Christmas term for the last art session. This time he chose card, which he had not done before, and used it to make a substantial reproduction of the 'good and bad' picture of the fourth session. This time the feeling was less angry and portrayed his ambivalence about leaving the hospital, unsure of the future but hopeful. He said that he could now talk to his parents about 'our baby', though it does make them sad. He also mentioned the issue of his second name, saying 'it's a tough name and I like it but it's not my name'. He could also now stop himself being sick and talked of returning to school where he thought he would be able to cope.

The final picture in the twelfth session was a Christmas tree in the shape of a woman, representing me and the end of therapy. It was attacked with red blobs which were presents. He then referred aggressively to his parents receiving more presents than he does and their reluctance to get up on Christmas morning. He was now able to be openly aggressive about the end of therapy and his parents' relationship, without fear of retaliation or their collapse.

Art therapy and parent/family sessions

The art therapist saw Peter for weekly sessions and the doctor and psychologist saw Peter's parents together fortnightly. Peter joined his parents for part of the later meetings when it was felt it would be helpful. He left the sessions after the issues concerning his twin had been discussed.

In the early parent sessions strategies for Peter's management were initiated and the therapists supported the parents' anxiety and anger as it arose. After the sixth art therapy session Peter agreed to the doctor's involvement in resolving the issues surrounding his twin. As therapists in separate disciplines our interest in each others' work with Peter encouraged us to share our thoughts about our work as it developed.

Peter's parents were relieved that he had expressed his anxiety through his artwork and felt better able to accept it this way. They no longer needed to fear being overwhelmed by their grief as Peter's need gave them permission to deal with their own feeling about the twin too.

In the art session prior to each parent session Peter was noticeably more anxious than in the intervening one. Gradually, as the issues were resolved in his presence at the parent sessions, Peter began to understand his feelings and those of his parents. The work of the art sessions showed that he had separated from his twin and was more in control (session eleven). During the last session he could talk of his ability to cope, and express sadness and aggression without resorting to psychosomatic symptoms. These changes were sustained with Peter's improved management and with support from the therapists. In this way the art, and parent and family sessions proceeded in parallel to a successful conclusion.

Conclusion

The parents of a surviving twin experience the difficulty of mourning a dead child and welcoming the survivor with all the attendant mixed emotions. Society generally, and even the medical profession, have in the past avoided referring to the dead baby, and the burial was often in an unmarked grave. Fortunately now parents are usually given the opportunity to see and talk about the dead baby. They are encouraged to ask questions, express anger, and share feelings about the child that might have been. It is important for the surviving child to have the opportunity to share feelings too. Elizabeth Bryan states that 'to be a survivor of a stillborn twin may be the worst fate of all'. She has found that these children's first drawings show a need to express their twinship either with a recurring second figure (sessions five, ten, and eleven), or with incomplete bodies (Bryan 1984). Peter's image of the twin boats with shared parts (Fig. 19.2, session five) was a turning point in therapy, expressing the existence of the previously unmentionable twin.

A remaining twin can carry into adult life feelings of guilt and loneliness concerning his own involvement in the destruction of his twin. He also feels anger toward the parent who allowed the baby to die. In Peter's case, anger was directed at his father as the destroyer (session ten).

Art therapy was helpful in offering a non-verbal means of expressing these unrecognized feelings of anger and guilt. Though the pictures were not brought to the family sessions, the material from the art sessions was made available with Peter's permission. The concrete nature of the pictures thus provided a focus through which the whole family were able to explore the sensitive issues which had previously been too threatening.

Peter was discharged with continued support. This included liaison with the GP, who agreed to give immediate advice concerning his fitness for school if the parents were unsure. The close cooperation of his school helped him to settle well there.

After three months his care was returned to the referring psychiatrist who continued to see the family. He arranged for them to receive the details they felt they needed concerning the delivery, etc. A year later he reported that the family had never been happier. Unusually, we also received a letter from the family saying they were now able to do things together which they had never thought possible and were very happy with the outcome.

Art therapy had enabled this family to communicate their feelings concerning the dead twin, lay to rest disturbing images of the day of the birth, and become a happy normal family at last.

Acknowledgements

My grateful acknowledgements to Dr Gillian Forrest, consultant child psychiatrist who was responsible for Peter's treatment, and Dr Jackie Small and Mr David Westbrook who conducted the family therapy.

References

Bryan, E. (1983) 'Death of a twin', in Bryan, E., *The Nature and Nurture of Twins*, Bailliere Tyndall, London, pp. 156–65.

Bryan, E. (1984) 'When a twin dies', *Nursing Times*, 7 March, pp. 24–6.

Forrest, G., Standish, E., and Baum, J.D. (1982) 'Support after perinatal death: a study of support and counselling after perinatal bereavement', *British Medical Journal*, 285, pp. 1,475–9.

Lewis, E. (1976) 'The management of stillbirth', *The Lancet*, 18 September, pp. 619–20.

Pincus, L. and Dare C. (1978) *Secrets in the Family*, Faber, London, pp. 9–11.

Name index

Subject index

Abstraction 118–19
ACCEPT 208
acting out 196
action representation 128–9
alcohol abuse 110, 207
anthropology 77, 86, 89
anti-psychiatry movement 88–9
anxiety 157
apocalypse 22–3
archetypes 119, 192
art: colleges 147, 186; critics 152–4; galleries 149–54; Moore on 10; 'primitive' 11, 54, 58, 113, 119–20
art therapy: case histories 202–6, 208–18, 220–9; development 76, 80; distinctive features 147; disturbed children 220; drinking problems 207–18; evaluation 172–5; family 110, 200–6; figurative 40; groups 110, 156–7; integration 170–2; models of 3; nature of 107, 155; professional recognition 169–70; quasi-scientific approach 2–3; supervision 175–7; training 147–8, 167; validation 172–5; verbalization 3, 183; workplace problems 168
artists: Freud's view xiii; pressures on 38; Winnicott on 18–19; work process 151–3
asylums 78–9, 86
avant garde art 21, 31–2, 38

Bedolina Map 119
Bethlehem Hospital, London 78, 80
bipolarity 192
blank page 157–8
body: female 24–5, 31, 56, 60; relationship with 193–4
boundaries 4, 108–9, 150–1
brain disease 87

British Association of Art Therapists 179
Bulgaria 180–2

Camunian petroglyphs 107, 114–25
Caribbean society 99
caricature 27, 31, 120
Cemmo 115–17, 119
censorship 161
charisma 86, 91
children: art therapy 111, 220; Lear's relationship 72–3; meaning of drawings 109, 127–41; pattern use 162; 'primitive' comparison 185–6
Christendom 17
cockerel 48–50
communication 114
condensation 39
configuration 128–9
confrontation 207
consecutive themes 201–2, 205
contact 125
control 27, 31
copying pictures 164–6
Cosmics 21, 23
cows 50, 120
creative power: individualistic 38; Kandinsky on 24; nature of 40; theories of 54
critics 152–3
Cubism 24–5
culture 16–17, 18

death, imagery of 55
defence mechanisms 110, 143, 146, 171–2
delusions 91
dependence 8
destruction 27, 31
developmental theories 1

235